MATCHING BAITFISH

MATCHING BAITFISH

Patterns and Techniques for Great Lakes Steelhead
and Lake-Run Browns

Kevin Feenstra

STACKPOLE
BOOKS

Guilford, Connecticut

Published by Stackpole Books
An imprint of The Rowman & Littlefield Publishing Group, Inc.
4501 Forbes Blvd., Ste. 200
Lanham, MD 20706
www.rowman.com

Distributed by NATIONAL BOOK NETWORK

British Library Cataloguing in Publication Information available

Library of Congress Cataloging-in-Publication Data available

ISBN 978-0-8117-3715-9 (cloth : alk. paper)
ISBN 978-0-8117-6684-5 (electronic)

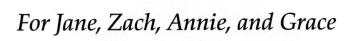

For Jane, Zach, Annie, and Grace

Contents

Acknowledgments

When I was a kid, my two brothers taught me how to fish. They loved to fish and took me fishing when they could. My mom also took me to the pier and fished with me on many occasions. My dad, who had little interest in fishing, knew that I loved to fish, and he selflessly took me fishing every chance he could. He taught me a lot about the birds and about nature, and never discouraged me at any time along the way.

When I graduated from college, it must have been disappointing to my parents that I wasn't moving on to grad school, yet they were always kind and encouraging to me. I thank them for the constant love and positivity throughout my life.

I made a lot of great friends along the way, as I moved from trout bum to committed fishing guide. I spent many days with guide Jeff Hubbard. Together we caught many fish, had a lot of fun, and learned how to swing flies for steelhead at a time when it was a shining new horizon in our Midwest fishing scene. Jeff remains one of the great anglers of this area, guiding on the Pere Marquette River. He is one of my best friends to this day. I thank him for the great times we had together.

I have learned from a lot of people over the years. Glen Blackwood and Bob Braendle, both great anglers, opened a lot of doors for me as a guide. Jerry Darkes and Jeff Liskay are also great friends who I always gleaned bits and pieces of knowledge from along the way. There are a lot of people that I can thank for adding so much to this experience for me, among them Jon Ray, Rick Kustich, Tom Helgeson, Matt Zudweg, Drew Rosema, and Nathan Hulst. Thank you, guys, for your friendship.

Someone who had a hidden impact on this book was my friend Erik Rambo, who helped me author some fishing videos and taught me a lot about photography. Some images in this book are a direct result of my friendship with him. He especially taught me how to make photos underwater.

The resources and studies put out by the Michigan Department of Natural Resources about the rivers around this state have been a big help in learning about various minnow populations. Our dedicated fisheries biologists manage our migratory fish populations, and I thank them for all their success.

I can't forget to mention my wife Jane, who has tolerated my passion for moving water and has always been positive and encouraging. She is a great partner, and has many talents. She has helped me a lot in organizing my time for this book.

Every day I see the tapestry of nature on the river. In my profession it would be difficult not to acknowledge the presence and love of a Creator. Thank you, God, for making such a beautiful world for all of us. The rivers, and all of creation, are yours. You have trusted us with these places, help us to take care of them so that our children can experience them. Please help us to be good stewards of the resource.

It is my hope that our rivers remain healthy for many years to come. This way, my son Zach can stand knee-deep in a trout stream and be awestruck by his surroundings. Hopefully his reel will sing and a steelhead will dance on the water in front of him.

Introduction

In the Midwest, we have access to a lot of fantastic natural resources. At the core of the region are the Great Lakes. These freshwater seas have matchless beauty and clear water. Beneath the hood, feasting on baitfish, are large gamefish. These predators move in and out of the many river systems of this region. Some of these gamefish are legendary and command the respect of anglers from near and far. I am one of many fishing guides who are committed to pursuing steelhead and large brown trout with flies.

As an angler, my passion for the last 25 years of my life has been swinging flies. With this passion, I have worked with a wide array of flies and have tried a vast array of patterns ranging from classic patterns to Atlantic salmon patterns to western patterns. At some point I came to understand that the migratory fish are different in the Midwest. In most instances the fish don't travel great distances to reach their destination. Upon arrival, they settle in to feed like the large trout they are. Thus, a lot of what we will discuss revolves around taking broader techniques, such as swinging flies, and assimilating them with food sources, such as baitfish. Though I fish an array of tactics throughout the year for migratory fish, this book will be heavy on swung-fly techniques, as it has been my focus for many years.

As a result of perpetual guiding and fishing, I need to tie flies just about every night. This has been going on from day to day, year to year. Over the course of a typical year, I will tie over 4,000 flies. These flies are the product of a lot of days on the water, along with some river knowledge. Most of them are stripped down to the core of what is necessary to catch fish. When I was a young guy, I would tie flies that I guessed looked like the baitfish that were in the river. I would get the pattern out of a book and hope that it would

Midwest rivers are amazing in their beauty, diversity, and gamefish. These rivers can be complicated and challenging, but fear not! This book will help you in your quest to catch fish while exploring our many miles of rivers. In its pages you will find information about the foods fish eat, the places they hide, and the stuff you need to catch them.

work in a local stream. Through trial and error, and by looking at images in books and on the internet, occasionally the flies came out looking like the fish that I now know they were imitating.

One early summer day, I first spent some time turning over some rocks. Later, I stuck a camera lens under the water. Moving from there, I started snorkeling the river with a camera. This forever changed how I look at my local river and the baitfish that call it home. It also changed how my flies are presented and created. It even changed where I look for fish. There are many fishing guides in my home state of Michigan, and a lot of us have been around for a long time and have lots of knowledge to share. This book about fishing baitfish patterns is my attempt to share an accumulation of knowledge with the fly-fishing community. Though this book is largely my personal experiences, I have incorporated some information from some of the most knowledgeable and well-respected people in the types of fly fishing that we will discuss.

I grew up in Grandville, Michigan, fishing a small stream every day as a kid. Like many in the fishing community, I was obsessed with fishing from a young age. Things were different then, and many kids would go to our local streams and fish. Fishing was considered a distraction from our studies, rather than video games and the internet. As a kid, I did some bait fishing but preferred fishing spinners and lures for brown trout and steelhead. I often tell people that I caught more big trout as a kid than I ever have since, and it is the truth.

One day, I saw a man with a fly rod catch a steelhead on Saturday-morning TV. In hindsight, I don't know who it was, but after seeing this, I really wanted to catch a steelhead that way. The internet has profoundly changed how we gather information. Only a couple of decades ago, if you wanted to learn about something, you would have to gain that knowledge from reading books. So I went to the library and read about steelhead fishing. The only books that I could find about catching steelhead at that time were West Coast books. I followed their advice and swung flies, and as a teenager caught my first fish swinging flies on the Rogue River near Rockford, Michigan.

The first fly I used was a red-colored Woolly Bugger, and I caught my first few steelhead and

lake-run browns on that pattern. It is unclear why that fly worked, but as my fishing experience grew, I tried a lot of different flies and techniques. Because of my background fishing lures and hardware, fishing glittery flies that look like fish has always seemed appealing to me.

I figure that most people come to a river and learn a little about fishing. They initially discover a spot where they can catch fish. After they have been catching fish, they start to see that there are other similar places around to fish, and so they learn to read a particular type of water. This book will help you read particular types of water with various forms of structure. Each of these types of structure draw in different smaller forms of food, often in the form of baitfish. The goal of this book is to show you how to fish various types of baitfish patterns around different types of cover. Another goal is to help you read water regardless of your fishing method. This will expand your knowledge of the various types of water in our river systems.

As I graduated from college, a local outfitter approached me and asked if I would like to be a fishing guide. His logic made sense to me; he said that I should guide for a year or two so that I could tell my friends about it later in life. The outfitter's name was Glen Blackwood. I took his advice and became a fishing guide. Now, more than two decades later, guiding is still my profession, but I have morphed from a trout bum into a professional guide.

When I started guiding, we were using film cameras to take pictures of our clients' fish. As the guide service was strictly catch-and-release, it was necessary to take pictures of fish and then physically mail them to a client. On one guide trip, I had a very difficult client. Not only was he rough around the edges, but there were a lot of illicit chemicals whizzing around his system. We were fishing in the pouring rain, and though I took some pictures of his fish, they did not turn out due to the weather. As a result, he was very unhappy, and this bad experience led me to purchase my first digital camera. In this way, I could always verify that we had pictures of the catch.

Once I purchased a digital camera, photography really started to appeal to me. I wanted to learn about my home river in the deepest way possible,

I spent a lot of my guide life fishing with these two guys, Jon Ray and Jeff Hubbard. They are respected guides from two different river systems. The two gamefish in the picture are the focus of this book. Although these two fish are radically different in some ways, they share the same water and eat the same types of food.

and cataloguing the different creatures I experienced helped me to assimilate an awful lot of knowledge about the river I have come to love. Much of what you will see in this book is the product of this constant learning about all aspects of the great rivers around West Michigan.

I got a late start on having children, and my wife and I now have a young son and two twin little girls. I still feel blessed to be able to spend almost every day on the water, though mostly locally now. Prior to the kids, I fished a lot all over the Midwest, and I believe that the knowledge I have gained and included in this book can be applied broadly to any river system that contains predatory migratory fish.

This book specifically covers two different migratory fish—steelhead and lake-run brown trout—and is aimed at presenting baitfish patterns for these fish. Initially, I considered including the various Pacific salmon in this work. However, as they are done eating after entering the rivers and don't pay much attention to natural baitfish

imitations (though they will crush attractor lures, etc.), they would miss the focus. So, we focus solely on steelhead and lake-run browns. These two fish are very different in some ways, yet they inhabit the same parts of a river, eat the same foods, and can often be taken with the same techniques.

One of the largest sections of this book covers how to read the water. As I write this introduction, I am coming off a tough guide day. We only hooked one fish today, but we did land it. I have been fishing this river for 25 years and have spent thousands of days on it. You would think that there would be some magical formula for catching fish, but no matter how much time you put in or whatever your skill set, there will always be days when the fish don't cooperate. It might be fishing pressure, it might be the weather, or maybe they just don't like your fly. A lot goes on below that water that we can't see: It could be that 50 fish chased your fly without your knowledge and none of them bit. Yet, no matter how much time you invest, there

Left: Steelhead are a Pacific fish and a close relative of rainbow trout. They are also the source of a lot of obsessive fishing behavior. This steelhead is in the wild and has ascended a tiny stream to spawn. Many Midwest rivers have wild, self-sustaining populations of steelhead, while others need to be planted. These fish have adapted well to our waters.

will always be days that just don't work out. This is especially true of migratory fish.

On the other hand, we did catch a great fish today. It was caught in an obscure spot that I would not have thought to fish even a few years ago. Fishing experience and reading the water helped to get that fish. My goal in this book is that it helps you find a memorable fish on a difficult day of fishing.

So, we set out to discuss two wholly different species of fish that happen to be in our rivers at the same time: steelhead and lake-run brown trout. These fish are both salmonids, and they like to eat the same food sources. However, their origins and their feeding patterns are different.

Steelhead are a fish of lore and legend, with origins on the West Coast. They are built for speed, with a sleek torpedo-shaped body, and have been in the Great Lakes for over 100 years. Most Great Lakes states began stocking steelhead between the late 1870s and 1890s. These stockings intensified in the mid to late 20th century to bolster struggling fish stocks in the Great Lakes.

Throughout the course of the century-plus that they have been found in the Great Lakes, steelhead have become a fixture in our river systems. There are many types of these fish throughout the Midwest, and some are genetically unique to our river systems. Most steelhead in the state of Michigan are Michigan strain, more commonly called Little Manistee strain, steelhead. These are a great fish that grow to large sizes and have a fall and spring run.

Steelhead have some advantages over other migratory fish and a few disadvantages. One of the advantages is that steelhead are a fast-moving fish that lives in shallow water or the upper parts of the water column in deeper water. This means that they are less susceptible to one of our unfortunate invasive species, sea lamprey. In the mid-20th century, sea lamprey devastated the native lake trout, which is one of the reasons steelhead have risen to prominence in our fisheries. As the lake trout declined, the need arose for gamefish to take their place, and not only for fishing purposes. At the same time the lamprey were having their devastating effect (which continues to this day), another invasive entered the Great Lakes. Alewives, a baitfish from the Atlantic Ocean, also came in. These baitfish littered the Great Lakes' beautiful beaches. With minimal lake trout to eat them, we needed more predators and thus the steelhead and salmon were emphasized. Lamprey do their damage to steelhead stocks for sure, but by and large they are less devastating to steelhead than to some of the other gamefishes.

Steelhead are also favored due to their ability to reproduce in our rivers. This is not a total win, as juvenile steelhead need to stay in their natal rivers for a year to survive before going out to the lake. In high-water-quality cool streams, this is not a problem. However, in streams with poor water quality, warm summer water temps, or limited food sources, steelhead reproduction does not fare well. For that reason, states in the Midwest employ heavy stocking programs. Many steelhead enter our coastal rivers in the fall and wait there until spring to spawn. This is a great attribute, as it gives us a long season to fish for them. In most rivers, this is a fall–spring time frame. In some systems summer steelhead, called Skamania, exist. In these streams there may be year-round opportunities to fish for steelhead. Steelhead can live up to eight years; however, in many rivers they make only one run before being harvested. The spawning process is rough, and many other fish die of exhaustion.

As steelhead enter our rivers, they have another often-overlooked advantage that plays well for fly fishing and sport fishing in general. Steelhead become territorial upon entering the river and after a few days will spread out a comfortable distance from other fish. If you think about it, if steelhead all gathered in one spot in a long river system, it would not make for great fishing. Furthermore, it would make the resulting fishing a circus. Instead, they spread out over the entire length of a river system, allowing them to be fished for miles on

end. It always amazes me that toward the end of the fall and through the winter, I can swing a fly in any likely spot over 4 feet deep in 46 miles of the Muskegon River and have a reasonable chance at finding a fish anywhere along the way. While spread out in each run, these fish acclimate to our rivers and feed.

One of the real advantages that steelhead have, and the focus of this book, is their great versatility as a gamefish. While out in the Great Lakes, steelhead will focus on any number of food sources that range from insects and crustaceans to a wide variety of baitfish. These baitfish will be a focus of one of our chapters, and imitating them is a constant learning process. I find that even as some stretches of river are pummeled by salmon eggs and their imitations, there are still fish that are willing to eat a good baitfish imitation. Not every steelhead likes to eat an egg, and that is a great thing.

Steelhead are a stunning gamefish with many favorable attributes. These fish fill a niche in our Great Lakes, and because of their ability to eat a lot of different things and reproduce in our streams, they will continue to thrive in a constantly changing environment in which less adaptable fish struggle. They can be taken on any number of spin-fishing and fly-fishing presentations, and are an awesome gamefish. On any day on West Michigan streams, anglers can be found fishing plugs, spinners, spoons, floats with spawn, and wigglers; fly anglers are swinging flies or fishing nymphs; and the list goes on and on. Fishing appeals to many people in many different ways; don't turn your nose up at any other type of angler. Some of my best friends guide with hardware and bait, and we have learned a lot about fishing for steelhead from each other over the years.

Though they will take a lot of different things, steelhead have marked preferences in how they like flies presented that differ from other gamefish. If someone asked me how to catch steelhead consistently specifically on a baitfish pattern, I would suggest swinging a fly. Steelhead have an innate curiosity about swung flies, and when properly presented, these patterns will elicit a vicious strike consistently, day after day. The strike of a steelhead on a swung fly is one of the most exciting things in freshwater fishing. The scenario that unfolds with this style of fishing is that you will fish for many hours on end, with freezing hands and aching bones. You question your own sanity, and your mind wanders from fishing. Without warning, the line goes tight as a large steelhead breaks the surface. This is awesome! In most cases, this means swinging the fly across the current without adding action to the fly once it is in the water. This technique is a dead swing, and it contrasts with the presentation for the next gamefish that we are about to discuss.

Another gamefish that has great attributes is the brown trout that migrate up and down our rivers throughout much of the Midwest. Though similar in some ways to steelhead, brown trout are from the other side of the world in their origins. The genus of the brown trout is the same as Atlantic salmon, *Salmo,* and our fish are indigenous to Europe. Though similar in shape, steelhead are a Pacific fish, from the same genus as Pacific salmon, *Oncorhynchus.*

Brown trout are a popular fish due to their innate beauty, their willingness to eat many baits that resemble a fish, and their widespread availability. They are also more tolerant of warmer water temperatures than rainbow trout, which gives them the ability to loiter in our rivers. They are a shallow-water fish while in the Great Lakes and will typically stay near shore or in harbors. This shallow-water environment contains a lot of the baitfish that they may see in a river. While in the Great Lakes, they feed on a variety of sources and their diet consists of a lot of the same things that a steelhead would eat in a lake. However, as a general rule of thumb, the larger fish consume a lot of baitfish. As brown trout enter our rivers, this predatory virtue continues and they are fish-eating machines.

One major difference between steelhead and lake-run brown trout lies in their spawning behavior. Brown trout spawn enter our rivers in the fall, and they can spawn from late September

Lake-run brown trout are an impressive-looking fish. Their fight does not rival that of a steelhead, but their natural beauty does. I hear stories of people going to faraway places to catch huge browns, but if you put your time in, you can find a huge migratory brown in many rivers attached to the Great Lakes.

all the way through December depending on the resource. Much like steelhead, they can spawn multiple times over the course of their lives, and have been found to live up to 13 years in the Great Lakes. Often they will be found in a river well into the spring, but unlike steelhead, they do not need to be there at that point. Post-spawn, these fish could leave at any time. For this reason, if a river is going to have a sustained period of lake-run brown trout fishing, it is necessary to have food sources that will keep them there. This food for the most part must be some form of baitfish, preferably large baitfish. If the food leaves the river in the winter or the spring, so will the brown trout.

Like any fish, there is a cost/benefit to staying in a stream for a brown trout. A lot of times the brown trout will leave a river after high water, provided their spawning is complete. Fighting heavy current is hard work for a fish. There is no reason for a fish to stay in a river and burn calories fighting a heavy current, when it can lumber out to its home lake and gain weight easily in the light currents of the harbor. Brown trout prefer slow river edges and flat rocky areas where they can feed on large baitfish.

By the same token, these lake-run brown trout are often genetically very similar to the stream trout. In many cases, the stream browns are the same strain as the lake-dwelling brown trout. In some cases, brown trout that live a portion of

Left: Wouldn't you think that a huge streamer-eating brown trout would be the most sought-after gamefish in our rivers? Instead, they are overlooked when steelhead are present. Though sometimes caught on a variety of baits, at their core they are a voracious meat-eating fish.

migratory runs of brown trout are left largely undisturbed, as the hype among anglers is with the steelhead. Steelhead are usually more abundant. In many places, the brown trout will take only a couple of different types of presentations, but the steelhead will take many. This is due mostly to their proclivity for eating large baitfish.

Fortunately, both steelhead and brown trout will take the streamer presentations that are the primary focus of this book. As mentioned, big browns are more fixed on large baitfish for food. There are also some real differences in their preferences in presentation and flies. One of these differences lies in the technique in which a fly is presented. If someone asked me what the best and most consistent way was to take a lake-run brown trout on a fly, I would without hesitation suggest stripping the fly broadside to the current with a sink-tip line. This broadside approach presents a wounded baitfish appearance to a trout and is the trigger it takes to get a big fish to bite.

Although steelhead generally take streamers more consistently on the swing and brown trout more consistently take flies on the strip, both of these fish will take these methods interchangeably, and that is why we cover them together in this book. This work also has broader implications, as the techniques and flies can be applied to an array of gamefish that live in our Midwest waters. Many of the baitfish that we will discuss are eaten by resident trout and the gamut of warmwater fish as well. Hopefully this book holds a little something for both the vastly experienced angler and the one just getting started on this adventure of fly fishing.

Please join me in the coming pages as we go through the types of baitfish that these fish will eat in the river and learn about reading the water and fishing the structure they live in. We will also discuss the techniques and equipment needed to follow through and fish for them.

their lives as stream trout might amble down to the lake, only to return as river trout. In the same way, a lake-run trout might choose to reside in a river for a long time after spawning or even revert to being a stream trout itself. This is all provided that the food is there to sustain them. A brown trout is pretty versatile and can make use of any appropriate habitat. This is great news if you are an avid stream trout angler who is moving into the realm of fishing for migratory browns. Migratory browns are the same as resident fish, only larger and frankly usually dumber.

You would think that huge migratory brown trout would be heavily targeted by all types of anglers. This is not the case, however, and often

CHAPTER 1

A Seasonal Approach to Baitfish

When you first start thinking about streamer fishing and swinging flies, these seem like very simple presentations. As you get out on the river and try doing it, however, you may find getting consistent results to be more difficult than you might have hoped. This book was made to address the subtleties of these presentations. Another goal is to give you an idea about how to mimic baitfish at any time migratory fish are around. Baitfish patterns really shine when the bite is poor or when the conditions are tough. They also are key to catching fish in the icy cold waters of a Midwest winter.

As you first approach a river or research it, you might look at the available food sources and determine which ones the gamefish might be eating. If you are streamer fishing, look to the bottom-dwelling baitfish that are in most rivers. They are a size that migratory fish like to eat and are found just about anywhere that has a few rocks. Furthermore, they are foods that are familiar to gamefish out in the Great Lakes. Large, fertile rivers have a lot of different food sources to choose from, whereas smaller, colder rivers have less. Rivers with poor water quality might be lacking baitfish, but that's OK because the migratory fish that are present will be hungry.

Thus, this first chapter will deal with the types of baitfish that we encounter on streams that are associated with migratory fish. Many of these types of baitfish occur throughout the country, so this information will be useful to you even if you are reading this in some faraway place, and might

Understanding local minnow populations has helped me in a lot of ways, and there is still a lot to explore. One thing is for sure: Learning the baitfish in your local river will take your fly fishing to the next level and will help you catch some amazing fish!

be helpful when fishing for other species as well. Please note that this is written from the perspective of an angler and not a fisheries biologist.

Every stream is different, and they each have their own food web. For many years I fished sculpin patterns and various other baitfish patterns without a clear knowledge of what the fish actually looked like. It took a lot of time to learn which flies worked through trial and error. If you really want to get to know your river and cut your learning curve a lot, you can do a few things to take your knowledge to the next level. One thing that you can do that takes little time and can change your perspective is to spend a few hours turning over some rocks of varying sizes along the edge of the river. In short order, you will have an idea of the colors and sizes of the bottom-dwelling fish in your river system. This is often a fun exercise, and if you have kids you may invite them to help you. An insect seine will pick up small baitfish, and this can also be a valuable tool in this exercise.

If you are so inclined, doing some underwater photography will take this one step further. It will really help you learn what is going on below the surface and will give you a reference when you are tying flies throughout your fishing adventures. For me, digital photography is a great tool not only to see what's on the bottom of the river, but also to take note of when I saw it. There have been times when I've wondered which baitfish I saw in the river at what point, and I simply visit old images for reference to what was happening in years past. Some of the image cataloguing tools, such as Adobe Lightroom, make referencing your photos a snap.

If you want to take learning about what is below the surface to yet another level, you can do some snorkeling in your local river. Always be careful when doing this, and it is a good idea to bring a friend along for safety. A warm summer day in your local river with a snorkel mask will reveal the underwater world to you in a way that nothing else can. Many types of baitfish are fast and difficult to sneak up on. When you are snorkeling, you become a part of their underwater world and they are more approachable.

This is a mature hornyhead chub. It is a large minnow, typical of the baitfish of the early fall. Big flies equal big fish in the fall. Many of these large fall minnows fall into the olive/yellow or gray/yellow color scheme.

This is an overlooked baitfish that I absolutely love. In the fall, spotfin shiners congregate around structure, often in the lower reaches of streams. At 2 to 5 inches in length, they provide a protein-packed meal for any predator fish.

Through fishing and using these various methods, I have formulated a yearly approach to the baitfish that are present. Following are some general guidelines on how to approach a year of fishing baitfish patterns in our Midwest rivers.

Fall

When migratory fish enter our rivers in the fall, the water temperatures in the river are typically warmer than the lake that they are coming out of. For this reason, the migratory fish are supercharged and, frankly, more gullible than seasoned fish that have been in the river for a while. As a result, they are often triggered by bright colors and flash.

During the fall months, color is typically more important than matching any particular baitfish with your fly. That being said, if you fish a lot, you will encounter a day when the fish aren't particularly grabby. This usually falls in line with a strong weather event or rapid changes in water depth and clarity. It is during these poor bite periods that a

natural pattern might take the one biting fish. Furthermore, even when using bright and gaudy patterns, the shape of the fly you tie on can help you be a more successful angler.

Some parts of our rivers have large congregations of shiner and chub minnows in the fall, and migratory fish will feed on these. I have seen steelhead and brown trout crashing these minnows in the mouths of our rivers, and there are many of them in other parts of our systems as well. A good shiner imitation will take a fish readily at this time of the year.

Migratory fish may pass upstream slowly. Delayed by low-water conditions, they might concentrate in these lower reaches of a river system for quite some time. For example, steelhead that enter a river system in the fall may have four or five months to reach the spawning waters. Many of them will stay quite low in the system, especially in years with low water levels.

The lowest sections of our rivers are ideal for shiner patterns. Downstream stretches of rivers are sandy in nature, and nymphs and crustaceans that require gravel to survive are not abundant in these places. The ultimate goal of a migratory fish is to get to gravelly areas, and so it makes sense that these lower stretches are lacking in gravel and rocks. Despite the substrate, there is enough food for shiners to thrive in these areas, and they can provide the best feeding opportunities for migratory fish.

Fall shiners tend to be on the large size, and mature shiners of several species can be 3 to 6 inches in length. One of the best shiners to imitate in my part of the Midwest is the spotfin shiner, which is often found around the sand and wood that is so common in these areas. A good spotfin imitation will catch many predators in the fall. Other species of shiners, such as common shiners, also thrive in these areas.

In addition, anglers may encounter lake forage species that come up into the river in large schools. Even if your local river lacks resident populations of baitfish near its mouth, lake baitfish will often be present. Alewives and gizzard shad are frequent visitors to the lowest ends of a river system that enters the Great Lakes.

Even in the fall, there are advantages to running a natural pattern while fishing for migratory gamefish. As a guide, I try to maximize the catch of everything, not just the target species. No matter where you fish a streamer for migratory fish, it is usually not a high-numbers technique, so access to other species of fish can keep the interest going when there is a break in the action. Using a natural-leaning imitation can give you a chance at other resident gamefish that the gaudy stuff might not. These include resident trout, walleye, northern pike, smallmouth bass, and others depending on your river system.

Some stretches of my home river, the Muskegon, have a limited variety of baitfish in the fall, so those stretches always get the sparkly, attractor-style fly selection. I love Flashabou and other glitzy

The Johnny darter is a common bottom-dwelling baitfish. It is often found around spawning fish and ends up in the stomach of fish that are eating eggs behind the gravel. When big migratory fish move gravel around, these baitfish break free just as nymphs do. Small bottom-dwelling baitfish are vulnerable and only move in short bursts. When you imitate this minnow, a good Hex wiggle nymph will suffice.

Similar to the Johnny darter, this blackside darter inhabits much of the same habitat and is imitated with the same flies.

materials, so you will never hear me discourage the use of attractor flies. However, other stretches have a wide array of gamefish, and I always keep a natural pattern on standby in these stretches. In this guide's mind, catching something is always better than catching nothing. A natural pattern helps with this. In the same way, if the fish are really on the bite, you might catch a whole theme park of fish if you imitate a natural baitfish. In a river that is diverse, when conditions turn right for them to feed, they all feed at once, and this can be some exciting fishing!

When things do get tough in the fall, you can always fall back on slowly presented baitfish patterns. One thing to know is that many rivers have weed beds during the summer months, and in these underwater forests, baitfish thrive. As fall arrives, much of the weed cover dies. Suddenly all these baitfish, which have been using the weeds for cover, are forced to fend for themselves. These include a variety of shiners and chubs. At the same time, big migratory fish, which have fed on large baitfish for years, have entered the rivers and, along with the resident predators, feed on the vulnerable minnows. Steelhead and lake-run brown trout are formidable predators. They feed on a lot of different things. By and large, however, they get big by eating other fish. Hunting a baitfish in a stream is something they are made for.

Fall is also the time of year when we have long days, abundant sunshine, and fishing pressure. In these conditions, a good option would be to fish a bright attractor, trying to trigger a fish that is fresh from the lake. There is definitely something to be said for the "bright fly and bright day" line of thought. (If you do follow this approach, try gold or holographic flash on your streamer!) Another approach is just the opposite: We would fish subtle natural patterns deeply, in an effort to find a feeding fish.

A lot of young-of-the-year baitfish are also present during the early fall. For example, when the salmon are spawning in the fall, there are many juvenile darters around their spawning gravel. These juveniles are remarkably similar in size and shape to a Hex nymph, which is a common imitation that is fished in almost every Midwest stream. Nymphing and swinging an articulated Hex nymph

in these areas, tied pale tan, is an effective imitation. Why mention a nymph pattern in a streamer book? A Hex nymph can pull double duty very effectively, imitating both nymphs and minnows.

A very common darter throughout the Midwest is the Johnny darter, which is dusky tan in color. Johnny darters are good fish baits, and if you see them in the water, their distinguishing feature is the markings that look like the letter *W* on their side. They are widespread, found in just about every steelhead stream, and they can tolerate a lot of variation in water quality. No doubt many Hex nymph imitations are eaten by fish thinking they are eating a darter.

Left: Pacific salmon contribute a lot to our resources after they die. Here an otter feasts on a recently deceased king salmon. Many animals feed on salmon, including fish, so bring a flesh fly. Salmon carcasses also attract minnows and crayfish, so the final resting place of salmon can be a great place to find a big brown.

points in their lives, even though they may not live where you are fishing. It is more likely that the fish sees the Hex pattern as a minnow, however. As you fish for steelhead and migratory fish, you will find that there are some flies that just work, that generically imitate a lot of different things. A Hex wiggle nymph falls into this category, and many other flies do as well. Many of the flies that we will cover in this book are close imitations of one baitfish but could vaguely imitate other fishes as well. As far as that goes, not every streamer that you use would imitate a minnow at all.

An example of this would be flesh flies. In rivers with large populations of migrating Pacific salmon, flies imitating decaying salmon can be effective swung flies late in the fall. Salmon carcasses tend to settle on the inside bends of rivers and also in areas that have remnants of weed beds. Though not a primary food source, steelhead will prey on them as they deteriorate. Slowly swinging pink or peach flies through these often smelly places is productive. These bright colors are natural draws, especially to steelhead. Steelhead might take a pink imitation as a piece of salmon flesh or may simply find it attractive. Either way, you can win with such a pattern. Migratory fish are not neurosurgeons, and so they will eat things out of curiosity.

Remember that migratory fish travel through a lot of unfamiliar water as they head upriver, and this environment is radically different from the Great Lakes environment. There is a whole world of difference between the river and the lake. The depth of the river is different, the current is different, the lighting is different, the clarity of the water is different, the water temperatures are different, and the food sources are a lot different than the Great Lakes. These are big adjustments for migratory fish. Upon entering a river, they encounter many foods that are specific to rivers that they need to get used to eating. I equate this

An underlying truth is, with a lot of patterns we are using, we just don't know what the fish is thinking at that precise moment when it takes your fly. In the case of the Hex nymph, it is possible that a migratory fish is familiar with these nymphs, and that is why it eats your fly. Steelhead and brown trout certainly encounter Hex nymphs at some to a small-town kid going to a big city and eating sushi for the first time. Some of the foods just take some getting used to. There are, however, some food sources that are ubiquitous to the rivers and the Great Lakes. These food sources are the most important when fishing for migratory fish.

Imagine that you are a steelhead or brown trout migrating up a river in the fall for the first time. You have left the comfort of the inland sea that you have thrived in for a few years. You are a lightning fast, experienced predator. In the stream environment, you are larger than any other fish you see. However, these surroundings are not familiar to you, and you need to eat. A lot of things in the river look tasty but are foreign to you. Yet upon closer inspection, you do see some foods that are indeed familiar, most notably sculpins and gobies, which had been a constant source of food for you in your former lake home.

Other things that we imitate with streamers that are not fish at all, such as crayfish, are also universal. A migratory fish enters the river and finds these foods it has eaten in the past. Using a universal food source as a pattern is a reliable choice for the fly angler.

Furthermore, there are other familiar baitfish that will migrate in and out of the rivers in the fall. I have seen alewives in several river systems, and have caught them as far as 40 miles upriver in one of them. Another visitor is gizzard shad. Young gizzard shad will sometimes move up rivers in amazingly dense schools. Both alewives and shad are familiar forage fish to migratory fish. It is always a good idea to have a large, slender baitfish pattern on hand in the fall. However, bottom-dwelling sculpins and gobies are the most reliable. These can be used in the fall, but really shine during the winter months.

Winter

In most streams connected to the Great Lakes, steelhead and/or brown trout migrate during the fall months and settle into the rivers during the winter months. The scenario for browns and steelhead is somewhat different, as brown trout enter the rivers to spawn in the fall, whereas steelhead do not spawn until the spring.

As such, the brown trout spawn and quickly become drop-back fish. Drop-back fish are fish that have completed spawning. The spawning process burns a lot of calories and diverts their attention from food. When this is complete, their focus shifts to survival, and they are ravenously hungry. Normally they are wary predators, but post-spawn hunger makes these giant browns easier to target. Unlike a big resident brown trout sipping on dry flies, they can be very unselective and once located will take a fly with abandon. They are by nature meat eaters, so they like the big flies that we present during the coldest months. Because they are focused on eating, they will lurk in the water that has the most baitfish. This is often the inside bends of the river or deep and slow areas.

Steelhead, conversely, have a different motivation. Steelhead are settling in to survive through the winter. Their biology won't let them pick up and leave in the middle of winter if they have settled in. They must have enough energy come spring to not only spawn but also return to the lake. In the early winter months, the water is cold, and the urge to spawn has not yet hit them. As such, they behave a lot like large winter trout, and the color of their bodies reflects their trout-like tendencies. Steelhead often hunker down in structure-laden areas, and this puts them in contact with the same types of baits that the brown trout pursue.

During the coldest part of winter, from above our rivers seem sterile. The surrounding trees are barren, and there is little to prove that anything is going on at that time. However, beneath the surface, our rivers are very much alive. The food sources tend to be either very large in the form of minnows or very small in form of insects and crustaceans in the winter months. Reproduction of most baitfish is limited to the mild times of the year, so juvenile fish are not prominent. The biology of the river seems pretty constant in the winter, and the food sources are relatively steady for months on end. This is especially true if your river's temperature bottoms out at around 32 and stays there due to freezing conditions. This is great news if you find a pattern that works well in late December, as it will continue to work well throughout the entire winter. Winter is a simple time of the year for fly tying, and for slowly fishing accurate baitfish imitations. It's the time of the year that knowing your baitfish really helps your success.

Much of the vegetation that exists at other times of the year in our rivers is gone in the winter. This means that any free-living minnows are forced to seek shelter around the same structure that the predator fish are. While lurking in the cover of rocks and timber, migratory fish are in contact with common minnows and familiar bottom-dwelling baitfish such as sculpins and invasive round gobies.

Sculpins have long been a favorite bait of mine, and I could write pages and sing songs extolling their virtues. My love affair with this bottom-dwelling, homely fish began when I was a teenager. When I was young, I spent a lot of time fishing the Rogue River near Rockford, Michigan. This river is a midsize, beautiful stream that is fast and rocky. Parts of it are undeveloped, but parts of it are also urban. It has become a heavily pressured river system but still yields a lot of great fish. Over the years, the Rogue has helped train several fishing guides.

One late summer morning, I learned a lot about the preference of steelhead. At the time, I was driving trucks for a moving company. The company had little on the schedule that day. The dispatcher knew that I loved to fish, and when I called him that morning and told him I had "salmon Ella," I could hear him rolling his eyes. This was my way of saying I am going fishing. He grumbled "OK," and I quickly diverted to the Rogue.

As summer was coming to an end, I was trying to catch smallmouth in the lower reaches of the river. I had tied an experimental sculpin pattern along

A master of camouflage, sculpins are tops for all kinds of big predator fish. They do well in any rocky stream with good water quality. Their subtle appearance is their best defense from big things that would eat them. They can only swim fast for short distances, and they have no body armor to protect them. All this adds up to a perfect meal for a fish.

with some crayfish flies. I cast the sculpin out into a pool, lazily gave it a twitch, and let the line swing across the slow-moving pool. The line made a slight twitch on the way across, and I thought, "That must be a small fish." Boy, was I wrong. The line swung a few more feet and then went extremely tight. Lightning traveled down the fly line. Suddenly, I was at eye level with a large summer-run Skamania steelhead and my jaw dropped. My rinky-dink college-student-budget Pflueger Medalist shrieked as if in terrible pain. With little tension to stop the fish, I began to run after it as it streaked downriver. I was a big kid and a bit clumsy, so I tripped over some rocks and swam a bit in the process of landing the fish. But I did land it 50 yards downriver, and admired its dazzling beauty as I released that magnum fish. Twelve pounds of chrome slid back into the depths of the river.

Though I had caught some fish swinging flies in the years prior to that fish, the experience radically altered my perception of what a steelhead might eat. I no longer held the illusion that steelhead would only eat a Green Butt Skunk or my old crimson Woolly Bugger. In an instant, streamer fishing for steelhead and lake-run brown trout became a viable, repeatable thing. Later that same year, as I began to guide on the Muskegon River, I started to fish this same pattern and had amazing results. At the time, there were few people streamer fishing for steelhead, and the ones that were focused on traditional patterns. Furthermore, the common belief was that steelhead would not eat a swung fly during the winter months. Thus, the cold-water months were uncharted and an exciting time of discovery and learning for me.

Time is a real gift when you are trying to learn new things. At the time I was a young fishing bum with no real ambitions save to learn how to catch more and bigger fish. So, I fished sculpins through many winter months, and they will probably always be at the top of my list for favorite things to fish for all species. During my first years guiding for fall steelhead, I relied heavily on sculpins for a wide variety of gamefish, and they will always be in the arsenal for catching something big.

The Midwest has a lot of sculpins. They are common in most rocky rivers, and a few species live in the Great Lakes. In very fertile rivers, a sculpin might be one of many baitfish imitations. However, there are plenty of rivers that don't have a large variety of minnows. Some of these rivers have environmental issues or lack substrate to support minnows. They might also be very warm during the summer months. Rivers with poor water quality don't typically support a large insect population, so the migratory fish will eagerly eat whatever species of baitfish that are available.

On the other end of the spectrum, some rivers are ultraclean. Some of the streams that connect to the Great Lakes are classic, cold freestone trout streams. These are the rivers that are wild trout and steelhead factories, and they don't need to be planted to sustain a great fishery. In fact, sometimes the progeny of migratory fish squeeze out resident trout in these places. Such rivers typically have other trout to eat as bait, such as young-of-the-year resident trout or salmon and steelhead fry in the spring. During the cold months, the main resident baitfish are sculpins. The epitome of such a river is the Pere Marquette, a famous stream located in northern Michigan. The Pere Marquette is fabled for its wild steelhead. It was also the first river in the United States to have brown trout in it.

I talked to one of the most knowledgeable long-time guides on the Pere Marquette River, Jeff Hubbard. Jeff says that the Pere Marquette has a great population of sculpins. These become one of his go-to fly types in the winter months while swinging flies for steelhead. When water temps drop, Jeff believes that steelhead and larger trout will key in on sculpin or goby-type patterns. When presented slow in slower pools and runs, it becomes a big meal that they don't have to work too hard to get. Jeff says that at these times, steelhead are opportunistic eaters that are not picky when something is presented in front them and they are in the mood to eat. In these freestone streams, sculpins thrive and are one of the primary baitfish species. Thus, whether you fish a big river or a small river, sculpins are a must for the Midwest angler.

Sculpins exhibit some traits that that you should know about. Their camouflage is extreme, and you could be looking right at one and not even know that it is there. Sculpins have a very flat head, which helps their body grip the bottom of the river where they are found as the current glides over them. The most common sculpin in this region is the mottled sculpin, and there are other sculpins such as the slimy sculpin as well. If you don't know what type of sculpin is in your river, don't worry: For all practical purposes, they all look very similar throughout much of the United States and their behavior is the same. Sculpins ranging from 1 to 6 inches in length are what we are concerned with when we are fishing for migratory fish.

Sculpins have traits as a baitfish that have implications as to how to fish them. They themselves are voracious little predators. They live on the bottom of the river, relying on their flawless camouflage to protect them and to help them sneak up on their food, which is typically insects, crustaceans, and other small fish. Furthermore, they are active at low-light times of the day.

Camouflage is the only defense that a sculpin has. One thing that has a real impact on fishing sculpin patterns is that they have no swim bladder.

A swim bladder is an organ that many fish have that helps them stay buoyant or neutrally buoyant. Without this feature, sculpins only have the ability to swim short distances quickly, which causes them to move with a stop-and-go action. They can move incredibly quickly, but only for a short distance. Salmonids like steelhead and brown trout are shaped like a torpedo and built for speed, so once spotted by one of these agile predators, a sculpin is in trouble. It may take them a moment to catch up, but just about any predator fish has more stamina than a sculpin and will catch a fleeing fish. Adding to their appeal, they have no scales, which makes them a nice smooth meal, full of protein for a migratory fish. And they are a sizable meal, often 3 to 5 inches in length. All of these aspects make the sculpin a swimming filet mignon for predators.

There is one thing about bottom-dwelling baitfish that you should keep in the back of your mind when fishing them, and it is especially true about

Many sculpins have a reddish tinge to their fins. Adding a touch of red flash to your sculpin patterns makes them all the more deadly! My favorite type of flash for sculpin patterns is cranberry Holographic Flashabou, which is a little more subtle than some of the other forms of flash.

sculpins. While snorkeling or turning over rocks in my local rivers, I have noticed something that is consistently true about these fish. The size of the sculpin that you find under a rock is directly proportional to the size of the structure that it is living near. This means that if you are turning over large rocks, you will commonly find larger sculpins, and vice versa. This plays a direct role in selecting the size of your fly. For example, if you are fishing a deep hole that has large boulders in it, you would select a large sculpin pattern. Conversely, if you are fishing near submerged gravel or a field of

Left: That reddish flash, imitating the fins of a sculpin, accounted for this great fish right after Christmas. Often, I describe my color combinations as corresponding to holidays. Right around Halloween, black and orange (or copper) are deadly. As we head toward Christmas, the holiday colors of green and red are the way to go.

cranberry Flashabou will make your winter imitations more attractive. For my purposes, an olive sculpin imitation with a touch of this dark red flash is about perfect for migratory fish. Over the last several years, this pattern has accounted for many winter trout, steelhead, and lake-run browns. In cold weather, it may very well be my best fly. As winter nears its end, sculpins sometimes develop a blackish head. Large, darker sculpin patterns work great throughout the spring for this very reason. Dark flies have a great profile and are easy to see. Steelhead especially have an affinity for dark flies. (Many sage old anglers have a common saying with steelhead: "Give me any fly as long as it is black!") When dark sculpins are present, take advantage of it and fish a darker sculpin pattern.

You should always take into account your angle of presentation when imitating sculpins (and really all baitfish). Few fish in nature are uniform in color on the top and bottom. A sculpin, for example, is well camouflaged on top but is cream, yellow, or pinkish from below. So then, it makes sense that if you are presenting your sculpin deftly along the bottom, you would use mottled, earth-tone materials when you tie your fly. If, on the other hand, you are imitating baitfish from underneath, you have to take into account their belly color. Thus, you might be tying sculpins that are a lighter, creamier color if you are fishing them more closely to the surface.

It is no wonder that many of the most successful stripped streamers for any number of gamefish are lighter colors such as white and yellow. Stripped flies typically run only a couple of feet below the surface in moving water. If you look at some of the most successful streamers on the market, you will see that the designers of these flies appreciated that they were imitating the underside of the forage species. They are commonly much lighter-colored than deep imitations.

smaller rocks, you would choose a smaller sculpin pattern. In a very generic way, you can match the size of the hatch.

Sculpins range a lot in color. Most commonly, I find them olive, brown, or tan. They often have a reddish edge to their fins, so a little red or

Note the cream-colored underbelly of the sculpin. Most baitfish have a light-colored body. When imitating fish high in the water column, lean toward lighter colors of tan, yellow, cream, and pink. On a cloudy, gray day, the underside will look exactly like what you see when you turn a sculpin over. However, on a sunny day, the underside will appear pink or yellow.

When viewed from the bottom, a sculpin can have a tapered, tadpole-like appearance.

The rule of thumb is simple: When fishing slowly and deeply, match the colors from the top of the species you are imitating. If you are not sure what their exact color is, just look at the color of the bottom of the river and match this color. Remember, sculpins are masters of camouflage, so they will take the color of the river bottom.

In this scenario, fish are at eye level with your fly. Such flies are often weighted to keep the fly at the bottom of the water column. When fishing high and fast, lighter colors often work better. With migratory fish I find that I do better imitating either the top or bottom color of the baitfish, but not both.

Sculpins also have a very large, flat head, and this is a necessary part of any good sculpin pattern. For swinging flies deeply, soft materials such as Ice Dub, Senyo's Laser Dub, and Australian possum work great. Somehow, you need to get that water-resistant fly as deep as possible, so choose your head materials carefully. In rivers with slow flow, this is not an issue. However, in large, swift rivers, a fly with good sinking properties can make all the difference, though this is not always an issue when stripping flies.

If you want to strip a sculpin close to the surface, you have many options, but deer hair does a great job with this. Deer hair is hollow and does not sink well, and its natural buoyancy will give the fly a lot of action as you strip it. Always remember the stop-and-go nature of a sculpin's swimming habits and you will do fine. If you have to strip a fly consistently very deep, a sculpin is not your best choice. No matter how you build the fly, in order to give it the right profile, it will have to be bulky and water-resistant. This wide-bodied fly will take a lot more work to get to the bottom than a narrower fly. If you do design the fly to be accurate and sink, it will be very hard to cast. If the fly is wide, currents in the river may prevent it from sinking even if it is weighted. This is especially true when the water is high or swift.

While we are on this subject, let's talk about how the design of your fly affects the speed of how you present it. If you are fishing a fly that accurately and exactly mimics the food sources on the bottom of the river, you can fish it very slow. Regardless of the speed of the presentation, it looks just like the real thing, so a fish will pounce on it, even as it gets a very close, slow look at it.

Sculpins take the color of the bottom. On a tough day, match the hatch by matching the riverbed.

Left: Sometimes it is easy to compare your flies to an actual sculpin. This one was so confident in its camouflage that I was able to place several flies side by side with him. This really helped me understand why some patterns work (and why others do not).

Accurate imitations work very well when the water temperatures are cold, because you are striving to keep the fly as slow as possible in the cold water. The drawback to fishing an accurate imitation is that it will not draw the attention of an aggressive fish from a long distance as much as a gaudy fly will. There is a trick to fishing the winter months, which you can see in the *The Deep and Dirty Swing* section in chapter 4 of this book.

A lot of anglers have frittered away much of their lives fishing, so there is a large knowledge base out there and many experts on the internet. Nonetheless, there is always mystery to fishing. Sometimes we think we know why a fish is biting, but at other times there may be multiple reasons. As mentioned, my favorite color combination for sculpin patterns is olive and deep red. If you look carefully at the colors of a male steelhead, you will notice that he exhibits these same colors on his head and cheeks. Though I believe I am accurately imitating a sculpin, at the same time this color combination might be triggering an aggressive strike from a fish, as steelhead can be territorial and that color combination might represent the colors of another steelhead in the area. As a result, a steelhead might strike a sculpin out of predation, aggression, or both. Either way, the angler is the winner in this situation. Using a fly that can trigger a strike for more than one reason will always add to your success as an angler.

A lot of times, the resident fish in the river will let you know when you have found a good, accurate winter imitation. Many Great Lakes tributaries have resident trout as well as steelhead and migratory browns in them. When you think about it, the residents are a whole lot smarter than their migratory cousins. They live in the river system year-round and are keen to their environment. Consider this: In a large hole in such a river, there may be a dozen trout but only one or two migratory fish, yet you are more likely to catch the migratory fish

Note the wide, flat head of the sculpin. This is something that should be part of any good sculpin pattern. It is important to choose your fly-tying materials carefully when building the head of your flies. This wide head can make the fly buoyant, and depending on your presentation, this buoyancy might not be desirable. In high or fast water, I would look to imitate narrower baitfishes.

because the resident fish are more in tune with their environment. For this reason, they are more selective. When trying new fly patterns, especially during the cold-water periods, you will know you have found a winning pattern if the resident trout will take the fly. Rest assured that if the resident trout eat a fly that is in the size range appealing to migratory fish, the migratory fish will eat it too. Tying flies that will take more than one species is another way to make a challenging style of fishing more exciting.

In contrast, gaudy flies don't typically work as well fished slow, but they garner a lot of attention when ripping across the current. For this reason, in the fall, when fish numbers are low but water temperatures are warm, it is good to add some razzle-dazzle to your flies (Flashabou is a good source for this). Migratory fish will travel a long way to get a

fly that draws their attention if the conditions are right. They are easily distracted by shiny objects, and if they were a dog, they would be chasing a lot of squirrels. Resident fish will seldom pay any attention to such a bait, but migratory fish will crush them. In the fall, you may be fishing some pretty quick areas. The idea of swinging flies in the fall is to get a predator to move quickly toward a fly and overrun it. The hard pull that you get from a fall steelhead is a result of this behavior. Gaudy flies trigger this sprinting behavior.

A fall sculpin imitation might be shaped exactly like a winter fly, but its coloration will be geared toward drawing a strike rather than matching the hatch. A fall fly is often skewed toward being an attractor, whereas a winter pattern is more likely to be a natural. This is true of any food source you are imitating, not just sculpins. Fishing natural patterns in the cold periods and gaudy patterns in the warm periods is an underlying principle that you can take to the bank.

Sculpins, for the most part, can be found under rocks during the day and due to their vulnerabilities will come out only toward evening and into the night. This is an advantage when you are fishing for migratory fish. They are a great early-morning or late-afternoon bait. Often on a bright, sunny fall day, fishing is a struggle during the brightest parts of the day. I have had a lot of guide trips that were saved by a late-afternoon change to a sculpin pattern. The large profile of a sculpin pattern against a fading sky, at a time when predators know that sculpins are active, leads to a violent strike. I mentioned matching the color of your fly in relation to what the fish are seeing (either the top of the baitfish or the bottom); however, when fishing in the early morning or evening, this flies out the door. In low-light hours, lean toward a darker-colored fly. The visibility may seem tough to you and in these low-light hours, but when looking up from the bottom of the river, a fish can see the profile of a big, dark sculpin pattern easily. In the low-light hours, the bottom of the fly is not illuminated, so you don't have to worry about imitating the color of the belly of the baitfish. For this reason, black and dark olive are deadly colors in these early-morning or evening hours.

I have taken steelhead well before sunup and after dark on water-plowing sculpin imitations. Their ability to save the day when other imitations have failed make sculpins a favorite imitation. However, a distant invasive cousin, which looks similar to a sculpin, occupies a large place in the winter fly box. This space invader is the round goby.

Round gobies invaded the Great Lakes and have elbowed their way into the food chain, in some places making up a large part of it. To gain perspective about gobies, you really have to start with a discussion about another invasive species, the zebra mussel. While invasive species have an impact on every river attached to the Great Lakes

In the winter, use more natural-colored flies to wake up a sleeping giant. Steelhead, like the one pictured, start to act more like river trout if they have been in the river system for several months. That is why a natural pattern might fool them more easily than a flashy pattern.

This is a typical round goby, or as fish call them, "dinner." Most invasive species have a really bad side. However, in my local watersheds gobies provide a familiar food source to both migratory brown trout and steelhead. Expect to find them anywhere the bottom is lined with zebra mussels.

in one form or another, I will use my home river to illustrate the changes that these nonnative species have made.

When I first started fishing the Muskegon River in the early '90s, it was a famous caddis-fishing river for the resident trout. It was an easy river to fish and guide, with constant cinnamon and green caddis hatches. When trout fishing, I could head to the river with flies imitating the life cycle of these caddis, and I would be all set. It was an easy, fun time to fish this great river. These types of caddis were filter feeders, gleaning small bits of food from the water as it flowed past.

Then suddenly, almost overnight, the river changed. This change made guiding a lot more complicated. An invasive species, the zebra mussel, had made its way into the river system. These filter-feeding mussels feed on the same things that the caddis do, and are better at it. Furthermore, they make the water extremely clear. Within a

year the caddis hatches were annihilated, and the water column, from top to bottom, was gin clear. A decade passed, and the water began to have a slight stain and the caddis hatches returned to a limited degree. It seemed as though the zebra mussel population had stabilized. "What had changed?" we wondered.

Then one summer day, I had a revelation. I was snorkeling the river, trying to take some pictures of sculpins. I took images of quite a few fish that I thought were sculpins. Underwater photography in current is challenging—things are often moving so quickly that I don't know exactly what I have captured on film until I get home and look at my laptop screen. In this case, when I got home and looked at the images, I was surprised to see that these were not images of sculpins at all, but were invasive round gobies. To this point, I had never heard of anyone mentioning gobies in the Muskegon.

Round gobies were first found in the Great Lakes in 1990. They spread rapidly through the region over the course of the next decade and are almost everywhere now. They are native to Asia, found originally in the Black and Caspian Seas. We presume they came here in the ballast of a ship that dumped its bilgewater into the Great Lakes. This is a common source of invasive fish in this region, and a difficult one to prevent. For the past few decades, fishermen in the Great Lakes have been at the mercy of wave after wave of invasive species. Each time a new one is found, we are faced with gloom-and-doom predictions about our fisheries. Such was the case with gobies.

As it turns out, gobies eat immature zebra mussels, and I think that they have helped stabilize the zebra mussel population. In one recent study, it was found that a goby can eat up to 72 zebra mussels in one day. Up to 60 percent of their diet may just be mussels. In a nutshell, we have gotten to the point where one invasive species helps to balance out another, and I guess this is OK. Gobies definitely seem like the lesser of the two evils.

It is, however, scary to think how far we might progress in replacing our native food chain with an exotic one.

As you might guess, gobies displace native baitfish, and some of the fish-eating birds have trouble with them (they can transmit toxins from the mussels to birds and this can kill them). In some rivers, this might mean that you end up with more gobies and less sculpins and darters. Gobies simply outbreed their competition. Many native baitfish spawn only for a short period, but each female goby can spawn once every 20 days for six months on end! On the bright side, they eat zebra mussels and gamefish love to eat gobies. It is for this reason that we must talk about gobies in the same vein as we discuss sculpins.

If you compare a goby and a sculpin side by side, they look a bit alike. There are some differences, however. Sculpins are always mottled, whereas gobies can be a solid tan. When spawning, male gobies are an inky, jet black. This coloration occurs throughout the late winter well into the summer.

A female merganser dines on a large goby. Until the river comes alive in the spring, gobies are a primary food source for a lot of birds and fish. Note the inky black color of this one. I don't know of any other fish that is this dark in color.

Gobies can tolerate poor water quality better than some other baitfish, and so it stands to reason that if you are fishing a river that isn't a sparkling, crystal-clear freestone stream, you will still have gobies. If zebra mussels are present, you will definitely have them. Many of our rivers that harbor migratory fish fall into this category. They are not true trout streams, and are only favorable for migratory fish because of the colder water in the fall and winter. If you have been fishing a river for many years and never had success with sculpin patterns in the past, you may want to give generic sculpin and goby patterns a chance, as gobies are a recent development.

Gobies tend to sit on rocks, whereas sculpins typically are under or around them. They also have a fused pelvic fin. Basically, whereas most fish have two small fins underneath their gills, a round goby will have just one disc-like fin. Think of this fin as a suction cup. I have observed gobies moving straight up the side of a rock, and they can do

Left: Juvenile gobies are extremely common in any river with zebra mussels. The high reproduction rate of gobies makes them always present in many waterways. Most people think of them as a big baitfish, but don't overlook imitating the smaller ones.

things that would make Spider-Man jealous with this nifty fin. If they come to an obstacle in the river, they simply putter up the side of it.

Gobies seem to be in any type of habitat, whereas sculpins prefer rocks and gravel. They populate an area by sheer reproduction, so they don't need to be as well camouflaged. Whereas sculpins sit under rocks and use them to survive and populate an area, gobies can often be seen at all times of the day on top of rocks or darting around the edges of the river. Gobies use their vision to avoid predators, whereas sculpins use camouflage. The visibility of this baitfish makes them appealing to all types of gamefish at all times of the year.

Though their behavior is a bit different, gobies bear some important similarities to sculpins, which can make the presentation very similar. Much like sculpins, gobies lack a swim bladder. This means that they can only move quickly in short bursts, making them a prime target. They also have a large rounded head, and though not as flat as a sculpin's, the profile is similar when viewed from below. Though not exactly the same, a good sculpin imitation may be "close enough" to a goby imitation, and you may have gobies covered if you have sculpins in your box. For all practical purposes, the presentation of sculpins and gobies is the same.

As a baitfish, gobies are very much a preferred food of many fish. In the Great Lakes, only Pacific salmon have not adapted to feed on them. There is a long list of gamefish that will prey upon them, however, which includes steelhead, walleye, smallmouth bass, northern pike, and brown trout. In the famed Manistee River, the brown trout will often eat so many gobies that they regurgitate them when caught. They have become superabundant, and if you fish a large waterway in the Midwest, you are missing out if you don't have a good goby imitation in your fly box. Like it or not, gobies have become a ubiquitous baitfish for all species.

In a strange way, we might owe gobies another thank-you. In addition to eating zebra mussels, gobies are filling a part of the food chain that is being vacated in the Great Lakes. The populations of some of the really prized baitfish in the Great Lakes—the alewives, smelt, and other long, shiny baitfish—have been fluctuating alarmingly in recent years. As a guide, this is an uneasy time, as apocalypse for our fisheries has been foretold many times. To this point it has been false prophesy, in part because of the gobies. Lake-run browns, lake trout, and steelhead have been able to take advantage of the gobies to fill a part of their diet that was vacated by these other baitfish. Gobies make up a part of the food chain and should be part of your fly box.

As previously noted, goby fly patterns can be used interchangeably with sculpin patterns. If you want to be goby specific, gobies tend to work best in larger sizes and in solid colors. Gray, tan, or gray-olive Craft Fur are great materials for imitating gobies. Gobies have a sheen to them, and Craft Fur is the perfect answer to this. I go through yards of gray-olive and tan Craft Fur throughout the course of a single year. Migratory fish goby patterns that I use in the winter can be recycled in the summer months, as the smallmouth bass love these Craft Fur flies.

Like sculpins, gobies have large heads and should be tied with a big head. Another feature that gobies have is large, frog-like, bulbous eyes. Bead-chain eyes, whether plastic or metal, will improve your success with these patterns. It might be helpful to think of gobies as underwater frogs. Their head looks like a frog's, and using short bursts of speed, they "hop" from rock to rock along the river bottom.

Gobies are always around, and their imitations can be used at any time of the year. For my purposes, they are at their best during the winter months. As water temperatures rise, rivers erupt with biological activity. At this point migratory fish

A chrome steelhead thrashes to throw a goby pattern. These flies are tied black with big eyes and represent a huge protein-rich meal. Often I will include black Flashabou in the patterns, as it is one thing that matches the gobies' sheen well.

This fish was caught in the dead of winter on a darter pattern highlighted with blue. Not only does blue work well in naturals, but it is also the most deadly color in attractor flies during winter.

have a lot of choices for food sources, and gobies become a minor one for a while. Gobies have become a part of our local ecosystem and provide food for many species, from reptiles to birds to, of course, just about every type of predator fish. I can tell that gobies are the main food source in the late winter months. Fish will spit them up, and birds and mammals like otters and mink are commonly seen eating them.

If you are looking for water where goby patterns are most effective, just look at the bottom of the river. If you have zebra mussels in an area, you will have a high density of gobies too. Thus, the highest concentrations of gobies are often below dams. Dams provide a lot of nutrients, so in these places the concentrations of zebra mussels can be very high. In these areas all the predator fish will be keyed on gobies. Another place where goby imitations take primary importance is near the mouths of our rivers. Any rocks, pilings, or bridges will have high concentrations of these fish, and

these places are a safe bet for their imitations. As you guessed, these are also areas with high concentrations of mussels.

In late winter, adult male gobies turn inky black in color, and you may find that whether you strip or swing your flies, jet black patterns can be deadly at this time. I know of no other forage species that turns this pure black color. Gobies can spawn multiple times throughout the spring and summer, so a black goby pattern will work for a good part of the year. Other baitfish such as sculpins are also black at this time, so late winter and spring are a great time to fish with a dark pattern. It is usually around late February that I see both dark sculpins and black gobies, and these darker color forms are around until mid-spring. As with the sculpins, if you are fishing from February to June, a black pattern should have a place in your box.

As mentioned, sculpins and gobies are around all of the time. As a busy fishing guide, I have tried to make sculpin and goby patterns that will catch

In the dead of winter, many of the darters will take on a bluish-green color. This can be imitated with peacock and olive color combinations. I buy huge bags of olive and peacock Ice Dub just to tie mass quantities of winter baitfish.

Darters are a diverse group of minnows, and I enjoy photographing them as much as I enjoy catching fish with darter patterns (well, OK, that may be a stretch). This image is of the largest darter species, the log perch, which is common in big, clean rivers. If you know they are present, tie a tan sculpin pattern tied with a narrower head or a cone head and you have it covered.

fish in all seasons. It is nice to have a good pattern in the box that will catch steelhead all winter and then turn around and catch trout and smallmouth bass as the year goes on. Even when I am fishing other types of imitations, sculpins and gobies are in the rotation, and I will fall back on them when all else fails. When I am investing time at the fly-tying bench, these are things that are always in the back of my mind.

In the cold of winter, another great baitfish to consider is the darter. I mentioned juvenile Johnny darters when we discussed fall. Darters are similar to sculpins and gobies in behavior, but have a narrower profile. As their name suggests, most species move very quickly, or "dart," along the river bottom. As they live in areas with really good substrate, such as rock and gravel, they are located in the same areas as steelhead and trout.

Darters come in a lot of varieties and are members of the perch family. They are a native baitfish. The largest species of darters, called the log perch, is found in many of our Great Lakes streams and can reach up to 7 inches in length. Other types of darters seldom get larger than an inch. For our purposes, we are talking about medium-sized species that live along the bottom. These fish are usually 1 to 3 inches, which is a common size for the majority of darter species. It is also an easy size range to imitate and cast. In many river systems, darters make up a large percentage of the actual baitfish population and are a familiar fish to any predator in the river.

The real advantage to fishing with a darter is that they have a nice, narrow profile. In the winter, you are trying to get your fly to the bottom and keep it there. For this reason, a weighted darter

pattern is tough to beat. The narrow profile max-imizes the ability of the fly to sink, and a narrow fly simply cuts through the water column better than a bulky fly. Darters by nature are a lot like stick fish on the bottom: They don't move much and use camouflage to their advantage. Thus, you don't need to add a lot of action to these patterns. They are at their best as a swung-fly pattern and work especially well with the deep and dirty swing discussed later in the techniques chapter.

In the winter months, a darter's behavior is pretty similar to a sculpin's or a goby's behavior,

Left: Though brilliantly colored in the spring, darters have more subdued colors in the winter. Many take on a cooler-colored appearance. Often they appear a peacock blue, which is true of a lot of bottom-dwelling minnows in the winter. Steelhead react well to blue-colored streamers in the winter!

As I am a fishing guide, there is a practical advantage to darter patterns. Due to their size and profile, they are generally easier to cast than an accurate sculpin/goby imitation. If a client is not a great caster, a darter makes the experience more pleasant for them and will catch equivalent numbers of fish.

Darters are a bit more attractive to smaller resident trout. When I want to have a chance at a migratory fish but also want to add resident trout as a bi-catch, I reach for a darter more often than not. Darters fall into a perfect size range. They are just big enough to catch a steelhead or lake-run brown, but small enough to catch everything else as well.

I fish two distinctly different types of water in the winter. One is the sandy lower reaches of the river system, and the other is the rocky upper parts. Though some darters are present in the sandy stretches, I find bigger flies work better in these places. Thus, I use darters in the rocky and gravelly stretches. This is where winter steelhead and migratory fish have settled in and are behaving more like stream trout. The species of darter that we are concerned with needs rocks and gravel to survive. The one I commonly imitate is the rainbow darter, which in the winter tends to be an olive or brown color, often with a hint of blue.

Darters are effective late into winter and well into the spring. Darter patterns have one further advantage: Their small size puts them in the same size category as some of the spring baitfish, such as salmon fry. This similarity in size turns a good darter pattern into a generic fry pattern. One of the flies that we use a lot in the springtime is the Inside Bender. This fly works well throughout the winter and into the spring. A Bender is a simple fly that is barred olive in color. In the water, it looks enough like a salmon fry that it could be taken as a fry as well as a darter. Salmon fry and darters behave radically differently, but they do have

and they are found in the same habitat as these other baits, moving around the bottom of the river near shoals of rocks. This is why I believe that a fish that would take a sculpin would be just as prone to take a darter imitation.

This image clearly shows the narrow profile of a darter. A lot of times, you can tie the same generic pattern interchangeably to imitate sculpins and darters. The darter would be tied narrow, and the sculpin would be tied wide. The advantage of darter patterns is that because you are tying a narrow fly, the pattern will sink better than a comparable sculpin pattern. With a wide water-moving head, a sculpin pattern will have more natural action, however.

Did you know that big predator fish will feed on a freshwater cod in some of the really clear rivers with high water quality? This eel-like fish is called a burbot, and I often find it while turning over rocks looking for sculpins.

some physical similarities. When you have one fly that can effectively cover more than one baitfish species, it can only be a good thing. If you fish a lot, it is nice to have a pattern that you can mass-produce on a day that you aren't fishing that you know will work for a long season.

Darters are one of the most neglected food sources in our rivers as far as fishing goes. They are just as appealing to fish as sculpins but get no press. They are extremely abundant and available everywhere. If you fish in the cold times of the year, you should consider a darter pattern in your box. Soon the rivers warm, and they become one of many food sources in the fly box.

SPRING

Whereas fall and winter have declining or steady biological activity, late winter strides in the opposite direction. In the warmer months, submerged vegetation provides cover for small baitfish and other organisms in a lot of rivers, but as those weeds recede in the fall, the baitfish are exposed and their numbers decline or remain steady in the winter. Insect activity is also steady in the winter, and there is little hatching to excite the gamefish in our rivers.

As air temperatures rise, melting snow initially cools the water. Often the first thaw around a river feels great to people outside fishing, but it actually puts the river into a deep freeze. Many rivers have a United States Geological Survey (USGS) gauge that transmits real-time data to USGS offices, which is then posted on their website. This site (https://waterdata.usgs.gov/nwis/rt) is an extremely valuable source of information. Watching the data from a particular stream, it is apparent when you have a snowmelt day and the temperature on the graph plummets. If this happens, revert to winter fishing tactics. If you have a really big melt event, you may end up with cold, high, dirty water. This is a really bad combination for fishing, and it may have some impact on whether you fish and where you fish.

Eventually, the slowly lengthening days and reduced snowmelt allow our rivers to warm. This can happen quickly in shallow rivers or in rivers with a dark bottom. Darker riverbeds absorb more light and warm up more quickly, which may very

well attract fish on a cold winter's day. On rivers that have hydroelectric dams, the water will only warm after the ice has melted on the lake behind the dam. When this happens, a chain reaction starts in the river, as biological activity explodes.

At first, as the water temperatures reach the mid-30s, early black and brown stoneflies migrate toward the edges of the river. These are common insects, found on many rivers throughout the United States. It is during this time period that trout and steelhead are gorging, and a good tactic is to use a peacock-colored Woolly Bugger for any number of presentations (if you add a little copper flash to it, it will be even better). Early stoneflies are extremely vulnerable food sources. If you have ever seen these insects trying to hatch, you can see why the fish get so excited about them. Stoneflies need to crawl to dry ground to split their skin and hatch. In the cold waters of late winter, this is an awkward process for the insects as they break free from the bottom and wiggle throughout the water column. They are easy to see and have no defense from predation. This initial eruption of life in the river makes the fishing frenzied on the good days but productive even on days where the fishing wouldn't normally be good.

A benefit of this insect activity is that it draws more predatory fish out of the dark winter depths into water 3 to 6 feet deep. This is the prime depth range for any streamer fishing tactic. If you fish through the winter months, toward the end of winter it often seems as though the numbers of fish aren't all that good. Suddenly, the water warms a little, and there are a lot more fish around. Many of our big winter fish have moved into very deep water and become stale over time. These are fish that have seen a variety of baits, and have sulked over the winter months. Perhaps they have been sitting in ultra-deep water or have been jammed into the heaviest structure. Regardless, as spring gets closer, the eruption of food and the desire to eventually spawn draws the fish out of their lairs. As they move out of this water, they are now in the perfect depth for streamer presentations. The stoneflies create a cascade of biological activity that works its way to the top of the food chain. This hatch will help your streamer fishing, even though you are not imitating a stonefly.

When stoneflies wiggle to the shore to hatch, they set off a nuclear reaction of activity in the river. As part of this food web, the fish become aggressive as the river erupts with life. As the stoneflies move toward shore, they are preyed upon by juvenile salmon and other minnows. In turn, the steelhead and brown trout feed on the minnows and the stoneflies.

Not every predatory fish will feed on stoneflies, or stoneflies alone. Sudden insect activity has an amazing effect on the food chain. As stoneflies start to move, minnows are drawn out of the depths to feed on them. This also adds to the frenzied activity and gives you something else to imitate. These minnows may be chubs or shiners, and they contribute to the frenzy.

Early spring is an exciting time of the year. At the same time that increased insect activity is happening in the late winter, another food source is waiting in the wings. Many of our rivers attached to the Great Lakes contain salmon fry. As water temperatures head toward the upper 30s, these fry begin to pop out of the gravel. This can happen as early as January or February in a warm year. In a cold year, this might not occur until April. (In my neck of the woods, I get nervous if I haven't seen fry by April, as our king salmon population

is mostly dependent on wild fish—if they are born too late, they might not make it to the lake before the water gets warm.) Salmon fry quickly grow to an inch in length, and they stay in that size category for a while, providing the perfect bite-size meal for a roving predator.

Often the steelhead and trout become so keyed on the size of this food source that it makes a profound impact on the streamers that you use with any method. This is a lesson that is sometimes learned the hard way. If you use your typical steelhead-sized streamer in March and April, you will get the occasional tug on those 2- to 4-inch-long patterns. However, if you drop that pattern to 1 to 1½ inches in length, suddenly you may get a lot more bites. This is true whether you are using an accurate fry imitation or the most garish fly in your box. There is a simple way to tell how big to make your streamer fly in the spring in rivers with salmon fry. Pull to a quiet spot on the side of the river, and look along the edges. Salmon fry don't fight the current well and will accumulate in these areas. Compare the size of the fry to the flies in your box. If you match the size of the fry, bingo! You are in business.

One of my favorite attractor flies for steelhead is a black and copper leech pattern we call the Halloween Leech. In the fall, this pattern is at its best when tied 2 to 4 inches in length. In the spring, if I fish the same pattern in that size, I will catch the odd fish. However, if I drop that attractor pattern to the size of the salmon fry, suddenly it becomes a deadly weapon at that time of the year.

In spring, it is common to have high water and a lot of runoff. In these conditions the natural reaction is to use the largest, ugliest, sparkliest fly to try to get a fish. If fry are present, fight that impulse and carry an array of smaller patterns as well. Even in the high-water conditions, predator fish will find your fly. This is especially true if the water is high and clear.

High water has another impact on your fishing in the spring. By and large, salmon fry don't use structure very well. As a result, when water levels rise, they are pushed to the edges of the river. If you are stripping flies, this can lead to some bonanza-like fishing along the edges of the river. Flies tied with a flank of mallard wing with some blue incorporated into them can be deadly in this scenario.

Spring fry patterns can be very specific and natural. There is a general rule of thumb for fishing fly patterns that are less than 1½ inches in length: The more natural the small fly pattern that you present, the slower and deeper your presentation must

Salmon fry feed on dead salmon carcasses and just about anything else as they try to survive the early months of their life. Though not native to our fisheries, salmon contribute a lot to Midwest fisheries while both living and dead. They also take fishing pressure off the steelhead and brown trout, and that can be a really good thing.

The Queen of the Waters, an age-old fly pattern, is still a great fry imitation. With a little help from modern materials of flash and sparkle, this fly is a killer pattern. A lot of old patterns can be adapted very well to fishing for steelhead. They are usually very easy to cast, which is a great advantage.

When you see a steelhead or salmon fry on the bottom on a sunny day, it is easy to understand why an orange wet fly is so effective. Think of it as the equivalent of imitating a sunny-side up egg.

King salmon fry have a higher survival rate than many other salmonids. Many Midwest rivers get to be very warm in the summer. Since kings leave the river by June, they avoid catastrophic temps. For this reason, they are often found throughout a river system as they work their way out in the spring. This one was in the lower sandy reaches of the river.

be. For example, if I am using a bright Halloween Leech that is covered with flash and is 1½ inches in length, I can still present it quickly. However, if I am using a small natural fry pattern, it has to move much more slowly and naturally around the bottom. The sparkly and small patterns are great for covering water; however, the natural patterns can catch large numbers of fish, as the concentrations of fish are high. A small natural pattern will require more precision in presentation.

There is a segment of anglers who love to use classic wet flies to catch steelhead and trout. Some of these classic wets imitate a steelhead or salmon fry very well. I like to use these patterns as well, and they are often a secret weapon in the spring. One of the very best of these patterns is the Queen of the Waters, which is orange with a duck wing feather over the back. Other classic patterns, such as the Rusty Rat, Lady Caroline, and Knudson Spider, are local favorites as well. In their classic form,

these flies work well. One of their components, the duck wing feather, has natural markings that imitate the markings of the fry very well. If you are willing to break from tradition just a little, adding modern synthetic materials, such as Ice Dub or Krystal Flash, to these flies will add to their effect.

As salmon fry grow, they form large clouds along the edges of the rivers. They become less concerned about safety and can be found in the middle or upper parts of the water column. Throughout much of their lives, salmon are an alpha predator, but when they are young, they are little more than dumb food that everything gorges on. In larger sizes, they are a prime food source for trout and drop-back steelhead. In one study on the Muskegon River, salmon fry comprised 40 percent of the food of resident brown trout. If resident trout prey heavily on salmon, you can bet that the larger predators make them a large part of their diet as well. Salmon fry are so universal that they can be fished successfully on the swing, on the strip, and using a variety of different nymphing techniques.

Heading into spring, keep an eye on the edges of the river for other things that might be happening. Depending on the river, there may be eruptions of other forms of aquatic life. An example of this is crane fly larvae. Often in the spring we have a day or two where crane fly larvae can be heavy. These are large and clumsy wormlike insects that wiggle in the current. I photograph a lot of underwater food sources; crane flies are a boring subject, as they are just blobs of wiggling protein. They range from olive to brown in color. Slowly swinging olive, chocolate, or black Woolly Buggers can take steelhead and trout when this is happening.

There is a terrestrial food source that makes an appearance in the spring that can be imitated with streamer patterns. During high-water conditions, earthworms are frequently washed into the river. In this off-color water, I have had great success with peach- and pink-colored leech patterns. Steelhead seem to prefer them in certain conditions. These flies work very well but must be swung close to the bottom. This is a great challenge in high water, as earthworm patterns are bulky. There are times when this is the only food source the fish will take. Often peach combined with a dirty yellow is a good combination for success.

If you don't believe steelhead will key in on earthworms, talk to some of the more experienced float-fishing guides. Under floats, many of them suspend pink plastic worm baits through the winter and early spring, and do so with great success. It may seem weird but, yes, steelhead like worms!

Soon the steelhead begin to spawn, as water temperatures reach the 40s. By this point, migratory brown trout have left the river, and the fishing is for steelhead. It is during this time period that the absolute maximum number of steelhead is present. It is conventional wisdom that 20 to 40 percent of our overall steelhead arrive in the fall and end up wintering in the river system. In the spring the remaining 60 to 80 percent of the fish arrive, and the rivers are full of fish. During the peak of spawning season, when the maximum amount of steelhead is in the river, you would think that the streamer fishing would be epic. This is not the case in many rivers, however: Often there is a lull in their desire to chase a fly, as they are concentrated on other things. Spawning activity also increases angling pressure and makes it difficult to swing flies, with many boats or wading anglers concentrated in the areas that hold fish. As spawning activity peaks and then starts to decline, another feeding pattern emerges as the fish drop back to their inland sea.

LATE SPRING

As steelhead drop back to the lake, their feeding pattern changes. Drop-back fish are ravenously hungry and take on calories as quickly as possible. Spawning is no longer a distraction, and the desire to survive by putting on calories takes over. This means that they will always be found around the most food, and they will be less selective than your typical migratory fish. This is true not only with steelhead but with just about every other predatory fish. When lake-run browns complete spawning in the fall, they go on a similar meat-eating frenzy, as do walleye and bass in the spring.

In my home river, the Muskegon, there are some really interesting changes in steelhead behavior as they drop back to the lake. You will typically find drop-back steelhead in one of two types of water at this time. They will typically be in proximity to a large concentration of eggs or in deep water. Now, if they are around eggs, they do not necessarily need to be steelhead eggs. Steelhead love sucker eggs as well, and a high concentration of suckers will have steelhead and predatory browns in the vicinity.

Suckers don't necessarily need the same types of gravel that steelhead and salmon do, so you may find great fishing in reaches of the river that you wouldn't think hold a concentration of fish. There are many varieties of suckers, and predators have a distinct preference for various species of sucker eggs. Most fish, when they spawn, like gravel that is easy for them to move around. For example, a king salmon is a powerful fish and can move around large gravel and small rocks. On the other end of the spectrum, suckers have weaker bodies and need fine gravel to spawn on, such as pea gravel. These smaller forms of gravel are often found in parts of the river that other fish do not spawn in, such as the lower parts. As they are scattered along a river system, they are the perfect food source for fish returning to the lake. For the streamer fisherman, catching migratory fish along these sucker beds can be very exciting. Sucker eggs must taste very good, as fish will jockey among themselves for access to them. This makes these fish very aggressive and willing to pummel a well-presented fly. In these same gravel areas, many salmon fry are often present, so this would make a good starting point for choosing an imitation.

The really interesting thing about these drop-back fish is that the females are by far the most common takers in the upstream reaches of a stream. Another interesting aspect of drop-back fish is that they are much less territorial than your typical migratory fish. Often they will school together as they drop back, and if you find one such school, you can have some fantastic fishing. If you find a single drop-back, it is best to work the runs in proximity to that one, as you may find a lot of fish. You may also want to step slowly through such a spot and come back through with a different fly pattern. If you get a pull from a drop-back fish, it is a great idea to make a point of returning to that area later in the day. There is a good chance this fish will take the fly again. Drop-back fish love to eat.

In rivers with little food, migratory fish will head back out to the lake pretty quickly after spawning. Lake-run fish are a big fish with high caloric needs; they will head to the best food source, be it in the river or in the lake. The spawning process combined with the strain of migrating makes for some hungry fish. Thus, if enough food is present

Some drop-backs come in and spawn quickly, maintaining their chrome appearance as they head home. I was fishing for stream trout when this fish abused me on a 6-weight. This is a pretty common occurrence during the late spring in many streams. Many of our large trout streams are ideal for swinging flies for trout, which is similar in style to how we target steels. It is no surprise that steelhead encounters are common.

When you fish around shiners, you will find that some species will move quickly near the surface, while larger species will gravitate toward the bottom. In this image, smaller rosyface shiners dance quickly above a school of common shiners. This has important implications for how you would imitate these fish: The surface shiners would be imitated with colors imitating their belly, but the common shiners, at eye level with the predators, would be mimicked from the side.

and water levels are stable, they will meander downriver much more slowly. In my home area, it is common to find spring drop-back brown trout into February and March and steelhead all they way into early June.

As the annual steelhead run concludes, steelhead go through the process of becoming a lake fish versus a river fish. If the fish has been in the river for a long time, it will have darker coloring. However, these colors start to fade and the fish will become an emerald color as they "resmolt" or "rechrome" as they approach the lake. As this occurs, they start to look for large food sources once again. In May these include sculpins, gobies, and spawning baitfish such as brightly colored darters and shiners. Drop-back fish become the dumbest of trout, and if you target them, feel free to use liberal amounts of flash, as these fish will

travel a long way to attack a large shiny object. If the water rises into the 50s in the spring, you do not have to worry about getting your fly deep anymore. Drop-back fish will move an extremely long way to get a big meal.

As a side note, no matter what kind of gamefish you are targeting, typically they will feed a lot right after spawning. This is true of all the coldwater species such as steelhead and trout, but also true of walleyes, pike, etc. Sometimes in mid-April it is difficult to keep the walleye off the line, as they are hungry after concluding their spawning run. Their bite is a pecking bite, and the line slowly gets heavy when they are connected. The ensuing fight of a spawned-out walleye resembles reeling in a leather shoe.

A really good formula for success with the remaining steelhead and trout in late spring is to

Common shiners take on a copper color when spawning. When this occurs in the spring, be prepared for great fishing with copper-colored streamers. These fish take trout flies and are often mistaken for chubs by local anglers. As their name suggests, common shiners are abundant throughout the Midwest. It is worth your time to learn about this fish.

look at the spawning baitfish and try to pick their primary color. As you tie your flies, tie them the size of the baitfish that are present but amplify that color.

A good example of this is the common shiners that are in most Midwest rivers. In May the adult shiners are 4 to 5 inches long, with rosy copper sides. Common shiners are exactly what you would think—they are, well, common. They are found in a majority of streams that have migratory fish. Trout anglers often catch these fish and mistake them for chubs. They are abundant, vulnerable food sources

Left: Even as the migratory fish withdraw from the river, spawning baitfish are very important all through the summer. These rosyface shiners are a prime baitfish for resident trout and bass in June and early July.

that are readily preyed upon by predatory gamefish. As they spawn, they are oblivious to anything around them. I have come to pods of these fish with my underwater camera and have been able to stand within inches of a large spawning mass of bait. These spawning baitfish are a dream come true

for a drop-back fish. If you were to imitate this fish for steelhead, you would tie it 4 to 5 inches long, but you would amplify the copper color. For me, this means a lot of copper- and pink-colored flash. This is one of the few times that I use a ton of flash to accurately imitate something in nature. However, if you want to make a more subtle pattern, cinnamon Craft Fur also matches their color well.

Drop-back fish take a stripped fly really well, and these steelhead are a common bi-catch when fishing for resident trout in the spring. One of the flies that will be covered in the fly patterns chapter of this book is called the Queen of the Muddy Waters. This fly carries the rosy copper color that is associated with these spawning shiners. Copper is always a great color to use to add attraction as flash to your baitfish flies. In the spring the attraction to copper stripped flies is amplified by the presence of these fish.

Shiner species as a family are colorful in the spring, and you can do well to pay attention to whatever varieties are in your river system. Another one that I encounter a lot is the rosyface shiner. These baitfish have a red head and a bright silver body. A red and white streamer can work very well going into spring.

Though not as prevalent in the western Great Lakes, emerald shiners are a common baitfish in Lake Erie and its tributaries year-round, so a good emerald shiner imitation can be deadly! Understanding the local shiner populations is always an asset when fishing this region.

Yet another example of spawning baitfish is a very common, brilliantly colored baitfish called the rainbow darter. We mentioned these earlier in the winter section. In the spring the male rainbow darters change from a dull olive color to a brilliant orange, red, and green. They spawn in areas that the steelhead have also spawned in, making them an easy target for fish feeding around the gravel, especially the drop-back steelhead. They also like to spawn in pea gravel areas, so they are

One of the most beautiful things in nature that most people with never notice, this rainbow darter is a snack for trout and steelhead. They are superabundant in many rivers and live in fine gravel or smaller rocks. Other darter species can also be brilliantly colored.

Regardless of when you fish darter patterns, as you tie flies you can think of them as shaped like sculpins, except with a narrower, more conical head. Their fins and texture are similar to a sculpin's.

While male darters of several species take on a brilliant color pattern during the spring spawning periods, the females have a muted color scheme. They are the tan, larger darters in these images.

a great baitfish along any sucker spawning areas. They are one of the most spectacularly colored fish, with their red and green stripes. The colorful males are territorial of their spawning area, which makes them vulnerable to predators. Often in the spring steelhead, trout, and smallmouth bass can be found regurgitating rainbow darters, and they are usually the colorful males. Rainbow darters can be stripped but also work well on a swinging, twitching retrieve. This is one of the last true baitfish patterns that I use as the steelhead retreat to the lake.

Though not technically a baitfish, crayfish should be mentioned when discussing spring fly options for steelhead or any migratory trout. One of the most common forms of crayfish in Midwest rivers is the rusty crayfish. Crayfish are native to the region; however, the rusty crayfish is a prolific invasive species that has annihilated the native species in many systems. Contrary to popular belief, not all crayfish dig burrows in the fall and winter, and they can be found under rocks at any time. I have been really surprised in the middle of winter to find numerous crayfish under the rocks. In mid-April the crayfish become very active, and large predators will feed heavily on them. I have a friend who occasionally will keep big trout, and he tells me that he will often find crayfish in the bellies of big trout species in this time period. Sculpin imitations with split tails can generically imitate crayfish, but they should always be fished in the bottom of the water column.

Crayfish can be imitated in a lot of ways. They are an invertebrate, and for that reason they need

Though we most commonly imitate them in the spring, crayfish are always present. A misconception is that they are not around in the winter, but the invasive rusty crayfish remain present under rocks. I took this one's picture when the water temp was 32 degrees.

Given the choice between a large, heavily armored crayfish and a smaller one, most fish will refuse a large one and take the lesser bait. This smallmouth bass refused this large crayfish only to binge feed on smaller ones. This same principle applies even more strongly to steelhead and brown trout. Unlike the smallmouth, they are not equipped to do battle with heavily armored crustaceans.

This picture shows a sculpin and a crayfish side by side. You can see the similarity in their earth-tone color. A good generic imitation can cover many different earth-tone species. These colors include olive, tan, and brown. There is never a day throughout the entire year that I don't have these colors in my box.

to shed their skin in order to grow. Predatory fish know this and will key in on crayfish that are shedding their skin. When this is happening, lean toward crayfish patterns that look soft, utilizing such materials as grizzly marabou, Craft Fur, etc.

Though they are abundant at a different time of the year than sculpins and gobies, crayfish fall into a more broad category of baits we call the "earth tones." Many of the creatures that live at the bottom of the river are olive, brown, or tan. A good generic fly can imitate a sculpin, goby, or crayfish at the same time. One example is the Emulator pattern found in the fly patterns chapter of this book. I tie it to imitate sculpins, but I have no doubt fish will eat it as a crayfish imitation as well. Bob Braendle, a great local angler, once said, "You can catch any big fish with olive or tan." I believe him!

Sucker and steelhead fry are often overlooked but deadly baits. The sequence for fry in many rivers is first salmon fry, then steelhead fry, and then toward the end of spring, sucker fry. If your river has self-sustaining fish of any variety, it will have fry at some point.

As suckers mature, most species take on a mottled appearance. These mottled suckers are another species you probably imitate when you fish basic sculpin patterns. You see, a good sculpin pattern can imitate sculpins, gobies, crayfish, suckers, and many other earth-tone fish foods.

Another great earth-tone baitfish that is over-looked and constantly available in the spring is juvenile suckers. Hog suckers and many other types of juvenile suckers are constantly present and look similar enough to sculpins while on the bottom of the river. Though we are often imitating a sculpin, darter, or goby, it may be that a fish is eating your pattern thinking it is a sucker. Again,

any time you can imitate more than one food source with your fly, it can only be a win.

As migratory fish leave the rivers, other fry have now hatched, among them steelhead fry and sucker fry. These baitfish are tiny in the spring but can be found in huge numbers, which makes them another prime food source. By this time, lake-run browns have long since left our rivers. However,

At the same time that steelhead fry and sucker fry are in our rivers, many of the rocky streambeds also have mayfly nymphs that dart around the current as well, such as this *Isonychia* nymph. Often a good imitation will not only cover minnows but generically imitate these swimming nymphs in the spring.

Notice how this *Isonychia* nymph is shaped just like a minnow. They also swim just like a minnow.

While descending a river post-spawn, migratory predators may encounter a wide array of baitfish. In West Michigan, spotfin and spottail shiners are always on the menu.

The majority of the steelhead I catch are on one type of baitfishy pattern or another. As they head to the lake, it is a treat to find one on a dry fly. This small hen was my last steelhead of 2019, and it took a dry fly while I was trout fishing.

steelhead feed heavily on these foods as they head back to the lake. Additionally, resident trout and smallmouth bass feed frantically on these defenseless fish. Scaling down your presentation can lead to a mixed bag of migratory and resident fish. In late May and into June, this is very exciting fishing!

Imitating these tiny baitfish usually involves an active presentation of a wet fly being twitched or a small pattern being stripped. Some very good small, accurate imitations work well for these types of baits, and some classic wet flies imitate them as well. Two such flies mentioned in chapter 6 are the Copperhead Fry and the Queen of the Waters.

The spawning run eventually winds down, and the steelhead and brown trout fade back toward their lake habitat. As they finally approach the lake, on the final leg of their spawning run, steelhead and lake-run browns will find themselves in a position to feed on the minnows of the lower reaches of our river systems. Much like in the fall, these can include a wide array of minnows, including alewives, spottail and spotfin shiners, and gobies. In late spring the river explodes with food, and this helps the steelhead recover from a spawning run that puts a lot of miles on their bodies. With the help of this wide array of baitfish, many of these fish will live to fight another day.

In summary, migratory fish will eat a lot of different kinds of baitfish, and having a seasonal approach to selecting flies is a great way to be successful. In the coming chapters, this book will show you specific techniques and patterns for each season of fishing for these great fish. We will also discuss reading the water, which is critical for success in this game.

Left: No matter what you pursue, a good slender baitfish is likely present in your waters. Here a great brown struck a shiner imitation. There is a lot of information on the internet about the shiner species available in many rivers. Finding out the general size and color of local shiners is a big help. Typically they range from 1 to 5 inches, and their size can vary a lot depending on the time of year.

CHAPTER 2

Reading the Water

In order to understand how to attack big migratory fish on your local stream, you first need a basic grasp of how to read the water. The real trick to being a good angler is to force yourself to be dynamic on the water. If you want to improve your angling skills, what you want to avoid is fishing the exact same water the exact same way every day. Even if you only have one accessible spot in your area, there are always new things to try: different fly lines, different flies, different colors, and different spots.

This chapter deals with the choice of where you fish. Probably the easiest thing to do as an angler, whether you are new or old to the sport, is to go down to your local river and fish the most likely-looking steelhead-holding areas, excluding the more nondescript areas. Yet it is these unlikely areas that hold many untouched fish. Even in instances where they don't hold the most fish, they could save the day when the river is busy or when lighting conditions are poor. By forcing yourself to fish these areas, you can have a more successful day and you will become a much better angler.

Fishing streamers for big migratory fish, in its most basic form, is a great way to find these new spots to fish. Even if you prefer to fish with nymphs, etc., understanding how to swing a fly or strip a streamer is a great tool to have in your box. Why? Well, because these techniques allow you to fish through water quickly without ever touching the bottom with your fly. Even if you aren't die-hard about streamer fishing, there is a great advantage to doing it. By fishing a baitfish pattern through unfamiliar water, you can often determine

Reading the water is an essential skill for consistently catching any fish. Once you understand the basics, you will be able to find fish on any river system. Steelhead and brown trout are looking for the same types of cover and the same currents, regardless of whether the river is large or small.

Right: I love the solitude of winter. The rivers are quiet, and the fish are big!

where the fish are and come back with a more precise method on another day.

Each year, throughout the fall and winter months, I swing flies for steelhead. Winter is my time to fish, as the other seasons are very busy with guiding. By the end of winter, swinging a fly through every nook and cranny has revealed where the fish are concentrated. As the water rises with snowmelt in the spring, we switch to nymph-fishing methods for a period of time. Because of all the time streamer fishing in the winter, finding spring fish is not a mystery despite totally different methods. When steelhead bump or pull on your line or flash at a streamer, they reveal their current location and more. A lot of times you find nondescript areas while streamer fishing, and you can come to your newfound spot time and time again and be successful.

A side benefit of streamer fishing with baitfish patterns is that your fly is fished above the river bottom. This allows you to fish your fly above snags. Every river has places that you just can't fish with traditional nymphing methods but can fish a swung fly or strip a streamer. Learning how to be productive with baitfish patterns opens up a lot of water that just doesn't fish well with nymphs, and this makes fishing more mysterious and enjoyable. Large tracts of waters that would cost numerous flies if solely nymph fishing can be probed effectively with minimal tackle loss using streamer fishing methods. Furthermore, you can approach a new river with these various streamer methods and feel confident that you have a chance at a fish. All that you will need is some basic knowledge on how to read water, which hopefully this chapter can cut the learning curve on. As we discuss in other parts of this book, there are ways to combine streamer and nymph fishing.

Another real advantage to fishing baitfish pattern is that you are using gear that would be considered heavy-duty if you were nymph fishing, etc. Because minnow imitations tend to be large, it is not uncommon to use tippet strengths of 10 to 20 pounds when fishing around structure. I am convinced that you can use even heavier line

than that in some instances. This is especially true if your fly is moving no slower than the current. Furthermore, there are other steps that you can take, which we will discuss later in the book, concerning hook selection and knots that can really help you when you are fishing along deadfalls and timber. Attention to small details is a great way to increase your success in the low-numbers game of streamer fishing.

As a rule of thumb for any type of stream fishing, the colder the water is, the slower and deeper you need to fish a fly. As you slow the fly down, the fish get a better look at the fly and your tippet, so the weight of the tippet should reflect this. A very heavy tippet might be used in the fall, as the fly swings over the fish quickly; however, fishing some of those same runs in the winter would require the fly to rub the river bottom, slowing it down. As you slow that fly down, the fish get a better look at your fly. Furthermore, the water is typically clear in the winter and the fish have been in the system for a while. For these reasons, you would use lighter tippet. We will cover equipment in more detail later in the book.

Before actually getting into the exact techniques, there are fundamental principles to keep in mind whenever you go fishing. They provide a framework for catching any type of predator fish on any river.

Structure and Strategies for Reading Water

Like any other predatory gamefish in a river system, steelhead and large brown trout relate to cover. They do this for several reasons. As a constantly foraging fish, they position themselves with easy access to food sources. Never is this more apparent in the Great Lakes region as when there are migratory fish, such as salmon, suckers, or other steelhead, spawning. Frenzied spawning activity draws hungry fish to the area. Steelhead will still relate to cover, using depth and gravel bars to stay comfortably close to the source of caviar. For example, you may see steelhead feeding actively near salmon during the morning hours, but then they disappear when the fishing pressure increases. They have not left the area; rather, they

are almost always in the structure and depths in that proximity. They will use the different forms of structure and different currents near food to sustain themselves when conditions are right, and they will hide when they feel vulnerable.

SIMILAR WATER PHILOSOPHY

To catch fish consistently, I use a simple strategy to cover water. The basic idea behind this philosophy in reading the water is that if you get a strike in one spot near one particular type of cover or current, you should continue to match that type of cover or current at a similar depth wherever possible. For example, if I catch a fish behind a 4-foot-deep boulder, for the rest of the day I will continue to look for other boulder fields in similar depths as I head down the river. I might also try to resist fishing more conventional spots while seeking this similar water. If the bite is crazy good, fish anywhere; otherwise, stick to this plan. Often anglers will catch a fish out of a spot and fail to note the structure and currents in the area.

If you are planning to fish a large stretch of river and you have a lot of choices in where you fish, this idea can be particularly effective. In most cases, we really have little idea what is actually going on below the water. All rivers are complex. There may be a type of food that is concentrated around a particular type of structure at a given depth that is drawing fish to that type of area. If you figure out a type of food and structure that is working, it is a good idea to roll with it.

This line of thinking can also be applied on the larger scale. On one of my favorite streams, I found a really nondescript area that held a lot of steelhead throughout the fall and winter. No skill was involved in finding this area. Rather, since zebra mussels had entered this stream, its clarity was excellent, and I happened to see quite a few fish in this spot. Coming back the next day, we fished that area and hooked several steelhead and trout.

I was quite young at the time, and this was a revealing moment. Despite fishing almost every day, I had no idea that these shallow to mid-depth gravel bars would hold fish during the winter. They just did not look like your stereotypical steelhead spot—they were not located in a pool and did not have a head or tailout. Because of continuing success in that spot, it became a model for future fishing. This also inspired me to look for new types of structure that hold fish. Through that entire fall and winter, I found spots on that river and others by looking for structure similar to the structure in that one spot. These spots were miles apart but had the same trait that attracted fish. I found similar spots 20 miles downriver and later found them on other rivers. By learning one type of cover that holds fish and applying it to other areas, you can have a better understanding of any stream.

ALWAYS BE ON THE LOOKOUT FOR FISH

This brings up a tip that I would offer to any angler in any body of water that has clarity: Keep your eyes open! There is a longtime guide on the Muskegon River where I guide. Though our fishing styles are different, I always had respect for him, and I remember watching him on the river when I was a young man. Whenever I would see him, he was seldom looking forward when heading down the river. Instead, whenever possible, his eyes were riveted down into the water. Over the years, I have found myself constantly staring into the river, and a lot of spots that I would have never considered fishing in the past have been added to the arsenal for no reason other than the fact that I happened to catch a glimpse of a big fish with a square tail while peering into the water.

A good example of this is in October, when migratory fish start to enter our rivers. In many of the Great Lakes streams, we have large runs of Pacific salmon, which were brought here during the 1960s and have flourished. The salmon appear in great numbers while the steelhead trickle in, so it can be tricky finding a desirable fish. Often I will drive the boat downriver, passing pod after pod of salmon. Salmon have a forked tail while steelhead and brown trout have a square tail, so the goal is to find a fish with a square tail in the bunch.

Salmon are dangerous to be around if you are a steelhead! This one chased the steelhead away and clobbered this goby pattern. Surprisingly, if I do happen to catch a salmon while targeting steelhead, the most common fly they take by far is a sculpin or goby pattern. I suspect that salmon recognize these baitfish as a threat to their eggs.

As long as it is not too bright, the feeding fish will be brazen and will be found pretty close to the salmon. Any trout species in proximity to spawning salmon are there for a reason: They are feeding. Salmon are dangerous fish, often attacking other fish that stray too close to their spawning area. If you see a Pacific salmon acting in an agitated way, it may also be an indication that one of our target species is in the area.

Because of the element of danger, if you find a visible trout or steelhead near a salmon, you can be confident that this fish is feeding. A steelhead or trout simply will not risk injury by salmon unless there is an overwhelming food source. You have a great chance at hooking a player in such a spot. Certain conditions such as fishing pressure or light conditions may make them more wary and are factors in approaching visible fish.

TWO TYPES OF WATER

If you fish a lot for migratory fish, you will find that it all boils down to two types of water. Some spots will have migratory fish in them any time they are available. These are areas of the river that contain the types of structure that are attractive to a fish, which are covered in the next chapter. These spots are the most common type of place to fish for migratory fish. A secondary type of spot is a place that holds a lot of fish for a short period of time while they are migrating. These spots are usually adjacent to some better holding water. They are very useful in helping you understand the progress of a run of fish.

As I write this, it is late October and we are having a nice run of chrome steelhead in our local rivers. Today I fished with two clients in a shallow run in a part of the river that is not heavily used. The run is very obscure, and it is near some nice winter water. Its flow is nice and there is some structure, but there is little food and quite a bit of current.

A few days ago we hooked three nice steelhead in this spot, yesterday we hooked two, and today we did not hook any in that same stretch of water. The fish stayed in this area but were slowly thinned out. This tells me that the run of fish that we had a week ago is waning, and I will need to fish deeper holding water for the coming week until new fish arrive. This type of spot is gold for catching fish when they are moving, but it also tells me a lot about what is going on in the area. If I catch fish in one of these transient spots, I may catch other fish in similar transient spots throughout that section of the river system. Such a transient spot would indicate a good number of fish in that section, and it would be wise to fish all types of water in that area thoroughly.

Even if I have not caught a fish at one of these transient spots for a while, I will still try to incorporate at least one into my daily guiding routine. Sometimes a small push of fish will move through and you just bump into them. Occasionally there are those golden times when a large group of fish has entered the river unannounced, with no change in water levels. Only by fishing these transient areas will you know that they are even around.

Not every spot will hold fish throughout a season, and it is important to understand the seasonal nature of some places. In summary, some places you fish for migratory fish are temporary, and some hold fish any time they are available. It is good to be able to distinguish between these two places. As you become familiar with your favorite streams, you will no doubt come across such areas. You could waste a lot of time fishing vacant areas during the late fall and winter, while you fish under the assumption that there should be some fish there.

SMALL RIVER VS. LARGE RIVER

Many anglers will find reading the water much simpler in smaller rivers. As we discuss some of the types of runs, talking about the parts of a run may be much less significant in a small river. For example, on a small stream, the head, gut, and tail of the run are so close together that you would fish through the whole thing. However, fishing brush, seams, crossovers, etc., are all similar in large and small rivers.

Big bodies of water are intimidating. For one thing, they are often physically more dangerous than smaller rivers, with strong and mysterious currents, and wading can be a challenge. Beyond that, they can be overwhelming to read. I remember driving my old beat-up car to the Muskegon River for the first time as a teenager. As I looked out over the river, it was overwhelming. I had no idea where to start, and did not catch anything (yet I knew I wanted to come back!). The best advice I can give to any angler is to break up the river into smaller sections and figure out each section as though it were a small stream.

Most of our rivers in the Midwest get significant runs of migratory fish. These fish are territorial and will spread out—they simply don't like being on top of one another. This is actually good: It means that if you fish methodically through an unfamiliar stretch of a big river, your fly will eventually go over a fish.

LIGHT CONDITIONS

As you learn how to read the water and master fishing structure, you may feel as though you can catch fish anywhere or anytime. However, there is one fly in the ointment that could ruin this master plan and bring you to your knees while on the water. No matter how many fish are concentrated in a run or how well you are fishing a run, many times they just won't take a fly if the sun is directly in front of them. One of the main reasons we are looking at how fish relate to structure and current goes hand in hand with how fish react to various light conditions.

Light has a profound impact on the life of any river fish. There is one simple thing to keep in mind whenever you fish for any gamefish: They have no eyelids. When faced with bright conditions, direct light is overwhelming to a fish. For example, if you are fishing down and across to a fish, facing downstream, and the sun is to your back, chances are the fish will not be able to see your fly very well. In these conditions, a fish might very well hide in the brush or just simply be inactive. Brown trout may flee to the densest of places, coming out only at night to feed. They may also seek to avoid you entirely.

These problems are amplified on large rivers, where any shade given by surrounding trees might not make it to the place that you hope to find a fish. To make things worse, fishing pressure, which often accompanies bright and sunny conditions (aka "a beautiful day for fishing"), will make fishing tough.

There are a few things that can really help you when lighting conditions look bad on a given day. If you must fish on a sunny day during the brightest times of the day, try to put the sun behind you whenever possible. If you look directly upstream from where you are fishing, remember that this is what the fish is seeing. Fish will always face upstream in straight current.

If you have an opportunity to fish water that has broken light, such as light coming through trees, this is a pretty good scenario. Not only does the broken light make the fish less wary, but it can often do nice things to illuminate a fly. Often when fishing in broken light, using a fly with some form of flash can really help. On my home river, I always keep some flies with holographic yellow flash in the box for those side-light areas. In many bright conditions, fishing yellow, gold, or a light copper mixed into your fly will cover this "bright day, bright fly" scenario. Remember that sunlight is warm in color, and a lot of the baitfishes reflect the color of the sunlight. Migratory fish, which have spent most of their lives chasing reflective baitfish, will be looking for that warm reflection on a sunny day.

Another option for fishing really bright conditions is to bring the fly down into the face of the fish. When the sky is high, and the river is pressured, the fish become sullen. This is where an accurate minnow baitfish imitation will really come into play. Fishing deeper rocky areas with a slowly presented sculpin pattern is a way to get fish to bite in bright, pressured conditions year after year.

If you are having a really hard time in bright conditions, just avoid them and look for shade. If you are fishing with a boat, this might be a matter of covering more water in bad light conditions. On a normal, dark fall day, I might cover 6 or 7 miles when guiding for steelhead from a boat. However, when it is a bright and sunny day, it is not uncommon to cover more than 12 miles. The reason for this is that I will simply exclude any spots that don't have the right lighting conditions. If you are wading, choose a stretch of river where you are not restricted to fishing exposed areas. Almost all rivers have bends and oxbows. These changes in the direction of the light coming through the trees and will make shade more accessible. If you select a stretch of river with frequent bends and it is surrounded by trees, sunlight will be less of a problem.

Don't be put off by the size of a river. Break it down into a small section and read it just like a small river. If you are fishing a swung-fly presentation, look for water that is 3 to 6 feet deep. Anywhere you fish for steelhead, this is considered a prime depth range.

I would rather fish to a spot that has two fish in ideal lighting conditions than fish areas with much larger numbers of fish, knowing that they are less likely to bite. Not only are the fish more wary of your presence, but chances are you are not the only one that would try to fish a prime spot. The sneaky spots with only a couple of fish will save the day. When it comes to migratory fish, there is often a dominant fish in each run that will respond to a fly. Whether there are two fish or a hundred in a spot, this active fish would be the one to take a fly.

If you hop into your beat-up fishing truck to go fishing and see on the weather report that it is going to be a bright day, a great way to overcome this problem is to choose a small river system versus a large one. Smaller rivers will have more broken light than large ones, as the surrounding hills are usually closer to the river and the woods are closer on both sides, breaking the light.

If you are fishing a bright day on a broad river, you may want to consider bringing other types of fly-fishing equipment for the slow parts of the day. Steelhead fishing with streamers will be slow during the brightest parts of the day. During these times, you may have the opportunity to fish for trout or steelhead with nymphs. This is a particularly good option if you don't have the luxury of picking and choosing your spots.

If you choose to fish a streamer in these conditions, use a heavy sink-tip and weighted fly, and try to bring your fly right into the face of a fish. This may present an opportunity at a meal that a big fish cannot resist.

Another bright-day adjustment has to do with timing. Timing can mean everything when you are fishing. If you are fishing an entire day, you may simply avoid an area during midday, knowing that it will fish better in the evening. Rather than going

Early winter mornings are great for photography but not so great for fishing. If you are going to fish during the shortest days at the coldest times of the year, it might not be a bad idea to sleep in. Water temperatures tend to vary more in smaller rivers that have a dark bottom. As the sun comes up and warms the river, water temps will rise. That little bit of heat should jumpstart the fish.

When I look in the rearview mirror in the morning and see a red sky, I know that a storm is approaching. I also know that in front of weather we stand a better chance of having a great day. It was particularly exciting on this day, as I knew a few steelhead were just coming in. Chrome fish + ideal conditions = great fishing.

down the river in a fixed way and fishing every spot you come to on a bright day, time your fishing so that you are in the right place at the right time and this will increase your odds at the big strike!

An example of this is how we often approach guide trips in the fall. If the day is bright, we will time the fishing along with the lighting conditions. I fight myself to avoid fishing some great spots in broad daylight, saving them for the way back upstream when lighting conditions are better later in the day. In a spot where the sun is upstream in the morning, it will be downstream in the afternoon. The sun always rises in the East, and sets in the West. A poor spot in the morning is a great spot in the afternoon and vice versa. As you fish your local river, pay attention to which spots have sunsets and sunrises directly ahead of the fish. These are the places that you want to avoid at certain times of the day.

If you are intimately familiar with the rivers in your area, a sunny day might be the best time to approach areas that are less well known and therefore have fish that are less likely to have the traffic. Undisturbed fish are more likely to take a fly in all conditions, and this is particularly true on a sunny day.

You would think that crystal-clear water and sunshine is the hardest condition to confront. However, I often find that sunny days when the water has particulate, or stain, in it is the hardest condition to face. This particulate will give the river a bronze color in the face of sunlight, and getting a fish to strike in these conditions can be mighty challenging. This is one of the few scenarios that I find switching to a lighter tippet can make all the difference, and I will try to do anything I can to get out of direct sunlight when this happens.

A lot of anglers schedule their week around their work. When deciding when to fish, choosing the morning or evening on bright days will make a lot of the discussion on lighting less important. Also, use weather reports to find lighting conditions that make the best use of your time.

Sunlight can sometimes work to your advantage. Fish will typically migrate in high-water or low-light conditions. When I was a kid, I fished a small creek called Buck Creek in Grand Rapids, Michigan. During daylight hours, you might not see any fish migrating at all, but as soon as the sun went down a little, you would see ripple after ripple in the shallow areas. These ripples were caused by migrating steelhead, salmon, and brown trout. Usually fish won't move upstream in bright conditions.

You can use this behavior to your advantage. Imagine that you come to a great spot while working your way downstream. The sun is shining brightly, and you still manage to get an aggressive strike from a fish. On a bright day, fish are not likely to migrate during the daylight hours. Because you had an aggressive strike at this spot, you *know* that the fish will still be in this area when you return upstream. This would definitely be a spot to try running your fly through before the end of the day. If it is a small, obscure spot, your chances of success are great.

When talking about light, you also have to remember that the seasons have a lot to do with fishing. For example, when guiding for steelhead in mid-October, the days are long, so the extra hours of bright sunshine will have an impact on the fishing. When the weather is nice and the days are long, you may also have more fishing pressure. It is on these long fall days that the sun gets high in the sky and has a greater impact on fishing.

Contrast this with fishing in the dead of winter. On these short days, a bright sunny day would be less of a concern, and possibly a benefit. During the winter the sun never gets very high. Furthermore, if the water temps are very cold, a little radiant heat from the sun might be just what is needed to perk the afternoon fishing up. The sun will have a more dramatic effect on dark-bottomed rivers or in lower volumes of water. Fishing pressure is often light in the winter, so the bright conditions have not made the fish wary of wading anglers or boats passing by.

Winter fishing would also negate what we mentioned about fishing in the early morning. Water temps might be at their absolute coldest in the morning hours, and you might encounter slush on a morning after a clear night. When choosing a low-light time of the day to fish in the winter, always lean toward the afternoon, when water temperatures are at their maximum for the day. Afternoon water temperatures usually won't drop until late in the afternoon.

Light conditions are always tied to the weather. Keep an eye on the weather report, as it can also help with other fishing decisions.

WEATHER

Weather is another factor that you should take into account when reading the water. It goes hand in hand with lighting conditions but also has its own impact. A part of me wishes that we could accurately predict when fishing will be good in given weather conditions. As a guide, however, that might be disastrous, as this might keep people away on the days when the bite might not be so good.

To my knowledge, there is no silver bullet to fishing around the weather. At the end of the day, fish are in the survival business of eating things. Even if conditions seem terrible, there should still be a fish that wants to eat something somewhere at some point during the day. Our rivers are full of food, concentrated in different places. Even if the weather is unfavorable for feeding fish, a locally active food source could trigger a bite from the target species.

Looking back over many years of fishing, the most likely time to have great fishing is when foul weather is approaching. The most frenzied bite periods of fishing are often right on the cusp of bad weather and continue into the bad weather itself. Steelhead and big trout are notorious foul-weather fish, so expect good fishing when you are most uncomfortable.

Over the years, the most challenging fishing trips I have had have been on the back side of weather, in high pressure after a storm front has passed. This is true with many warm- and cold-water species. The barometer itself has an impact on the fishing after the passing of the storm. High pressure also produces some of the most brilliant sunny days, which bring out more anglers and make the fish more wary of your presence, so these factors also contribute to often poor fishing in the wake of a storm.

One of the old salty anglers in my area always claimed to keep a goldfish in a bowl by his front door. If he looked at the goldfish in the morning and it was swimming around the bowl actively, he would know that it was a good time to fish. If the fish was sitting stationary on the bottom of the tank, then perhaps it was a good day to do something else. I can't attest to the veracity of this technique, but there is no doubt that the barometer has an effect on migrating fish.

Note that I have had great fishing behind a storm front, and really bad fishing when weather is approaching. No matter what weather conditions you are facing, you just cannot predict when the fish might turn back on or you might come across an active fish. If you are on the river, keep fishing and don't give up! Ultimately, the best time to fish is whenever you can.

As a general rule of thumb, fish through water quickly when the bite is good and conditions are good and cover lots of water. When conditions are poor, slow down your presentation and the amount of water you are covering. Take smaller steps as you work through a run. Allow the fish to get a good, deep look at your fly when the bite is poor. Methodical fishing produces when the bite is bad.

WATER TEMPERATURE AND FISH MIGRATION

There is another aspect to weather that ultimately impacts fishing for migratory fish. In a nutshell, we are paying close attention to the intricacies of a river system, but in the back of our mind we need to always think about their home—the Great Lakes—and what is making these fish enter our rivers.

All of the Great Lakes, like any other lake, get warm during the summer months. They are stratified by water temperature and the warm water stays on the surface, while the colder water, which is much denser, settles to the bottom. During the summer months the water near shore is usually pretty warm, and salmon, steelhead, and brown trout have little reason to come in toward shore and ultimately the river mouths. That 70-degree water that is nice for humans to swim in is no good for coldwater salmonids.

In any of our rivers, we wait with eager anticipation in the fall for events to occur that bring in migratory fish. In order for this to happen, two things need to occur.

First, on the river end of things, the water temperature has to be favorable for migratory fish to enter the river. If the river system that you are fishing has naturally cold water, this is less of an issue. Many Midwest rivers fall into this category, but even more do not. Thus, a lot of migratory fish runs are delayed by the length of the summer.

To illustrate how river temperatures affect migrations, consider our king salmon runs in West Michigan. I am on the Muskegon River, a tailwater, with warm summer water temperatures. In a typical fall, you won't have king salmon here until mid-September. Just an hour to the north, the Pere Marquette River flows. The Pere Marquette is a classic, colder trout stream that exists without any dams. The salmon will enter the Pere Marquette as early as August. Another small West Michigan stream, the Little Manistee, is even colder, and it often has salmon by the Fourth of July. Though salmon are a bit different from steelhead and browns, the water temperature of their natal rivers affects them the same way. Water temperature has a big impact on migration of all cool-water fish.

Second, in the bigger picture, weather has a lot to do with moving migratory fish into the river. As mentioned, our Great Lakes are stratified, with the cold water, favorable for migratory fish, being on the bottom. This is covered by a layer of warm water, which can be very warm early in the fall. If we have a weather system that blows from the direction of the shore out over the lake, it will push the warm water out and bring the cold water in near the shore. If you have a cool river and this turnover of water temperatures, you can have a lot of fish migrating into it. Our rivers around the Great Lakes flow in many different directions, so the wind direction required to make turnover happen would differ based on your geography.

This event kick-starts our fishing and can help you decide when and where to fish. If you are looking at your calendar for the week and are considering where to fish, and you see a reversing wind coming on the weather forecast, this is an indicator that it would be a good time to fish the lower parts of a river system. If your local river is currently warm, you might seek out a cooler river system that may get a better local run under these conditions.

A lot of times, people comment about how there are no fish in a river or that we are having a bad run. Some will point the finger at the baitfish populations and bag limits. At the same time, others will blame the fisheries management, etc. However, this may have nothing to do with the numbers of fish that exist, only the numbers that are willing to enter the river in poor conditions.

This is especially often true about steelhead. Steelhead have pretty stable populations in many of the Great Lakes, so whether they are in the river in numbers has more to do with migration conditions. Furthermore, steelhead have a large migration window, often spanning from September until early May. They do not *have* to migrate in the fall. This contrasts with brown trout and Pacific salmon, which must spawn in the fall.

A couple of years ago, we had a very warm summer, and by early October the water temperatures in many of Michigan's tailwater fisheries were approaching 70 degrees. We had some rain early in the fall, but the river remained warm and few fish came in. At the same time, the nearshore water of Lake Michigan was also warm. This was a bad combination, and many anglers griped about the lack of fish in the rivers.

We had a typical winter and spring that year, with below-average numbers of fish. With no big weather events, the fish were never motivated to enter these rivers. By mid-April, we assumed the fish weren't coming en masse, and it would be a "ho-hum" sort of a spring. Then early in May, a violent storm hit with some high water. Soon the river was flooded. It was also flooded with chrome fish. Conditions were finally right, and the fish, which were in the big lake all along, finally arrived. It is likely that we had a large run overall that year—it just didn't get here until everyone was done thinking about steelhead.

In order to have good fishing, you have to have fish in the river. The next section deals with where fish will hold in a river system.

Left: Some of the hardest days of fishing will be on the back side of weather and the high pressure that follows. Additionally, the sun is now out. If it was a storm front, the fish have adjusted to low-light conditions.

Understanding the Lies and Preferences of Migratory Fish

Having a working knowledge of river structure and a dynamic view on reading water will always help your success. If you fish a local stream throughout the course of a year for the other predator fish that are available, such as resident trout and smallmouth bass, you may be able to effectively apply this second principle: the principle of understanding the lies, or holding areas, of gamefish. As stated earlier, after entering a natal stream, steelhead become a predator just like any other.

In a river system, all gamefish relate to ambush spots in the river. These prime ambush spots, often called "prime lies," give predatory fish access to various food sources such as nymphs, minnows, etc. The best of these ambush spots provide for feeding and provide comfort, such as access to warmer water and resting water. A prime lie is such a good spot that the top gamefish in the area always occupies it. Such a spot may hold a large

trout in the spring, a smallmouth bass in the summer, and finally a steelhead or lake-run brown trout in the fall.

How does this apply to fishing for migratory fish? Steelhead and brown trout enter tributaries in the fall, winter, and spring, often when the water is high. The structure in the rivers is invisible, and it would be very difficult to see any fish around them. Even the keenest of anglers might overlook a good spot if they don't know what's on the bottom of the river. Often when you catch a steelhead you may know where they are but really don't know why they are there.

By learning a river during the low-water times of the year and fishing for other species, you can have a greater understanding of the prime lies in the river. When you return to fish your river for migratory fish, the rocks and structure that you learned during the low-water periods will no longer be a mystery. The places that held the largest trout or other predator species in the summer will

This brown trout is waiting in ambush in a prime lie. This is such a good spot that it is occupied by resident trout in the spring, smallmouth in the summer, and brown trout and steelhead in the fall. If you are a year-round angler, pay close attention to spots where you find large predator fish in the non-migratory season. Often these very same spots will produce the dominant migratory fish during the peak season.

Smallmouth relate to a lot of the same cover that steelhead do. When I catch a big smallmouth out of 3 to 6 feet of water, I always make a mental note and later apply it to fishing for other predator fish. Fishing for smallmouth in the summer helps me find a lot of great steelhead spots in the fall and winter.

hold the migratory fish in the fall. If you want to take this to the extreme, go snorkeling during the summer in your local stream. I guarantee that over the course of the day you will learn more in a day than you might in a week of solid fishing.

You would think that warmwater fish such as smallmouth bass have little in common with steelhead. However, smallmouth are one of the most helpful fish for me when looking for potential steelhead spots. In the summer, some smallmouth bass migrate into many of our rivers while resident smallmouth become more active. If I can find a large smallmouth in 3 to 6 feet of water, it is often a red flag for finding migratory fish (especially steelhead) at other times of the year. I have found more steelhead spots by fishing for smallmouth than I have ever found while fishing for trout or any other type of fish. If I catch a big smallmouth in a spot like this, I make a mental note of it and think, "This will be a great spot to try for steelhead in the fall." More often than not, it is!

DEPTH

When you ask most avid streamer anglers who target trout or steelhead what depth they like to fish, they will typically answer 3 to 6 feet. As we talk about the types of structure and reading the water, keep that 3 to 6 feet in mind.

Migratory fish, with the exception of Pacific salmon, are almost always located on the bottom of the river, usually around structure. The reason for this is that the water is slower on the river bottom, as the structure and rocks break the current and provide resting areas. Because of the way migratory fish are colored, they blend in surprisingly well with the bottom of the river, which gives them the advantage when ambushing food. The substrate of the bottom is also what is going to produce much of the food for feeding fish. Bottom-dwelling minnows, insects, and crayfish all live around the riverbed.

Living near the bottom of the river also provides a great vantage point for spotting minnows and other types of food above. Certain types of bait-fish, such as salmon fry, steelhead fry, and some species of shiners, will be located near the surface. Looking up from the bottom against a glassy sky allows fish to see and attack these baits. In the spring it is common to see drop-back steelhead, lake-run brown trout, and other predators herding schools of fry and viciously attacking them. Often it is reminiscent of a saltwater fish chasing bait near a shore and can be splashy.

As you can see, many gamefish have a vested interest in living near the bottom of the river. It provides rest and access to food. If the fish are near the bottom, it is a good idea to bring your bait down to their level.

There are practical considerations for getting your fly to the bottom that really constrict successful fishing to these moderate depths of 3to

6 feet. In many rivers, any streamer presentation is going to require that you use a sink-tip to get down to them. Reaching fish at this target depth would require an amount of tip that is usually not that pleasant or practical to cast. This is not a disadvantage, however, as most rivers in the Midwest are of reasonable depth and it is not hard to find fishy water in a suitable depth range.

Another practical consideration is that we are often fishing in cold water, especially through the winter months. The extended cold-water scenario is what distinguishes fishing in the Midwest from many other places where you might catch migratory fish. The metabolism of gamefish shrinks a lot during the winter, and your fly has to get deep and stay deep. It is key to give the fish a chance to see the fly, at a speed at which they can respond to it. In cold water, if you can just get the fly in

River speed affects a lot of aspects of fishing for migratory fish. Fast currents made it necessary to use a fly with a tungsten head to sink to the level of this early-winter chromer. The more weight you add to a fly, obviously the more quickly it will sink. The trade-off is that you will rob the fly of some action with all that weight. It will also be more difficult to cast.

front of the fish, often they will respond. Once they commit to feeding, it's game on! It is much easier to control your depth and speed if you are fishing moderate depths.

This depth range is a prime feeding range for fish, and you will find that they move in and out of the deepest areas, where they rest, and into the moderate-depth areas, where they feed. Tied directly to the idea of depth is the speed of the current that you choose to fish.

RIVER SPEED

Before we get too carried away with talking about the types of water to look for when fishing, we should also consider the speed of the water that we are going to fish. River speed and river temperature have some correlation. If you are swinging flies for steelhead, it is often said to look for "walking speed" water to fish in. This speed of water is typically at its best through the bulk of the fall when targeting migratory fish. However, when fish first enter a river, you may find them in some of the fastest runs; these spots may provide security to fish that are accustomed to life in an inland sea. If the water is uncomfortably warm, riffle water may also hold more oxygen.

Heading toward winter, this changes significantly. Both the steelhead and the lake-run brown trout will often look for water that is slower than walking speed. The speed of the water has a lot of implications for your rig. For example, you may use a heavy sinking line to get a fly down in the fast runs, but you will have little control over the speed of the line. Thus, in the winter when you are presenting a fly and line control and speed is more important, you might opt for a floating line instead.

River speed also has implications for your fly selection. For example, a chunky sculpin pattern with a big head will fish well in slow or moderate currents, but fishing such a fly in fast water will require a heavy sink-tip and may crush the profile of the fly. If you are trying to get a fly down, certain fly-tying materials should be avoided. For example, if your fly has a deer hair head, you will have a hard time sinking that fly deeply, especially over short distance. As a result, you will be forced to use a very heavy sink-tip or possibly some weight on the line to sink the fly. In faster water, a fly with a narrower profile will be much more practical to sink.

As this book discusses baitfish at length, river speed has a further effect on fly selection because certain types of baitfish will be present in slow water and certain types will be present in fast water. A big sculpin would be found in the slow, rocky winter water; shiners might be found in the faster stuff; fry are found along the edges of the river, etc.

In summary, the speed of water that you choose to fish goes hand in hand with your equipment selection and your choice of flies. River speed is always a consideration when you are picking a type of structure to target.

TYPES OF WATER THAT HOLD BIG PREDATORS

Migratory fish use a variety of river features or cover in a river system. In order to fish streamers successfully on a regular basis, you should learn to view all types of cover as potential steelhead water. Most steelhead anglers who have taken up the swung-fly method of fishing have spent extensive time either nymph fishing or spin fishing with bait for steelhead. When you use these methods, typically you look for clean, obvious runs that have a distinct head and tailout area. These classic runs are very productive for steelhead fishing in general and will produce steelhead with the swung-fly method.

Streamer fishing produces thunderous strikes for migratory fish, and there are many benefits to fishing this method. One of the best things about fishing baitfish patterns is that you can target secondary spots that would not be ideal for other styles of fishing. Learn to fish both the classic steelhead run and the stand-alone forms of structure (funnel areas, submerged gravel bars, boulders, logjams, and brush). This will help you increase your chances at these elusive gamefish.

The Classic Deep Steelhead Run

If you were to define the typical steelhead run or pool, it would probably consist of a throat, which gradually drops into the deep area, or gut, of the run, and then a tailout. These classic steelhead runs

often have a lot of rocks and boulders in them, which are great hiding places for bottom-dwelling baitfish such as sculpins. For swinging flies, the throat and tailout areas will be of particular interest. In smaller rivers, the head and tail of a run are so close together that it makes good sense to fish the entire spot. However, larger rivers may have

100 yards of river in a run, with some very deep water in the middle. In these circumstances, break the spot into its different sections.

The very beginning part of a hole, often called the throat, is a great place to catch steelhead or other feeding migratory fish. In many runs, the throat is a good place to catch steelhead with a

Left: The head of a classic steelhead run is often easy to wade and is an obvious place to look for migratory fish. The head of a run often has immediate access to food sources dropping off the shallows, and the fish hanging out in this section are likely to be feeding.

is all the more desirable. If the river is turning at the top of the run, this can add a nice, deep seam with access to resting water, and this too can make the head of a run more appealing.

The throat of a run or big hole is often best at the start of fall. In some areas of the Midwest, the throat often begins at the end of a series of gravel bars. As steelhead arrive in September and October, king salmon and brown trout are spawning on these gravel areas. Depending on the depth of the preceding spawning areas, the steelhead, which relish feeding on eggs, may avoid close proximity to the spawning fish, particularly if the spawning areas are shallow. Directly downstream from the spawning area is shelter for the fish, the beginnings of a deep hole. When no other structure exists, the only thing holding fish in the head of the run is the availability of food. If you encounter this situation, you are a lucky angler. Fish found in these circumstances are often happy fish, just waiting to eat your fly! Regrettably, after the spawning fish leave and the egg supply runs out, the steelhead quickly leave such a spot unless other foods are present. They may simply drop into the other parts of the same run.

If you are fishing in the evening and the fish are migrating, perhaps due to water temperature or an increase in water flow, look to the throat of the run. Many migratory fish, including steelhead, migrate in the evening. When passing through an area, they will move to the front of the run in which they are holding in the evening, in preparation of moving upriver. If there is shallow water upstream from the run, they won't want to migrate until darkness or bad weather provides safe passage.

In deep holes or pronounced bends in a river, you may come to a deep, slow area. We consider these deep areas to be the "gut" of the run, and they frequently hold large numbers of fish. In smaller rivers, you may fish every inch of a given run, as the slow part may be very small. In a large

swung fly on a year-round basis. A main reason for this is the depth of the beginning of a run. By definition, the throat of a run is an area that is going from shallow water to deeper water. The shallow depth of such an area makes it very easy to sink the fly to the fish. If the throat of a run contains structure such as boulders or gravel bars, the spot river, however, there is difficulty in fishing this part of a deep run. For one thing, these fish are often in the deep part of the run for a reason. If you were a fish, you would choose a spot like this to hide or to rest. It is deep and slow, and you are protected from any possible predator. Steelhead in such a spot may be fleeing river pressure, hiding from the sun, recovering from being caught previously, recuperating from spawning, or simply resting. These fish in many instances are better targeted with a nymphing approach, if at all.

Another reason to avoid the gut of a run if swinging is that even if the fish in this part of the run are active, the gut may be too deep to fish effectively. Complicating things further, in large rivers whirlpool or eddy currents make a good streamer presentation impossible in some areas. As a guide, I look to keep the anglers in my boat interested as we fish from spot to spot on a river system. Fishing the deep, slow areas might lose the attention of my customers, and losing their interest is the kiss of death to a fishing guide.

Yet one more reason to avoid the gut of a run is the logistical part of it. In the deepest part of a run, you might need an extremely heavy-duty outfit to get your fly to a fish. Casting a very heavy line into the most dismal part of a run is not usually my idea of a fun way to catch fish.

There are a couple of exceptions to this, however. The inside bends found in the gut of a large run will often accumulate baitfish, such as shiners. These fish can form impressive schools during the cold times of the year. Stripping a fly through these areas provides an opportunity for a lake-run brown trout. One of the mental blocks to fishing the inside bend of a run is that the bottom composition is usually sand. Though a steelhead would not prefer this, a brown trout has no problem in this type of water and their coloration gives them some good camouflage. Furthermore, brown trout are fall spawning fish, and they are recovering from their spawning activities. The slow current on the edge of a deep hole is the perfect place to regain their strength.

Another time the deepest, darkest parts of the run have a moment of shining glory is the late spring. At this time of the year, steelhead are working their way back to the lake. If your river has

them, salmon fry might also accumulate in these areas. A combination of food and deep resting water provides a formula for finding many post-spawn steelhead in these deep areas. In some rivers, these fish may linger for weeks or months as they gorge before they return to the lake. Fortunately, these fish are very active and very hungry. Even though they are located in the deepest parts of a run, they are willing to move some distance for a fly. For this reason, you will not have to swing your fly too deeply to be successful in this area.

Approaching the end of a run, you come to an area that becomes shallower. This area is frequently referred to as the "tailout" of the run. When approaching an unfamiliar area, I can give you no better advice than to pay special attention to tailout areas. They are the perfect starting point when trying to read water in a new stream. Steelhead really like tailouts. They not only hold many fish but also frequently hold some of the most active, aggressive fish in a run. When you approach these areas, be careful to begin in the final parts of the gut of the run and fish all the way down to the very end of the tailout. It is not uncommon to find a steelhead in 2 or 3 feet of water at the very end of a very deep hole.

Regardless of the type of structure available at the end of the run, steelhead prefer them, especially tailouts with large boulders. Tailouts with available spawning gravel will also be attractive to steelhead any time there are eggs around to eat. This applies to the fall when salmon are spawning, and also to the spring when steelhead are spawning. The first time I fish an unfamiliar river, tailouts are a ubiquitous target, as they hold fish in almost every river I have encountered.

It should be noted that if steelhead are on the move, you may find that there are more fish available in the tailouts in the morning than in the evening. At these times of the day, the migrating steelhead move to the throat of the run. This is especially true if you are fishing a part of the river that has little structure or food to hold the fish—a common scenario when fishing the part closest to the lake. In many rivers of the Great Lakes region, steelhead quickly pass through these areas. They are en route to the gravel upstream, which affords structure and spawning areas.

As this angler approaches the end of the bottleneck of a run, a piece of structure marks the end of the spot. In this case, it is a piece of timber. If you fish it properly, a bottleneck will regularly produce a fish at the very end.

Tailouts also produce very well in the morning and evening for another reason. As fishing pressure is light early and late in the day, this is a prime feeding time for big fish. In these places, they can access food and drop into deeper water when fishing pressure increases or when conditions aren't good for feeding.

Each part of a large run will have food sources that are specific to the bottom cover. If the run is covered with big rocks and boulders, expect large food sources such as sculpins, gobies, and crayfish to be present. In the head or tail of a pool, there may be submerged gravel bars. These will have smaller food sources present, such as darters and insects. The inside bend of the pool will have a different assortment of baitfish, composed of shiners and sometimes fry and parr depending on the time of the year. The composition of the forage is always something to keep in mind as you work through a run.

Fishing the Bottleneck

In the last section, we discussed the tailout of a large run. An exaggerated form of a tailout is called a bottleneck. In a typical hole or run, the deep spot of a run might start and finish at the same width. However, this is not always the case. Sometimes as a run tails out, the current pushes closer to the deep side as it becomes shallower and shallower, forming a deeper, narrower tailout toward the end of the run. If you are wading, this is really obvious because you will have to wade farther and farther out in the river in the constricted part of the run to keep your fly in the target depth.

Bottlenecks are a great place to corner a fish. Coming from your typical fly-fishing background, you would think that cornering a large fish might make them scared and not prone to biting. Sometimes this is the case, sometimes it is not. Essentially, you put a large predatory fish in a scenario where it is either fight (or "bite") or flight. You want to give the fish a chance to hit the fly, or run. The main idea with this is that you slowly and methodically push the fish with your fly. If you go too fast, the fish will simply flee, go bolting past you, and reposition upstream of your position. On many occasions I had been fishing a bottleneck in clear water from the boat, only to see the fish swim right past the boat as I got to the tailout. This was likely a failure on my part, or the fish were in a spooky mood.

For years I watched guys back-pulling plugs and other hardware, forcing a lure down in front of a fish until they would bite. I would see them catching large fish while fishing close to the boat, in mid-depth water. The idea is similar here. The goal in fishing a bottleneck is to constantly make your fly present itself to a fish. You want there to be no break in the fly's being in the water. This tactic is effective when wading, but deadly from a boat. The boat creates a barrier that the fish do not want to cross, as they sense that they are vulnerable when approaching a boat. As you move fish in this way, if the concentration of fish is good, you may see them occasionally porpoise as they become more concentrated with each step downstream.

The tactic for fishing these areas is straightforward: Using a swung-fly tactic, you cast your fly down and across through the bottleneck. Ideally you would use a substantial fly, such as a sculpin or goby pattern. These patterns have a wide head and push a lot of water (usually I keep some wide-bodied flies in the boat for just this scenario). It is best to keep your fly in front of the fish as much as possible, so you would not strip in your fly until after each step you take through the run. When fishing from a boat, having two anglers fishing at the same time helps your chances, as it makes it less likely for a fish to slip by your position. I am always watching my clients' lines in this situation to make sure that one is still presenting while the other is casting. I will not move the boat until the timing is right with their presentations. This is one scenario where the person in the downstream end of the boat is the most likely recipient of a strike.

As you approach the end of a bottleneck, your presence and your fly has probably forced the fish to move down the river in front of you. Many times the end of the bottleneck comes as you approach

a large boulder, a piece of timber, a gravel bar, or a peninsula jutting out from the shore. As the fish become increasingly agitated, you might get a plucky bite or two. If there are a lot of fish in the run, and the run is shallow, you may start to see fish breaking the surface. As the fish are pushed to the very end of the run, they are forced to flee past your position, or to attack the fly. Some of the hardest strikes can come under these conditions!

Always plan on fishing constricting tailouts all the way to the very end. Many of these spots have a weird aspect to them: If you don't start a ways above the fish, you will never catch a fish. At the same time, I can tell you from experience that a lot of these places won't produce a bite until the very end of the run. As a result, you must fish the entire tailout in order to get the final reward of catching a fish. There are a lot of areas that I fish with clients that I know we will not get a bite until the conclusion, yet I must fish a part of the run that is time-consuming in hopes of the final reward.

And so the takeaway for fishing bottlenecks is this: Always fish until the absolute end of the run, and always fish your fly all the way around below you. So many times, it is the last cast in a bottleneck that gets the fish.

Runs with Uniform Depth

Not every run that you come to will be the classic style of run. Sometimes you will come to places in the river that have a favorable depth for fishing a streamer, but may just be long and flat. Often such places are in long, straight stretches of a river. This may be a natural occurrence, but it may also be the product of intentional straightening of the river. This was pretty common in the logging days throughout the Midwest. In such places the river may lack any features and may not even have a lot of cover, but they are a comfortable resting spot for the fish. If they are in proximity to a spawning area that the fish will eventually use, the fish may stay in this area until the spawning season.

In a uniform run with good substrate such as rock, the good news is that you may find that it maintains a good fishing depth throughout its entire length. However, the bad news is that you may find that there is no consistent part of the run that produces from day to day. You may catch a fish in the upstream part of the run one day, in the tailout the next day, and somewhere in the middle the day after that. This means that such a spot will take a large investment of time to make things happen. If you are anything like me, it will become difficult to fish patiently through the entire run. Even though it seems very slow and meticulous, fish such a run from the very top all the way to the very end. Because the water is a constant depth and you will be fishing pretty close to the bottom, you may move a fish a great distance down the run, pushing it down to the very end. At the very tailout of the run, this angry fish, pushed all the way down from the top, is now ready to strike. I have fished through such places many times, only to have a fish violently strike on the very last cast at the extreme end of such a pool. From top to bottom, it may have taken hours to get to that point. Be thorough and you may just be rewarded.

Sometimes you will come across a long, straight run that has adequate depth, but the bottom composition is not good for food sources (sand is a good example of this). Such a run might have very little rock or other structure in the middle of the river. In such a place, downed trees and branches along the edge will break the current in a way that is favorable to the fish. These trees and branches will create the seams and foam lines that migratory fish love.

These long, straight areas are some of the most tedious spots to fish, and this is a drawback. It can also be a benefit. In most rivers, there is a form of common courtesy that prevents people from fishing on top of one another. This is especially true of migratory fish, and if you drop in on someone who is fishing a run, you would be accused of "low holing" and might be run off the river. These spots really shine if you are going to be on the river on a day that you know will be very busy. If you go to one of these long, tedious runs on a busy day, you will have a great chance at catching some fish and will be able to fish for quite a while without

Complex currents make it impossible to fish some runs efficiently. In this case, it is a deep back-swirling hole in high water. However, the areas that surround these spots can be productive when fish move in and out to feed. Mornings and evenings are a great time to check these nearby places.

bother. On the days that I know are going to be very busy, I may flee to this type of area first thing in the morning. This is something you might think about as you plan a day on the river.

In a similar fashion, this type of spot is more nondescript than some of your larger and more obvious runs, and this too might allow you some undisturbed hours on a river on a busy day. These spots are usually pretty easy to fish, as they are even depth. You can confidently fish such a spot with a sink-tip.

The types of flies that you would use should directly reflect what is on the bottom of the river. If the bottom is pea gravel or sand, you will have more small food sources available, such as darters and shiners. If the bottom cover is mostly rocks, sculpins and gobies would be a great choice.

The Deepest and Darkest Eddy

In contrast to the classic steelhead run, many places that look like fantastic places should just be avoided when streamer fishing for migratory fish. As a new angler, you might come to a river and find a deep, dark, swirling hole and think that this would be the perfect place to catch a very large fish. These spots tend to look very fishy. A lot of them are more like a pothole than a run, with a steep initial drop-off and no distinguishing tailout. No doubt, these very deep and dark places hold their share of fish. However, a lot of becoming an efficient streamer angler involves not just knowing where to fish, but where not to fish.

If you see a spot with strange hydraulics, or a reversed current, coupled with deep water, this might be a place that is best avoided. The sheer depth of such a place is reason enough to avoid such a spot, but there are other reasons as well. These hydraulics are usually caused by a steep drop-off of some form, followed by deep water. The drop-off might be caused by a large rock or a change in bottom composition. Another common place to find strange hydraulics and currents is a steep drop-off behind a gravel bar. Furthermore, due to the swirling currents, there probably is not much structure on the bottom of such a spot, and the bottom is often sand or clay.

One reason that fish in such a place are difficult to catch is that many times, because the current is actually moving upstream, the fish will be facing downstream and your fly will never be in a good position for them to strike. Often I will see steelhead, trout, and predator fish facing downstream in such a place. Over the years I have spent a lot of hours trying to catch those fish, and most of those hours have been wasted.

Furthermore, the fish that are at the bottom of such a deep and dark place are there because they are resting, not feeding. Active fish will be in the best feeding lanes, commonly in 3 to 6 feet of water, which is also a great place to present a streamer.

There is, however, a part of these spots where you may find a fish. Look at the current in such a place: If there is a point, often at the very tail end of the run, where the current straightens out, this will be your best place to present a fly to a fish. This tailout can often be short and steep, but will usually contain a fish that has slid out of the depths to feed.

If you are stripping flies through such a spot, you may find a big brown along the slow edges, as in the gut of a classic run (a good way to think of these places is as the gut of a run, without the bother of a head or tailout). However, if you are fishing from a boat, one of the biggest challenges will be simply rowing through such a spot, as the reversing currents will be an issue. If the fish in this area are using the spot to hold in, they may move in and out to feed.

Deep Runs as a Mother Ship

Though these deep areas might be horrible for actually presenting a streamer and thereby catching fish, they usually have some overall significance to the area you are fishing. A deep run might hold a lot of unreachable fish on its own; however, this same deep run may be in proximity to moderate-depth areas upstream and downstream of the run. These next runs upstream from a deep, dark hole will often be where a migratory fish slips out to in the morning and evening to feed. Targeting these areas in the low-light hours of the day can produce great fishing opportunities.

It is easy to think about a hole that contains fish as the home of the fish, but in most systems migratory fish will have a range that they move in to feed at various times of the day. Streamer tactics are a great way to approach these mobile fish.

Egg Repositories

In talking about reading the water, one thing that plays a key role in the fall and spring is where the food eventually ends up. When you fish at a time of the year when some fish are spawning, be it steelhead, salmon, brown trout, or something like suckers, and you see the run declining and reach its end, you may notice that the migratory fish, which have been feeding on the eggs, will stick around the area for quite a while after the spawning has ended. Many times these areas are faster spots that don't seem to quite fit the mold of the perfect gamefish spot.

This is because loose eggs remain in the area for a while, often breaking free from the gravel until they settle. They are denser than water, and won't go too far. A lot of times, these free eggs are taken by the current and are deposited in a specific area. This glut of food keeps feeding fish present for a long time after the actual spawning is completed. As the fish are competing for food, this is a great place to catch one. When you fish, look for places where loose food will settle—this is another way to read the water and find a feeding fish. These eggs can settle in a lot of places, often at the bottom of where the current is funneled.

For my guiding in early fall, in the presence of king salmon, I spend a lot of time thinking, "Where do the eggs go?" As I was going down the river this past October, it occurred to me that a lot of spots where I might fish a streamer pattern are these egg deposits in the river.

Funnel Areas

Funnel areas are left largely unfished and are another inconspicuous area that holds predatory fish. Funnels are usually located in the center of a river. By nature, most anglers would rather fish one side of the river or another, whereas a funnel is usually found dead center.

Funnel areas are often narrow, gravelly spots in a river system and are shallow on the edges of the river but deep in the middle. These areas are frequently found below spawning gravel where the river forms a dip in the gravel between the sides of the river. In these places, the gravel bars are usually a little more downstream as they get deeper. In this way, they form a natural V from each side of the river, and food is forced down the middle. They can also be formed when rock formations or logs on both sides of the river force water to the center of the stream. Man-made structures, such as an old washed-out dam, can also constrict the current into a funnel. A funnel can also be made up of a combination of gravel bars, logs, man-made structure, etc.

In a funnel area, the predator fish will use the gravel bars or other structure as a break in the current, and they will dart out into the funnel to grab food. Though some funnel areas produce fish throughout the year, they are at their best when an abundant food source, usually eggs, is available in the area. When I fish for migratory fish in the early fall, I look for places where the salmon eggs are concentrated or forced through if they did not find a place on the bottom. Look for steelhead in the heavy currents at this time of the year.

When exploring a new river that has a spawning population of salmon, always try to imagine where the salmon eggs are going to end up. When it comes to eggs, remember that migratory fish and resident trout aren't the only one eating them. Other smaller fish are also in the vicinity, such as chubs. A large trout in the area may choose to feed on eggs or may feed on the minnows instead. This can help with streamer fishing. Also, if there are several migratory fish behind a spawning fish that are competing for the eggs, this can also create a scenario where a big fish is willing to chase a streamer out of aggression.

Gravel in the Larger Picture

Even though you may not be fishing around spawning fish, always remember that migratory fish have their eyes on the prize and are in a river system to spawn. This means a few things for you as you consider where to fish.

First of all, the lower reaches of a river system, which typically hold less gravel, will always be temperamental compared to the upper parts of a river. A fish migrating up a river will stay in the lower parts only as long as they have to, and are always looking to go to their natal spawning areas. If the habitat is poor, they will have more incentive

As a creek meanders for miles, it picks up many salmon eggs. The ones that don't cling to the bottom make it out to a small hole at the mouth of a creek. Places where loose eggs accumulate are great places to find fish, as this angler discovered! Eggs are denser than water and sink, and they will stay in one place for a long time once they settle. However, if taken by a strong current, they can bounce around until something eats them.

to blow by. If there is limited food in those places, or if the water temperature is warm, they will move upriver quickly. A migratory fish expects the headwaters of a river to have cooler temperatures and to have better feeding habitat. In reality, this is not always the case, as our rivers have man-made dams, pollution, etc. Nonetheless, this is how these fish are programmed.

High water will bring new fish in to these spots, but it will also clear the old fish out. Fish will surge as far as they can upriver when the water is high and conditions are right. They will also travel more quickly in warmer water conditions. If you have warm water temperatures early in a run and have a high-water event, expect to find fish as far upstream as they can go. Conversely, if you have high, cold water, such as in a winter storm, the fish will still enter the water but they will move upriver more slowly. This is a good scenario if you like to fish in the low parts of a system. Cold-water migrations can make for well-distributed fishing opportunities throughout a river system. You can have some of the best fishing in the bowels of a river, but you can also have the worst.

There is another practical consideration for the fish as well. The lowest ends of many rivers have a less desirable substrate for the fish. This means that the river bottom is composed of sand. Sand bottom is not conducive to the lower forms of life in the food chain such as minnows and insects. Moving upriver may be a matter of hunger as well as spawning desire. If there is food in such an area, it is most likely to be in the form of minnows. The minnows in these areas are the suspending types, often common shiners, sand shiners, and emerald shiners.

Though these marginal food areas are less desirable for holding fish in the long run, in the short run if you find them in such a place, you are likely to get a bite. Imagine you are a big trout, sitting at the bottom of a sandy run, with little food around you. Suddenly, a sparkly shiner imitation glides over you. It is the most delicious-looking thing that you have ever seen. Yum! You are so hungry, you don't think too much about it. You strike it! In this way, areas with limited food often produce the most jarring bites from the least-discriminating fish.

There are exceptions to what I have just written. Many times, you may look at a part of the river that appears sterile and think that food sources are insignificant. However, if you look closely along the shore of such an area, you may see that the bank is composed of silt or clay. These formations hold a deceptive amount of food. Silty banks will hold lots of swimming nymphs, such as hexes and dragonfly larvae. Clay banks are a cornucopia for crayfish and gobies, which hide in the crevices. In this way, the bank of an inconspicuous spot can attract fish even when the bottom of the river itself looks unattractive.

Some rivers have longer distances to the spawning areas. In such rivers the fish may move through the lower reaches more quickly, as they are somewhat territorial and will move upriver until they find more fish. If the migratory distance to the gravel is short, the fish will likely use the lower reaches of the river system more.

Heading closer and closer to the actual spawning period, the fish will spend a much shorter time in the lower regions of a river, even if migrating conditions are not ideal. As the migration continues, fish numbers become lopsided toward the gravel parts of the river system. This is especially evident in rivers with upstream limitations such as a dam. The fish will migrate up to the gravel stretches near a dam and find that there is no farther to go. For a short period they are concentrated, but they will then drop into any area that provides the types of structure outlined in this section in proximity to spawning gravel.

Most gravel areas in any river have deep water upstream and downstream of them. As a run of fish progresses, the fish are less picky about the type of structure and will heavily occupy these areas. These areas will have large numbers of dark winter fish as spring approaches. They may be superabundant, but they will often be stale fish after a long winter of waiting. Stale fish tend to be very moody; either you will get a bunch to bite or none at all. Conversely, the chrome fish at the lower ends of a system are more grabby, but less abundant. These are the things you must think about when you are choosing where you are going to fish.

A typical decision goes something like this: If I am fishing during the week, in bad weather, I know that the fishing pressure will be light and the fish may be turned on by the weather. In this instance, I might go to the area with the stale fish, as I know they might come out of their bad mood for a day in those conditions. On the other hand, if the sun is out and there is a lot of pressure on the water, I may opt to head to a more desolate place in the hopes of finding naive, grabby fish.

My point is, always look at fishing in the context of what is happening biologically with the fish. Fish numbers, and fishing pressure, will always be greatest in some proximity to spawning gravel at any time of the year. However, if you desire solitude and undisturbed fishing, fishing in obscurity might be better for you.

Look to the Center in Large Rivers

If your tactic is stripping flies, there is something that should be mentioned about large rivers. In general, you could fish any of the types of structure that we describe and have success stripping flies. You might pay special attention to the parts

about fishing around timber. For many who strip flies passionately, heavy cover is where it's at. If you fished a river that is only large enough to cast to one side of the boat at a time comfortably, you would be very accustomed to casting to the edges of the river.

Probably one of the biggest mistakes I personally make when streamer fishing for trout or migratory fish when stripping flies is that I will sometimes only read the shore side of the river, even though I know that there are a lot of fish sitting in the middle of it. I see a lot of boats go by stripping streamers for salmonids over the course of a year, but very seldom do I see them fishing toward the middle of the river. Often in wide rivers this area holds the larger fish, which are using the middle depths as an access point to shallower baitfish. As most people overlook them, they are less pressured and more likely to take a fly. At the same time, they are using the deeper water as a form of cover.

If you fish in a large river, it bears mentioning that in many of the Midwest's large rivers that

A crossover is a place where current is concentrated as it shifts from one side of the river to the other. These are consistently good places to find a migratory fish. They are also great places to cut through leaves and debris that are on the surface.

hold migratory fish, you may have better success fishing out toward the middle of the river, from the shore side. This is true in a lot of areas that don't look very impressive. A typical scenario is when there is shallow water on one side of the river and a slow drop-off all the way to the other side. In these places, the water column from one side of the river to the other side is shaped like a wedge. This is a classic spot to find a large salmonid, especially a migratory brown trout, in the middle of the river. If you are stripping a fly as you row down the river, consider the middle if you are having a tough day, as there might be some large fish in these overlooked places. On a busy day, when all the other boats are throwing flies toward the edge of the river, there are untouched fish off the other side.

This is true at any time of the year but especially during the spring, if you are fishing a river with salmon fry that is available. When stripping flies, fish holding in the river are easy to overlook. An example of a midstream area to find migratory fish is a crossover area. Crossover areas are important to all types of streamer fishing.

Crossover Areas

Crossover areas are one of the most sublime types of currents that hold migratory fish in a given area, and are easily overlooked. It is an area where the current shifts from one side of the river to another, typically a seam or bubble line that leads from the tailout of a run to the head of the next pool. Crossover areas represent prime feeding areas for the steelhead. Steelhead will lie on either side of the current in such a spot. As food enters, they can easily move in and out of the current to attack their prey. Crossovers are a type of current break or seam. If you are fishing a large river, these spots can be easily seen by the formation of foam lines.

Usually crossovers have a steady drop in depth as you move through them. The river is starting to bend at this point. If there is no visible seam, you may be able to see the river channel switching from one side to the other. Another scenario where you find a crossover is behind a big obstruction in the river, such as an island. Often the island will have strong current down one side that will cross to the other side once past the island.

Steelhead are the gamefish typically found directly in crossover areas. These are usually feeding fish that have come out of an adjacent pool or run. This is another good situation for fishing purposes. If you recognize such a spot, your line may soon be tight!

Another feature of a crossover is that they have a very distinct soft edge on their inside. During the winter months, trout and steelhead will often use the soft edge to rest. Steelhead will frequently be pretty close to the seam in this scenario, whereas trout will rest in the slowest of water if conditions permit. Often lake-run browns are found at the slowest point in such a run. If I am parked in the middle of the river and casting over a crossover into the slowest water, I know that if I hook a fish immediately after casting into the slow water, it is likely a large brown. However, if the fly has swung into the current and I get a heavy bite, it is usually a steelhead.

There are two times that I use crossovers in adverse conditions. In the fall, when there are a lot of leaves on the water, I will often fish a crossover. In these areas it is possible to cast a weighted fly across the current into the slower water, allowing the fly to sink before the debris interferes. Sometimes I think that leaves are the bane of my existence, and they can complicate the fishing immensely when they plague the river. For many of us who use jet outboards, leaves clog the engines and make things challenging.

In a similar fashion, in the winter when slush is on the river, you can think of it in the same way. A crossover will concentrate the ice, and you can cast over it to get the fly down and swing it beneath the ice. However, in the winter months, the fish are more likely to be closer to the slow water. In the winter you would have to take special care to make sure that your streamer sinks. A heavily weighted fly can be a big asset when this occurs. I often carry a few ultraheavy flies to get me under debris.

Wishbone Runs: Where Seams Converge

There is another type of current that we pay attention to—it is obscure but it happens often enough that I thought I would mention it. Occasionally you have a flat, shallow, straight area composed of gravel. Due to undercut banks, trees fall in the shallow water and form a seam on each side of the river. As the shallow area comes to an end and starts to get deeper, the currents unite to form one seam, typically on the deeper side of the river. As these seams merge, they create a flat spot on the surface of the river as the water depth drops off. This flat spot, located between two seams, is a great place to look for a migratory fish.

Think of this type of current being shaped like the letter Y, or a wishbone. One run comes down each side and just above where they converge, in the V part of the Y, is where you will find the fish. In this V section, there is a natural resting spot for the fish. If it is a steady drop-off, this area will be the perfect depth. In this instance, you would cast over one seam into the slow water in the middle. If you find this type of spot, it is usually overlooked by others and can be a boon for fishing.

AVOIDING DEBRIS IN THE WATER

As mentioned earlier, there are times you will be forced to fish around areas that have a lot of debris in the water. Early in the fall, this may be dying weeds. On windy days, you may have leaves in the water. As winter bears down on us, many rivers are riddled with slush as their water temperatures drop into the lower 30s.

One way to work around heavy debris in the water is to fish spots where it is most concentrated and go under it with a heavy fly and sink-tip, such as mentioned above when discussing a crossover. Fishing a seam behind a piece of structure would offer a similar opportunity.

If you are fishing with debris in the water, sometimes the opposite approach works very well. If you have a lot of water to work with, look for very broad areas of the river that hold fish and have no defined seam. In my home river, the average width is approximately 150 feet. If I was fishing on a debris fiesta type of day, I would look for areas of the river that are 175 feet wide or more. These areas would distribute the debris in a way that was much less bothersome.

A common type of structure that would present a good fishing opportunity on such days would be mid-river, deep, submerged rock or gravel bars.

Notice the steelhead in the front of the picture out in the open. This is a positive sign that the fish are active. Though the fish is out in the open, notice that it is close to the cover of a log. Often you get visual cues when you are on the river, especially from a boat. If I see a lot of fish out in the open, this usually indicates a good bite day. If I see very few fish in the open, we might be scraping for fish.

Both fall and winter can be challenging when debris or ice are found in the river. Approach them the same way. Use a heavy fly and go deep. You can also look for broad parts of the river, where debris or ice is less concentrated. Another option is to look to tight seams and crossovers where you can get your fly under and past the problematic area.

This type of cover holds fish but does not concentrate the leaves. Fishing such a place can provide less frustrating and more pleasant fishing experiences.

In summary, if you are trying to avoid debris in the water column, look for areas where the debris is extremely concentrated, such as a crossover. Another great option is just the opposite: Look for areas where the debris is spread out over a larger area.

GOOD SIGNS

Though fishing on a day-to-day basis is hard to predict at best, there are some things I notice on a daily basis. One of the best positive signs that I see is fish out in the open. If you are in a boat and looking at the bottom of the river, you may go down the river one day and see a lot of fish. Chances are, on that day you had a pretty good bite. However, the next day you may go down that same stretch of river and see very few fish out in the open. There is a good chance that the fishing was tougher for you on that day.

Often other anglers will say to me, "Yesterday there were a lot of fish here, but today they must have moved on, as I am just not seeing any fish." It is possible that the fish moved upriver or downriver, but if the main migration has slowed and there has been no change in water levels, this is not usually the case. As previously mentioned, when the bite is poor and the fish are inactive, they simply tuck themselves into the structure and they are sullen. If I don't see fish out and about, it tells me I should hunker down and fish the areas of high concentrations of fish meticulously. It also tells me that I should fish heavy structure like brush that day, as that is likely where the concentration of fish is.

WATER TEMPERATURE AND STRUCTURE

Water temperature is discussed quite a bit in this book. Understanding water temperature can help you choose which types of cover to fish on a given day. Furthermore, as our rivers get very cold in the Midwest, understanding water temperature can have a profound impact on your fishing success.

Understanding water temperature is key to success when conditions get tough. For years it was thought that migratory fish would not take an active presentation in icy water, but they will! Fish will feed on big minnows throughout the winter months. However, you have to be a lot more selective about where and how you fish during the challenging cold periods.

This is true throughout the fall but of particular interest during the coldest water periods.

As steelhead enter their natal rivers in the fall, water temperature usually is not a big factor. Indeed, for steelhead entering rivers in the months of September and October, the water temperature in many streams ranges from the low 60s to the mid-40s in some of the spring-fed rivers. In some very warm Midwest streams, you will find steelhead at the mouths of springs and creeks at the beginning of their run. These fish will back away from these areas as the water temperature drops.

As fall progresses, the steelhead relate to the forms of cover that were discussed earlier in this chapter. The water temperature now ranges from the high 30s to the mid-40s depending on the river system.

The steelhead's behavior changes in the fall and early winter, and this change affects how they relate to cover. If you have ever fished for trout in the winter, you will notice that they move to the quiet water, hugging the edges of the river channel. They may do this because of the food sources available, but there is another factor that influences why they are there. Cold water, by its nature, holds more oxygen than warm water. As the water gets colder in the winter months, the trout and also the steelhead do not need to stay as far out in the current as they would at other times of the year. The water in the slower areas is now rich in oxygen. This opens up a lot of new areas to migratory fish. Steelhead are conserving energy before they spawn in the spring, so it makes good sense that these fish would lean toward slower holding areas.

As winter progresses, the steelhead and the trout will move to the slowest parts of a run. The best of these places will also have access to food sources. In these slow, currentless areas, tiny food sources are active during the winter. These range from midges to scuds to caddis larvae. Many of the trout and even the migratory fish will feed on these sources, skipping a rung in the food chain. However, that middle part of the food chain, the baitfish, are also drawn to these tiny food sources. This provides an ideal scenario for fishing with baitfish patterns.

At the same time, fishing pressure decreases when conditions are most brutal. This can also contribute to steelhead being more brazen, and often being found in slower water or water with less structure. There are few predatory birds around in the winter, which also makes them less concerned about structure. Furthermore, winter flows are less than fall and spring flows, due to snow and ice absorbing much of the moisture. All of these factors combine to make the need for structure a little less urgent. In the spring and summer months, I fish an area that has a solid gravel bottom and is very nondescript. When you look at it, there is absolutely no cover there that would hold a fish. And yet during the winter, when the river is deserted, if I am careful I can catch a fish there every day.

SPRINGS AND FEEDER CREEKS

Another thing to consider in the winter is the presence of springs along the bank of the river or underneath the surface. Springs that provide cold water in the summer months now provide warmer water in the winter months. The boulders, brush, gravel bars, etc., that we discussed earlier that are downstream from such a warm-water source will hold more steelhead than those areas without it. Even when conditions seem perfect, these springs add attraction to fish, and many of the best steelhead spots I know have springs or groundwater quietly flowing into them.

Underwater Springs

Many rivers have underwater seeps that come in and sweeten the water throughout their length. These spots are very attractive to fish but are difficult to find. During the winter months, these spots are often some of the best producers of fish, and in some rivers they have a dead giveaway.

The dead giveaway is this: Other types of fish, such as suckers and other bottom feeders, will often congregate in these locations. If you find these groups of bottom-feeding fish you will find the spring and the steelhead. I used to go right past these areas in the winter, as they are often found in sandy stretches with little structure. However, when I looked closely, I commonly noticed the telltale square tail of steelhead mixed into the group.

The only draw to such a place is the favorable water temperatures. The bottom is sand, but if you

Left: Springs are a great place to look for gamefish. They provide a constant water temperature that is beneficial when the water in the river is too warm or too cold. These springs can be obvious but they could also be underwater. Springs and small tributaries will almost always have something good to catch near them.

think about it, this is a great place to look for a biting fish. Small fish as well as big fish are drawn to this type of spot. If a food source is present, it may be minnows or baitfish also drawn to the spot. These minnows will make the gamefish receptive to a well-presented baitfish imitation.

Winter water is usually some of the clearest water of the year. Ice has absorbed some of the water, so river levels can be low. Snow, as precipitation, does not cause rivers to rise as much as rain due to the lack of runoff. These clear water conditions allow you to see the bottom around springs. If you are in a boat, take a close look at these areas. Seeing fish in such places can reveal the sweet spots that are often overlooked.

Springs and High Water

Springs and tributaries have a lot to offer those who fish for migratory fish. But they also can be a repellant to fish. If a tributary has a lot of clay in it, for example, and there is a storm, the water flowing out of that creek might be repellant to fish, who don't like the clay and particulate in their gills. Often fish will shift to the clearer side of the river to avoid such places when the water gets high.

This is obvious in one of our local rivers. In the spring, as the water gets high, a large tributary will dump clay into the river. Typically, the best fishing would be right in front of the mouth of that tributary. However, as the clay integrates with the river after runoff, the fish will shift to the other side of the river, even though cover is limited on that opposite side. As water levels come up, all the anglers will shift to the clearer side of the river in that area. This is true of the bait, hardware, and fly anglers. It is not that the fish don't bite in this clay-infested water—they are simply avoiding it.

Not all particulate flowing from springs and creeks is equal in our rivers. In rivers with a constant stain of the same variety that flows from the springs, the fish adapt and will find a fly in constantly bad conditions. In rivers that are naturally clear, the influx of particulate into the water will have a greater impact. The fish will either adjust to the stain after a period of time or will wait until it leaves the area and clear waters return. These changes in water clarity are exacerbated when the sun is shining. Sunlight illuminates the stain and compounds already poor conditions.

GENERAL TIPS FOR HIGH WATER

If a spring is adding mud or particulate to your spot, there are ways to combat stained water when you are fishing. These tips for fishing around springs apply more broadly to fishing high water caused by runoff as well. The first thing that you need to do in any high-water condition is to slow down your presentation and make sure that your fly is right where the fish are. If a fish is having a hard time locating your fly, you need to make it easier for the fish to find it. This is especially true of swung-fly presentations.

Compounding the need to get your fly to the fish, you should understand that in high-water conditions, the fish usually have a glut of food in the system to choose from. Higher water typically scours the river bottom and breaks a lot of insects and other organisms free from the bottom. Furthermore, food sources from the banks of surrounding springs and low-lying areas will be washed into the river in flood conditions. Both steelhead and brown trout are known to eat terrestrial food sources. These could include earthworms, frogs, and mice. In the springtime, one of my favorite imitations in high water actually looks like an earthworm. Swung slowly along the bottom, this unusual fly has led to a lot of steelhead and trout over the years.

One thing you can do in poor-water-clarity scenarios is to incorporate things into your flies that will make them easier to see. This can include adding copious amounts of flash to your flies. Each river has its own formula, but dark-bodied flies with blue incorporated into them work well in this region. On sunny, high-water days, add some holographic materials to your flies. These will reflect light in murky conditions and may be the trigger needed to get a strike.

Another way to make your fly more noticeable is to give it more movement in the water. There is a tradeoff to this, as mobile flies often don't sink very well. In high water, whether this approach works will depend on the flow in your specific waterway.

Initially when high water hits, you may want to move as far as possible from the springs, tributary streams, as they will be adding a lot of dirt, tannin, and debris to the water column. Often I will fish a stretch of river with the minimum number of creeks or I will try to fish upstream from the creeks to avoid fishing the dirtiest water. On my local Muskegon River, there are certain tiny creeks that I will avoid at all costs when the water is high. Some of these tiny creeks contribute a lot of ugliness to the river when they blow out.

However, this changes quickly after a short while. Typically small creeks will recover their clarity more quickly than the main stream of a river. Thus, if the tributary creeks or headwaters of the river are open to fishing when the water is high, you might consider fishing these. Also, water that is smaller may be safer to wade when the system as a whole is flooded. A side benefit to fishing upstream is that the fish will often surge upriver as far as possible when the water is high, and this will lead them into small places. This is how migratory fish are programmed and is especially true of steelhead.

Another rising water suggestion is to fish the broadest stretches of your river when the water is high. In this way you are approaching dirty water in the same way as having leaves or ice in the water. In these broad areas the dirt and debris in the water column settles to the bottom of the river and makes the water clarity a little better. If the river is broad for some distance, the water clarity will become much better. Furthermore, the water flow is usually a little slower in these broad areas and the water is generally shallower. If you find a gravel bar that breaks the current or a run along the edge of a wide area, this may be a great spot to fish. Due to the generally shallow nature of these areas, it is also easier to get a fly in front of the fish and keep it there.

If you are an avid angler, you will become acquainted with high-percentage spots that you

In the spring, steelhead will go up into the tiniest of creeks. We leave them alone while they are there, as the spawning that they do in these small places is critical to having wild fish in our rivers. Steelhead need to stay in the river for a year before migrating out to the lake. If a river gets too warm in the summer, these small creeks may be the only chance for wild fish survival.

absolutely know contain fish, regardless of the water conditions. Approach these areas in high water and slow your presentation down. Use heavy flies, and present them slowly. If you are swinging flies, take very small steps and make multiple casts per step. This will ensure that the fish has the chance to see your fly and hopefully react to it. You do have one small thing in your favor when the water is high: Because the clarity is not good, the fish are not aware of your presence and are less wary of your tippet. This will allow for multiple presentations. Don't expect to be able to push the fish with your line or movements as you could in lower-water conditions.

If the river is blocked by a dam or other barrier, you will find high concentrations of fish just below the dam after high water. Often it is pretty obvious when the fish are in such a place, as they tend to draw a lot of anglers. They can also be seen porpoising downstream of such an obstruction.

Though dams provide high concentrations of fish, they usually have a lot of complicated currents and presenting a fly might be a challenge. As the water settles in and clears, the fish will become territorial. This leads them to distribute downstream from the obstruction, and you will find good fishing in the miles below a dam as the river clears. If you received a large surge of fish, this redistribution could stretch for miles.

A common misconception about migratory fish is that they move only upriver in the fall and winter. I don't believe this is true. In shorter river systems, steelhead will move in and out of the system several times if conditions aren't right. Their movements in and out will be more dramatic if the river system does not have good food sources for them. We mentioned particulate in the water column earlier. If there is too much particulate in the water column and it makes it difficult for fish to survive, they may simply move out of the river for a while, only to come back in when conditions are right. In the same way, fish will bolt upriver in high-water conditions, which are great for migrating. However, if the water becomes too low when the water drops, they will simply leave only to return closer to spawning time.

Even in large and fertile rivers, like my home river the Muskegon, the migratory fish will move upstream and downstream great distances prior to spawning season. Sometimes we can prove this because of the presence of other anglers on the river, as illustrated by the following story.

I'll begin by noting that many fly tiers can recognize their own flies when someone else finds one along the river. Due to the heavy tippet, fly consumption is usually pretty light when it comes to streamer fishing, but you do sometimes lose a fly to a tree, rock, or fish. One day in November, as waters were receding from a high water event, I was guiding two guys from out of state. A few hours into the day, one of them hooked a large chrome steelhead. The fly he was using was a large chartreuse and purple leech with a lot of Flashabou. It was distinctive enough that there was little chance that anyone else was using a fly like it. After a furious battle, the chrome fish leapt into the air and broke the line as it hit the water on the way back down. I heard some expletives come from both ends of the boat.

Two days later I met one of the excellent veteran guides on the river, who guides spin-fishing and fly-fishing trips, Jon Kolehouse. Jon approached me in the parking lot and handed me a fly—the same purple and chartreuse leech! When I asked him where he had gotten it, he showed me a picture of the fish—a very large steelhead—caught several miles *downstream* from where we connected with it. Fish will move upstream and downstream in a river system freely, especially prior to spawning season. As the desire to spawn becomes more urgent, they will stay in the upper regions of the river.

AVOID THESE SPOTS

We have covered a lot of different types of water, but there are some things that I avoid. More frequently than not, they consume the time you have to fish and are unproductive. There is a lot of inconspicuous water that holds fish, but there is also a lot of great-looking water that I have the luxury to avoid. Most of these spots are eddies that have tough currents for swinging a fly.

If you are specifically swinging flies, avoid any current that forces the fly to swing at an unusual angle. Often these areas are strong eddies behind a large piece of structure. A lot of times when the water is clear, I can see predatory fish facing downstream in these places while at rest. This is unusual because most fish will face upstream 95 percent of the time in Midwest rivers. These are similar to deep eddies, on a smaller scale. If you can avoid fishing these areas, it is often for the best. However, you can be successful if you find a straight current that will tow your line and fly out of the more complex currents.

There are workarounds for a lot of difficult fishing areas. As I said, I may just avoid fishing a difficult area when I have a lot of options while fishing from a boat. Sometimes, however, this might not be possible. If you come across a complex current that you are forced to fish, there are things that can be done to help your chances.

First of all, you may want to consider adding motion to the fly. For much of swung-fly fishing, you'd probably prefer a dead swing. However, in complex currents, slowly stripping the fly might be just what is necessary to make the fly appealing to a fish. Also, a weighted fly can at least help keep a fly swinging straight as your line tows it across a current. A floating fly line will be a good choice when you need to manipulate the fly as they provide more line control. Because they are buoyant, they can also pull a fly around if you have the right current. Floating fly lines will be discussed later on in techniques section of this book.

DON'T OVERLOOK THE OBVIOUS

Learning to read the water and understanding the forms of structure is an important step in becoming a good steelhead angler. Understanding how shade and water temperature impact these fish is also very important. Many of these spots in a river are sublime and take experience to recognize.

When fishing a river, using what is left behind by other anglers can help you recognize potential fishing areas. Human beings are messy creatures. Paying attention to the signs left by other anglers can lead you to good fishing areas. If you come to an inconspicuous area in a river that has a tree covered in spawn bags hanging over it, this may tell you that this is a good place to fish. Lures left in the water, footprints on the shore, and other signs are left by anglers leaving an area. They can tell you where the fish are but also can tell you what spots have been fished. If you know a good angler is fishing the river in front of you and you don't want to fish where that person fished, pay attention to the signs they leave behind. We also do this all the time from boats, where we listen to the sounds of motors around the bends in a river.

Reading the water and looking for the structure mentioned earlier in the chapter found some of the best areas in my local rivers. Other areas were found by seeing other anglers pulling out of a spot. There is no need for pride when identifying new fishing areas.

There is a real beauty to fishing streamers for steelhead. Few steelhead that you see in the river can't be approached with this method. For that reason, always keep your eyes open during a day of fishing. Many times I have floated down a river and have seen a steelhead holding in an unusual place. Fishing that same spot the next day, we often would catch a fish. Keeping your eyes open

can result in future success and sometimes immediate success.

Early in the fall, we often have clients that like to fish for steelhead. While West Michigan Rivers are loaded with a variety of migratory and resident fish during the early fall, steelhead can be difficult to find. As the number of steelhead and lake-run browns is very limited when they first come in, a common tactic is to move slowly down the river and look for a desirable fish, and then turn around and position upstream from it to try to catch it. But there is one difficult question that must be answered: How do you identify the steelhead or trout from the salmon, bottom-feeding fish, etc., which are seemingly everywhere? The answer to this lies in the tail. Steelhead and brown trout have a square tail, whereas most other fish have a forked tail. It is the one distinguishing feature that gives these fish away at all times of the year.

When you guide you have a lot of memories of great fish taken over the years. A few years back, I was guiding a client who desperately wanted to catch a steelhead, and early October was the only time that he could fish. There was a large slug

The tail of a steelhead or brown trout gives them away. Both species have a square tail.

of king salmon spawning in the river, and what few steelhead were around would certainly be in proximity to the irresistible food source, eggs. We started to traverse the river, fishing some likely runs below spawning areas, to no avail. As we moved downriver in the boat, our eyes were glued to the bottom of the river, trying to catch a glimpse of the target species.

As we approached and passed a large run of salmon, I could see that one of the tails of the fish looked square, even though the rest of the fish was obscured and looked a lot like a salmon. We positioned at a steep angle above the fish and selected a fly that resembled a natural minnow that would be kicked out by the salmon. Then we proceeded to swing a fly so that it skirted the back of the gravel.

The line swung around and as it passed the salmon, a chrome steelhead broke out of the pack and annihilated the fly! A furious battle ensued, but victory was ours. A large, bright fish was in the net.

This simple way to identify steelhead and trout has helped on many occasions. A combination of understanding structure and common sense are the real keys to reading the water.

Left: Sometimes fishing pressure is hard to avoid, but there are things you can do to give yourself a fighting chance when the river is busy. If you have the luxury of avoiding it, do that. Being able to read the water and understanding structure will make your fishing much more enjoyable. The obscure spots that you find will produce fish while other anglers jockey for a spot on the river.

FISHING PRESSURE

Learning how to read the water will help you find water that is not as heavily fished. Sometimes, however, there is just no way to avoid fishing pressure and you are forced to fish around others. Perhaps you are fishing a local river and word is out that the fish are in, or maybe you head to the river on your day off, which happens to be a holiday weekend, and you find the parking lot full of cars (I once guided on the Muskegon on Good Friday only to find 127 cars in the parking lot of the launch I was using). If you are caught in a situation that you know will be a busy one, there are things you can do to make the fishing more productive.

The main thing to keep in mind is that a skilled angler will often catch the most aggressive fish in any spot with any method. Thus, if you are working your way downstream behind a good spin-fishing angler or another angler who is nymphing, that person will often catch the active fish—which is often the fish you are after with your streamer—first.

If I am in a busy river situation, I try to start early in the morning and find a large spot to fish to myself. Often this means I will travel a mile or two rather than fishing and be caught in a crowd of anglers. A lot of times, I will avoid fishing an area where I have seen another angler fishing, only to fish the area on my way back upstream at the end of the day. Since that angler may have caught the active fish, I don't want to fish immediately behind him. The good news is that as long as a decent number of fish are present, another fish will soon become active and aggressive, and you should get a bite there later in the day.

It is a good idea to also judge the targeting method of the anglers passing down the river in front of you. For example, if you are fishing behind someone fishing live bait, which often catches more-passive fish, you may have a better chance at catching a fish than behind someone with an active approach, who may be casting lures and spinners. Lures and spinners will take the same type of aggressive fish that you are trying to get with your streamer-fishing method.

As a boat fisherman, I have learned to look at things in terms of how many rods have gone through a run versus how many boats. For example, if a boat with only one angler has fished through a run, then in my mind if I fished the same spot soon thereafter, the person in the front of my boat would now be only the second rod through. I am frequently fishing two anglers, so this would be exactly the same as if I had fished the spot first and the angler in the back of my boat had been the second rod. I would not have a problem fishing the run in this scenario. Thus, the number of rods that have fished an area is a bigger influence than the number of boats that have gone through. In the same way, if a boat pulling five different plugs has gone down the run in front of you, it might be best to pick up and go to another area. If it is a really good area, you can rest it for a few hours and come back to it.

As a guide, you learn to judge the quality of an angler from a distance. Sometimes I see a very bad angler in a very good spot in my home river. That angler, who is obviously not likely to be catching much, may be the perfect "placeholder" for a desirable place for you to fish after he has left. After his boat passes you and he finally leaves the area, it may be a good time to try that spot. A lot of times you will see someone fishing a spot from the wrong side or frothing the water with a new Spey rod. Yet another scenario is when you see someone in an area targeting a totally different species. This is common around here, as we have walleye and resident trout in areas that may not be located in the same depths as the migratory fish. These are places you can be confident at trying as the next angler going through.

FISH DISTRIBUTION

After some practice reading the water and honing your fishing skills, there are still things going on beneath the water that no one can predict. Fish distribution with migratory fish can be mysterious at best. For some intangible reason, fish seem to choose different runs on different years to populate heavily.

There is a beautiful spot that I love to fish year after year, a nice depression in the river in front of a large rock formation. It was so good one season, I could get a swung-fly steelhead every day out of that area. That year the run of fish was not very strong, so I came to believe that it was the most prime spot in the entire river. The next year, we had a very strong run of fish, and I was excited to fish my favorite spot. I thought it must hold fish, as every other run in the area was producing. Day after day I set up on that run with clients, and it looked exactly the same as it did the year before. I was persistent and too stubborn. We never caught anything there. Believing I had wasted a lot of time, I gave up on that area and never fished it until the following year.

I was in the habit of avoiding that spot—I was over it. Yet one day, I saw another angler throwing bait in that spot and he was obviously successful, as a large chrome fish was leaping out of the water. Soon I was fishing that spot again, and was elated to find that the fish had returned. My point is don't hesitate to try a spot that you once read as a good spot even if it has fished poorly at some point in time.

In my experience, early season fishing holds some clues to fish distribution. In late October, when our fall runs are typically light, I will cover a lot of water to find a fish in an area. More often than not, if fish begin to accumulate in an area early in the run, they will continue to populate that area throughout the entire fishing season.

SOMETIMES THEY GIVE IT ALL AWAY

This chapter has dealt extensively with figuring out how and where to find fish when you are out on your own. Sometimes, the fish really give you some help. Though they do not show in the same way as Atlantic salmon, sometimes migratory fish, specifically steelhead, will porpoise and give away their location, especially in the fall. This is a great sign, and if you see a fish porpoise in the fall, you should certainly run a fly over it. They tend to exhibit this behavior during the low-light hours.

Steelhead are territorial, and when they migrate they will sometimes become more populous in an area than they would like to be. This, in turn, can make them very aggressive. A porpoising fish is often in this situation. A tailout or bottleneck area is the most common place to find such a fish. A large baitfish pattern can really channel their inner animal. If you see a fish porpoise, and it is in a spot that is presentable, proceed to its location quickly and get a fly over it. The results can be amazing!

Springtime fishing leads to a different situation with steelhead. Often I am swinging flies with clients at that time of the year and see fish porpoising. A client will often see these fish and get very excited. However, they are mostly fish to be ignored. Male steelhead will spawn until they are exhausted and will do anything they can to maintain their proximity to the spawning areas. As they become tired, they will often porpoise to maintain their position. These are not fish that will bite. These same steelhead will also porpoise and jump as they are heading back to the lake. Again, these fish are highly unlikely to be takers, and we should leave them to their important business.

However, sometimes in the spring, I will see a female steelhead porpoise. They look obviously different from the male fish, with a slender, torpedo-like shape and a silvery color. Female steelhead spawn quickly and become ravenously hungry. In a river with lots of food, they will stick around and take a fly readily. This is a fish that we would swing a fly or strip a streamer over.

A common scenario if we have a late run of fish in the spring is that female fish will come

This is the typical drop-back fish. This one took a small fry pattern while trout fishing. It was a lot of fun on a 6-weight! Drop-back fish will leave a stream quickly if there is no food. Conversely, if food is abundant, they will gain their strength back quickly and leisurely work their way back down.

in, bright from the lake, and spawn very quickly. Shortly thereafter, they will start to feed. These are ideal fish, as they are sometimes dime bright and fight very well. The spawning process is easy on these fish.

For me, a really interesting footnote to spring fish is that as I fish in the upper stretches of my local stream, I catch mostly female drop-back steelhead in the spring. I have friends that fish in the lower reaches of the river, 30 miles downstream, and when they catch returning fish in the spring, the majority are males.

Male steelhead, after they spawn, are completely exhausted. They will drift downstream for miles, not resisting the current at all. Sometimes you will see them flopping on the surface as they back down the river. Finally, they will find a resting spot and will start to feed with abandon. In the spring, you may see a distinct difference in your local stream in the gender of the fish you are catching depending on what part of the river system you are fishing as you near the end of the migratory fish season.

This chapter was designed to help you figure out where to find a fish. The next one covers the techniques you can use to fish these places well.

Left: A large male steelhead lumbers out of a small stream after spawning to exhaustion. This fish is not one that will take a fly and will probably not feed much until miles downriver. I find that we catch a lot more female fish after the spawning run in the upper parts of the river, whereas the male fish split more quickly for the big lake.

CHAPTER 3

Fishing to Structure

Though this book has something for any stream angler, it is geared with the Midwest in mind. These waters are unique, and our rivers are lined with hardwoods. This creates a lot of structure in our rivers and makes the consideration of fishing structure a necessity when fishing for migratory fish. Our rivers have a storied history of logging, and many ancient timbers and remnants of the logging era contribute to the intense structure in some of our waterways. Wood is a common form of cover, but some rivers have vast gravel shoals, others have shale and boulders, and urban streams have man-made structure.

In addition to the structure, the migration of fish in the Midwest is largely easier than in other places in the world. In their native habitat on the West Coast, a steelhead might travel a very long distance to reach spawning waters. However, in a typical Midwest stream, a fish might migrate as little as a few miles or as much as 100 miles. In comparison to other places in the world, this migration is generally pretty easy. Our gradients are mostly pretty mild, though there are exceptions to this. After they migrate upriver, the fish associate with whatever cover is available and their trout-like instincts take over. Their colors change to darker river colors, they live in prime river lies, and they devour the foods that are available to any other predatory fish. Understanding their behavior and their habitat is a key part of being successful as an angler. This chapter addresses how to approach the various forms of habitat that migratory fish like to occupy.

Depending on the circumstances, large trout species relate to structure for other reasons. Structure provides resting areas for the fish, but also

Fishing around areas with dead or dying weed beds in the fall and winter months produces. Weed beds naturally shrink and die off in the winter, creating an ever-smaller refuge for the minnows that live in them.

A fin of a migrating steelhead pops out of the river. Migrating fish typically have a pretty easy voyage in the Great Lakes region. Steelhead are built for a long migration in steep gradient out West. Even in our longest rivers, these fish are not stressed by distance.

security. Migratory fish have few animal predators. However, any threats that they would have would come from above, and structure alleviates this stress on fish. One of the great threats to fish throughout their early lives is birds. Each year I watch as herons and kingfishers annihilate thousands of steelhead fry. Meanwhile, ospreys and eagles take larger fish from above, while otters swoop in from below. Even when they mature and are out of danger from wildlife, fish don't know that the shadows above them are not threats, so they need the structure to alleviate this fear.

Without a doubt, the biggest threat to fish in most rivers is man, another predator that approaches from above. Not all anglers are catch-and-release, and fish are wary of our presence. Structure can be an asset when simply avoiding people or fishing pressure. Water temperature is also a factor: As our rivers become very cold in the winter, finding structure or depth in relation to springs or warm spots in the river can provide for more active fish and greater success.

Structure, therefore, is very important to understanding migratory fish. It governs where we fish and what methods that we use to fish for them. If you understand how to read the water hand in hand with finding good structure, you will have everything you need to catch fish.

Keep Every Spot That You Fish in Context

When you are trying to learn a river, everything needs to be kept in the context of location. I fish some stretches of rivers that have numerous great hiding spots: They have gravel, rocks, terrific structure, and everything else that a fish might need. In such an area, I might not bother fishing a spot that does not look exceptional.

Other parts of a river may have poor structure and little in the way of food sources for miles. Eventually, as the fish move upriver, they will come to some great habitat. If you find the first good habitat upstream from some blank water, you will be in a good position to catch fish as they are migrating. Sometimes these spots hold the most fish!

In the fall, gravel bars are a great example of this. Steelhead zip upriver pretty quickly, with little to slow them down in many rivers. If other fall-spawning migratory fish are present, such as salmon or brown trout, the steelhead will move upriver and eventually come to the first spawning area. This might be near the lake, or it might be 20 miles upriver. Regardless, this first easy feeding station is an example of a form or structure that will hold fish and is an awesome spot to fish.

The Importance of Bottom Composition

Gravel is just one form of bottom substrate. As we go through this chapter, we will talk about different types of structure. However, there is an important aspect to reading water that has to do

with what is around the structure on the bottom of the river.

Let me illustrate: You might be fishing for migratory fish near the upper reaches of a river and find a rock or piece of timber to fish. If you go 20 miles downriver, you might find a piece of structure in the same depth of water that looks the same, but the fish will behave very differently. The reason for this is the bottom composition. Consider that the upstream spot is surrounded by rocks and gravel, whereas the downstream spot is surrounded by sand. Though the structure looks very similar, under the hood the composition of the bottom has a drastic impact on how the fish will behave.

If the surrounding substrate is made up of gravel and rock, a lot of food sources are present in the area. Not only will the structure itself have food for the fish, but so will the surrounding area. These are the types of areas where bottom-dwelling baitfish patterns such as gobies, sculpins, and darters excel. This diversity of food source will make migratory

In the sandy parts of a river system, food is at a premium and the fish will readily eat minnow imitations. These fish might also be more aggressive, even in cold water. One type of minnow that thrives in sandy areas is shiners. The one pictured is a sand shiner, but you may find emerald shiners, spotfin shiners, common shiners, and many others in these places.

Right: Fishing sculpins around boulders is a great way to find both steelhead and lake-run brown trout. Boulders are one of the most obvious forms of structure ubiquitous to the rivers that hold migratory fish. If you find a big boulder, it is likely to have big baitfish around it. Conversely, smaller fields of boulders have smaller baitfish.

fish trout-like, and they will be more selective of the choices that you present them and how well they are presented. Since a lot of different types of food are present in these areas, you have a lot of different fly options. This wide array of food sources can complicate your fishing. On the bright side, such a spot will hold good numbers of fish.

This is a common scenario in many streams as you move upstream into the areas where the fish will eventually spawn. This is no coincidence, as migratory fish are looking for places where their young will have immediate access to food. As winter approaches, these upper stretches become more concentrated with steelhead. The gravel in these upper reaches is the focal point of their migration. At the same time, lower reaches of many rivers may be jammed with shelf ice during the winter. For these reasons, we are often fishing these places during the coldest times of the year.

In such a spot, fish will move around the structure to feed. As a result, you will want to fish a larger area around the structure. The fish might be upstream, downstream, or beside the structure if a lot of food is present. Structure surrounded by a good feeding area is typical of a good fall, winter, or spring holding area.

In contrast, if the substrate around the structure is more sterile—composed mostly of sand, for example—the fish will be less selective. This is common in the lower reaches of many rivers. Food is at a premium in these areas, and the fish are not likely to stay there long. However, if you find them there, the fish will be hungry and may ravenously slam a generic pattern. If you have a general idea of what bait is present, they might readily eat it. They simply have less food to choose from and don't have the luxury of being as picky.

Furthermore, because food sources are not the main draw to structure surrounded by sterile substrate, the fish will be located close to the structure. Typically, you will find fish directly behind the structure, so your presentation can be precise. Structure surrounded by a poor feeding area will hold fish as they are migrating but will be less productive as the fish settle in for long periods of time.

Though not evident in the cold-water times of the year, it is really helpful to know where weed beds exist in the warmer times. Weed beds usually spring up in areas of silt and softer river bottom. They are everywhere in the summer months in many rivers, but die off during the fall and winter.

Weed beds tell you a lot about what is going on in a certain part of the river, even in the cold-water times of the year. As discussed elsewhere in this book, they provide cover for minnows during the summer months. In general, they indicate a richness of food that is very attractive to predator fish. Minnows are present because of the weed beds, but there are also a lot of food sources near the bottom of the food chain that use these areas. The weeds may be growing in silt, and silt is rich in food sources, including swimming mayfly larvae such as Hexes, dragonfly nymphs, damselfly nymphs, and crustaceans.

There are a few obscure spots that I have found while fishing during the winter months that hold steelhead and brown trout. These spots always made me scratch my head—I just could not understand what any fish would be doing there. They held little structure, and had only had minimal depth. The "aha" moment came when I recognized that these areas had dense weed beds during the summer months.

I pay special attention to medium-depth weed beds in the summer, because they may be great spots to hold migratory fish in the fall. They have a certain richness and substrate that is very appealing to the fish. The minnows that were in the weeds in the summer may still be present as a food source. Everything is intertwined in nature, and if you are on the river in the summer, you can apply lessons learned to other times of the year. In this way, you have a year-round approach to fishing.

Stand-Alone Structure

In many rivers, the places to fish for migratory fish are obvious. These are the classic runs that have a head, gut, and tailout that we previously discussed. In some rivers, however, the holding water is less obvious. Even in rivers where you do have obvious places to fish, it is a good idea to know about the secondary places to fish. It is these secondary spots that can save the day when the river is busy. Secondary spots might hold fish because of the structure that they possess, such as boulders, brush, or gravel bars. They might also be temporary holding spots such as spawning areas or my favorite—the funnel areas in a river.

BOULDERS

When you fish with nymphs or perhaps bait, you may find that fishing around boulders and brush can be difficult. With solitary boulders, you will often find that the current is uneven. Depending on how far they protrude, boulders produce a back eddy, or swirling current, thus making it difficult to get a drift around with these methods. Furthermore, nymph and bait-fishing anglers look for congregating fish, but a solitary boulder may only hold a lone fish. For this reason, boulders are often overlooked as holding structure, although boulders in general are great places to find baitfish, especially things like sculpins, gobies, and darters.

When you fish streamers, however, boulders often represent a perfect target for presenting a fly. Streamer tactics are used to look for active, aggressive fish. Furthermore, you are looking for feeding fish. It also helps when you swing flies to target areas that are of reasonable depth and can be quickly covered with a fly. All of these traits make boulders an ideal target for the swung fly.

If you are fishing specifically for steelhead, a boulder represents a desirable fish resting spot. Being territorial fish, a migratory steelhead or trout will take up its place there and will defend it. This makes such a boulder a great place to fish a gaudy fly—one that represents a violation of the fish's territory. Swing a fly close to a boulder and keep it there, as this may draw a vicious strike.

Boulders are also a great ambush spot, and this too makes them a great place to swing a fly. In rivers with large baitfish populations, steelhead will hold next to a boulder not only for rest and shelter, but also to launch an attack. In such places, swinging natural baitfish patterns such as sculpins, shiners, or chubs produce vicious strikes. If the boulder is not dominated by a steelhead, you may encounter a stream trout, migratory fish, or even a bass or walleye depending on your river system. The dominant predator will always dominate a good ambush spot.

Whether you are targeting aggressive fish or feeding fish, boulders are often located in areas of depth that are ideal for swinging flies. In a large river, boulders located in 4 to 6 feet of depth may lend themselves well to presentation. In smaller rivers, boulders in 3 to 5 feet are ideal. In some unique midwestern streams, the runs are very shallow and holding water is at a premium. In these streams, boulders represent an ideal form of cover to target.

When you are fishing a streamer, you are covering water very quickly. A likely boulder is an easy target for a quick flurry of casts. If depth permits, predatory fish may position themselves in front of a boulder or beside it. Large boulders may form a run on either side, thus creating two separate channels worthy of checking out. The most likely spot for the steelhead is the most obvious, behind the boulder. Paying close attention to these areas will help you find more fish.

In many rivers, the rocks that protrude from the surface will have only one seam behind them, which forms the obvious lie for the fish. However, if you have a very large rock, or piles of boulders, this large structure will form a seam on both sides of the boulder. If the depth is good on both sides, it can be productive to fish such a boulder from each side, as each seam will have potential for fish. In such a situation, you would want to cast your line over the seam and swing or strip across it. Usually the eddy behind the rock will allow your fly to sink for a moment before it is carried into the faster water of the seam.

Sometimes multiple large rocks can be found in an area, and such areas often form a nice pocket upstream from the structure. The water is slowed by the presence of rocks and scours a deep pocket. This is always a prime lie. Some of the very best spots I can think of are formed by multiple rocks.

In smaller, freestone-type rivers with good gradient, rocks may be the best cover available. In these rivers, rocks will form "pocketwater," which are great places to hit with a streamer. In these places the holding spot is very small, and there is a lot of current. It is essential that you use a weighted fly, as you have to get your fly down to the fish and fishing in the shortest time possible. You can place yourself in close proximity to these pockets in order to control the line and keep the fly in the pocket for as long as possible.

Some small rivers have good runs of migratory fish. The holes and deep water are restricted in these places, and because of their territorial impulses, the fish will spread out. If you have a good run of fish in a small stream, they will occupy any reasonable pocket. The holes in such rivers just don't allow for many fish, so they are pushed out into any reasonable cover. Such streams are a lot of fun to fish, and you should be willing to fish anyplace that looks like it might hold a fish. Because holding water is limited, you can look to smaller pockets and shallower areas than you would normally fish.

BRIDGES

There are some large-scale structures in a river that you can think of as a large rock. One of the most common would be man-made bridges. Many of our streams are urban or suburban and very few, if any, don't have bridges that cross them. Bridges are supported by pylons that strike the water in deep and shallow areas. Where those columns hit the water, it creates a seam in much the same fashion as a rock. If the current is straight downstream from such a column, it can create a great spot for fish to rest.

If the water comes up and fish are migrating, such structure may create a highly desirable resting spot for a bunch of fish. It is during these high-water periods that rocks and timber might be fully submerged. A bridge is a bridge, however, and will break the current. Great numbers of fish can be found around man-made structures when no other current break is available. Always look at the river when it is high in a different light and ask yourself, "If I were a fish, where would I be able to rest?" No matter how obscure, if it looks like it might hold a fish, it probably does.

If you are fishing a bridge column that has deep water in front of it, this is also a prime place for a fish to reside. Even though they may be lurking behind an underwater rock or other form of structure, they still like to be in proximity to a bridge, which provides a quick escape if they feel uncomfortable. They can also then slip in behind a bridge if they need to rest.

On bright days, bridges provide a break from direct sunlight, and fish will slide into these areas when the sun is high.

ISLANDS

Like bridges, natural and man-made islands also provide a great spot for fish to rest. Islands are present on many rivers, and you can often think them as a large form of structure, like a huge rock. In large rivers the island will form a seam on either

Whether natural or man-made, large structures such as islands can have great opportunities for fishing baitfish patterns. Islands create converging seams where they tail out, and these areas often provide a resting spot for fish. In times of high water, islands might be the only form of structure that breaks heavy current.

side, which is often very obvious as it passes the island. This seam will be on the downstream side of the island. Much like a bridge pylon, an island can become a great refuge if the water is high. High water may make the rocks in the stream less comfortable; however, if there is an island around, it will have an increasingly desirable seam if the water comes up.

On the downstream end of an island, a deeper spot is found. This deep spot is just like the eddy found on the downstream side of a rock. If the island is made up of rocks, it can be a really deep spot. However, if it is composed of sand, it won't be nearly as deep.

If it is a large island or in a river with lots of flow, fish may sit on either side of the island. Often one side will have some deeper water with brush and timber that make it a great place to look for fish. In tight spots like this, wading may be the best way to approach them versus fishing from a boat.

DAMS

Do you know what the steelhead said when it hit the concrete wall? The answer is . . . "dam." I'm sorry, I couldn't help myself. In seriousness, though, dams represent the epitome of man-made structure, and the water they release and the currents that they form have a profound impact on the fishing in a given area. Hydroelectric dams are often found on larger rivers and have a huge impact on the ecology of the river and the distribution of fish. Hydroelectric power is considered to be a "clean" form of energy because it does not generate emissions. However, dams have a lot of environmental implications and block fish migrations, so few new dams are being built.

For this reason, most of the dams were built a long time ago. Like a highway or any other piece of infrastructure, these dams need more and more maintenance as they age. Throughout the Midwest, these structures were built at a time when

A few dams have fish ladders to pass fish. Even with a fish ladder, the fish are concentrated as they figure out how to pass the obstruction. Here a hen steelhead passes a fish ladder. Dams are great places to fish and often have excellent access; however, this can make for a heavily pressured spot to fish.

the impacts of their design on the environment were a minimal consideration. As a result, many of these dams have a negative effect on the river system, adding unnaturally warm water to the system in the summer months. This unnatural addition of warm water is called "thermal pollution" and it has an impact on migratory fish, as warmer water reduces natural reproduction. It also affects the growth rate of fish that are in the rivers.

One other effect of the dams is that they change the migration patterns of fish. Typically a dam forms a lake, or pond, behind it. Ice forms on these lakes, and it may take a while for it to go away. As a result, it takes the water behind the dam in the lake longer to warm up in the spring, which in turn makes the river cooler and delays any spring runs of fish. In the same way, after a hot summer, the water behind the dam is warm, and it takes a long time to cool down. This creates warmer fall and early-winter water temperatures and later fall runs.

On the bright side, dams do have some good attributes. They may halt the upstream progress and propagation of invasive species, protecting the waters above them. Dams will often create an accessible spot where fish are concentrated. In most cases, these dams have public shore-wading access. When I was a teenager, I spent a lot of time fishing below various dams and caught some memorable fish there.

Depending on the design of the dam, they can block or delay migrating fish from going upstream. This concentrates fish and often anglers in one area, sometimes creating a bonanza-like atmosphere for fishing purposes. The bonanza may turn into a circus, and if that happens, I would leave the area.

Most hydroelectric dams have two sides to them. One side has floodgates, and the other side has turbines that actually generate the electricity. During normal flow, the floodgates may be turned off and all of the flow may be used for generating power. In between these two areas is a berm, which separates the two sides. During normal water levels, one side of the dam is usually pumping water through and the other is not. When one side of the dam is in use, it creates a nice channel, and this side is attractive to migratory fish who follow the current upstream until they can go no more. Fish that have been in the river a while will make themselves at home in the slack side of the river, often chasing the variety of baitfish that are provided.

In recent years, dams have concentrated zebra mussels, making the bottom of the river very sharp. These zebra mussels have in turn attracted gobies, which are by volume the most common baitfish by many dams. In addition, the dam itself will bring unsuspecting insects and baitfish through its turbines, providing disoriented food for the gamefish below.

When very slow water on the side of the dam not in use meets very fast water on the side releasing water, a very strong break in the current forms. This seam, or foam line, often proceeds from the berm on the dam. It is an awesome spot for a fish to hold, with very good resting water, along with some of the best food sources in the river. These seams can carry for a long way downriver, and following them down as far as possible will give you great chances at fish. Not only are dams a barrier to fish, forcing them to congregate, but they are also a rich spot for food, and this makes for a good combination.

The current side of dams is very good for swung-fly methods, and the seam that feeds them is a prime area for sure. The concentration of fish may make them aggressive toward brightly colored flies, so come prepared for that. Even if fish are not migrating, they will be drawn to the rich food source at a dam. As the fish settle in and there are fewer fish migrating upriver, it is a great idea to fish with a more natural fly pattern, with a goby pattern being on top of the list. Many of the gobies around dams are the mature spawning variety, so large black or tan ones will do the trick. Other baitfish such as common and striped shiners are abundant at dams, and these imitations are useful as well.

The slack side of the river provides a different challenge. Because of the lack of current, the swung-fly method is out the door. However, this is a great place to slowly strip a big baitfish pattern for the lake-run browns or steelhead that would be holding there. The scenery is not that great at these spots, but they are nonetheless fun to fish, as you never know what you might catch. In addition to the migratory fish, you might find pike, catfish, drum, walleye, carp, and really anything else. If you

This large school of common shiners was found on the downstream, slow side of a point. Shiners survive by reproducing in huge numbers. This group was not too wary, and I got very close. Imagine if you were a giant brown trout or a steelhead migrating through this spot!

want to catch variety, lean toward a slow-moving earth-tone imitation.

There may be some strange currents in these areas, so it will be necessary to keep the fly moving at all times. Be aware that most dams have sharp debris around them, and fly loss may be more than expected. Again, a goby pattern is a great bet, but crayfish and shiners are always present in these areas so those are good options as well.

The slack side of the dam may be some of the slowest water in the entire system, so it may require a lighter sink-tip than other parts of the river. In these slow conditions, the strike is often subtle. If you feel the line get heavy, set the hook!

POINTS AND BAYS

When I was a kid, I loved fishing, I absolutely could not get enough of it (in that regard, you might say that I am still a kid—my wife says I am a big kid all

the time, but I digress). In the 1980s, the internet was nonexistent, so I spent every Saturday watching Jimmy Houston, Roland Martin, and a wide cast of other fishing celebrities catching fish on TV. These fishing legends were always talking about fishing around points in lakes and rivers. One of the concepts I had a really hard time with as a kid was the idea of fishing around such points. It was only after a lot of years as an angler that it finally clicked what the significance of this kind of cover was. Points are exaggerated in the scenario of a river and create congregations of baitfish, resting places for predators, and bays that are ideal for catching gamefish.

As the current rushes down a river, it is constricted in places by rocks or gravel that juts out from one side of the river. At the spot where the current touches the point, the river is narrowed and very fast, but as you move past the point, it creates a seam directly off its tip, followed by slow water on its downstream side. This slack water can be slow for a long distance. It is counterintuitive, but a lot of times in high-water conditions, the water behind a point may be slower than it would be at normal water levels.

In a fast river lacking in timber, a point may provide the only resting spot for fish, big and small. Juvenile fish concentrate in these areas, as do any minnows that exist above the bottom of the river. These spots won't congregate bottom fish such as sculpins; however, shiners and salmon or steelhead fry are commonly found in such a place. Large predators will use these places to feed on bait throughout the year. In the summer I rely on slow water created by points to catch some of the largest smallmouth bass. As the water cools, these same places are where predatory migratory fish lie.

If the water is high, even more large gamefish will be in these areas to escape the current. High current for a fish is like a windstorm: They need to hide behind something to get out of the wind. The main problem with current for fish is that they have to work hard to fight it, which in turn burns calories. The unnecessary use of calories is a dangerous proposition for any fish that lives in current. The goal of any fish is survival: A large brown trout will be trying to gain calories to get back to a lake, and a steelhead will be using the break in current to preserve the maximum amount of energy for the spring spawn. Both of these gamefish are highly motivated to stay out of the current, and the presence of baitfish is an added incentive to these fish.

Some of the best runs that hold fish throughout the fall, winter, and spring are created by a point. Furthermore, the seam created by a point will serve as a conveyor belt of food for the fish living in the slow water behind the point. Seams create perfect places for brown trout and steelhead.

Most Midwest rivers have stretches lined with trees that provide great cover for fish when they fall in. A newly fallen tree will immediately form a great seam for catching fish if it is in deep-enough water. Some of the best spots I have ever fished were formed by a fallen tree. However, such a spot has a finite life, as the tree will eventually blow out during high water or will simply deteriorate with time.

In addition to the seam that is created, the returning water downstream from the point creates a bay that is often a wider part of the river. The slowest part of the bay may be an ideal place to strip a fly. If the water below the point is deep, it may create a backswirl. In this whirlpool current, stripping a fly may be the only practical way to catch a fish. Eventually this wider part of the river narrows down. This constriction of the bay creates a perfect place to swing a baitfish pattern for a predator fish.

As we mentioned, a point creates a seam. Initially the slow water in the bay is quite a ways from the seam, but as you go down the bay, eventually the seam and the shore get closer together as the bay narrows. When swinging flies, you would cast a weighted fly into the bay and work your way down the seam. As you work your way downstream, the fish may also work their way down in front of you. As you reach the end of the bay, your fly is swinging right into the face of any fish, and the fish will strike!

Points and bays create an awesome place to find a fish. Often the slow water below a point becomes the resting place for timber and old logs, which have washed down from other places. Timber is another important type of structure in our rivers.

BRUSH AND TIMBER

As mentioned at the beginning of this chapter, our rivers have a long history of having a lot of timber in them. Understanding fishing brush and timber will become an even bigger part of fishing for a lot of gamefish in the next decade or two. Our rivers are constantly affected by many different invasive species, notably sea lamprey, zebra mussels, and gobies. However, most of us have overlooked a subtle invasive that has profoundly impacted a lot of our rivers in the last few years and will continue to do so for a while.

An invasive insect called the emerald ash borer has invaded much of the north-central United States, and in so doing, has killed much of our ash forest. It is an environmental tragedy. These hardwoods are common around our rivers, and their demise is making many waterways a lot more brushy than normal. The only silver lining is that there is a lot more timber in our local river systems,

and this will continue for the foreseeable future. Downed timber is an exceptionally large part of the fish-holding cover in this region right now.

In addition to the natural timber that falls in our rivers, in the late 1800s the logging industry clear-cut most of the Midwest. Without modern automobiles and trucks, our rivers were the highways for these logs. Millions of logs were floated downstream, and some were embedded in our river bottoms with great force. These logs are still on the bottom of our rivers. They will continue to provide cover for fish for many years to come, and are often found in parts of the river where natural structure is absent.

Some of these logs lie in shallow fields in flat areas of our rivers. In normal fishing conditions and low water, these logs would seem to be a horrible place to look for migratory fish. This is true in ideal fishing conditions, but if we have a high-water event, this timber will flood, in some cases becoming 3 to 4 feet deep. In such a place the timbers on the bottom moderate the flow, and migratory fish will gravitate toward this spot.

I know of one such area in a local river. It is near a public access site and close to my house, so I fish it often. Throughout much of the year, the steelhead and trout will concentrate on the opposite side of the river from this flat, submerged timber area. However, as the river rises after rain or snowmelt, the typical fishing spot becomes a ghost town for fish. It took me years of fishing to figure out that the fish simply moved across the river to the flooded timber when the water got high. This particular stretch has been an ace in the hole for me many times when no other area would produce in high water. If you are in a large river, expect many areas to become difficult to fish in high water—but a few spots, especially these flooded timber spots, will become better fishing.

Using the water philosophy laid out earlier in this chapter, I have found many similar areas that also produce fish in adverse conditions. In addition to the actual logs that are in the river, old wooded structures such as wing dams and deflectors still exist after more than a century. These structures are common and were used to keep logs in the river channel as they floated downriver toward the mills. They now add lots of fish cover in parts of our rivers.

In some of the more extreme cases, some of our rivers were actually straightened in sections to allow logs to pass downriver without hindrance. These straight sections scoured the river bottom, and the only structure that remains is timber. In these places, learning to fish timber is vital to success.

You can see that there are a lot of good reasons to sharpen your game when it comes to fishing along timber. Furthermore, many rivers that hold migratory fish may have natural brush along their entire length. On smaller streams, fishing around brush is an everyday challenge. Because of the narrowness of the river channel, any log that falls will provide some possible fishing opportunity. This is very common in streams that run through forested areas.

Larger streams and rivers are less affected by deadfalls, as they are initially located near the bank. But these same streams, as they lose their rock formations, become increasingly brush-infested as they head down into the estuary areas. Because of this influx of brush, the historical timbers, and all the normal decay of trees caused by old age and flooding, fishing brush is very, very important.

Fishing brush presents a different challenge than other forms of structure. Wood, when found in a river, is often neglected by anglers pursuing migratory fish. Most anglers who have been fishing for migratory fish for years with nymphs or conventional gear have learned to find fish around cover that is out in the main current. Many times the timber that is in the water is found along the edges and seems too shallow to hold fish. However, when water levels rise, the main channel of many rivers becomes some pretty heavy water. The spots where you would typically look for fish have either pushed the fish out or are unreachable due to the water conditions. On the bright side, the

Lake-run brown trout love heavy cover and will use it extensively, especially in daylight hours. Lake-runs are identical to stream trout in many ways. However, when they first enter our rivers, they are pretty gullible for such a big fish. Living in the big lake for years does not introduce them to many flies.

wood along the edges of the river is now in the perfect depth range and also breaks the current nicely. It is a great place to look in high water. Many of us have been mentally trained to avoid fishing for migratory fish among the snags, but streamer fishing allows for it.

Wherever you fish, you will likely encounter a circumstance when you find steelhead or migratory brown trout holding around brush. Both species love brush, with brown trout preferring brush in slow to moderate currents. Many people avoid this structure, thinking that brush is not the ideal place to fish. This is kind of odd when you think about it. Most of us in the Midwest who love to fish come from a bass-fishing background, and everyone knows bass love timber. Yet for some reason we ignore this prime fish habitat when we fish for coldwater species.

This is frequently learned from fishing other methods near brush and experiencing numerous snags, etc. If you are like me, you grew up fishing various bait-fishing methods that avoided fishing brush in favor of fishing classic runs and holes in a river. After all, fishing around trees would mean that you would lose more-expensive fishing lures. This prospect was unappealing when clean runs were available and easier to fish. Now that many of our fisheries are becoming more pressured, the fact that this type of water is usually avoided by anglers is in itself a great reason to fish it. Brush holds many steelhead both for shelter and as an ambush spot, as with boulders.

Streamer fishing has a unique advantage as a presentation style—you can present your fly above the brush and sink the fly after you are clear. The strike from a migratory fish may be different around brush than it would be in a classic run. Often brush is located in sandy areas, and as a result, the predatory fish may not want to stray far to attack. Don't be surprised if the strike comes quickly after your fly hits the water.

I was reminded of this fact on a fishing trip to the lower parts of Michigan's famed Pere Marquette. After a good day of fishing in late December with a close friend, Jeff Hubbard, I was waiting with the boat at the launch. A large brush pile sat below the tailout of a sparkling run. The truck and trailer were a good distance away, so I stepped

through the run, fishing while I waited. As I approached the end of the likely water, I decided to throw a cast beside the tangled mess of brush. I could see the sand bottom beside the brush, meaning that any fish that would eat the fly would have to come directly out of the brush pile. I made the cast with little hope of catching a fish. Much to my chagrin, the line tightened immediately. I lifted the rod, fully expecting the deadweight of a tree limb on my line. The rod lunged and my despair turned to euphoria! A large buck steelhead erupted on the surface.

Just then, my friend appeared with the truck. Thinking I was snagged, he looked away. When he looked back, I could see his eyes get large as he saw the fish thrash from a distance. The fish came to net in front of the launch and ended a great day of fishing. Fishing heavy cover provides some of the most memorable strikes and some of the largest fish.

There are changes to your rigging that you should consider when fishing hairy parts of a river system. The fish in such areas are usually less pressured, so this allows you to do things to your equipment to make fishing more practical. Even with the ability to fish above structure that the streamer allows, you will still likely lose a lot more flies in brushy parts of the river if you use them the same way you would in other areas. I suggest that you do a couple of things to decrease your fly loss.

The first thing that you can do is bump up your tippet. In normal types of cover, 12-pound tippet is my typical choice. However, in heavy brush it is common to use 14- to 18-pound tippet. I have experimented with swinging flies with up to 20-pound tippet in heavy cover and have seen no loss in hookups. Make sure that you tie a good knot in these scenarios. A good knot to consider is the Eugene bend. It is a very strong knot that works well in these tippet sizes. As I stressed before, you are fishing for a limited number of strikes each day. A good knot will make each of these opportunities more likely to be successful.

How you build your flies for fishing in heavy stuff can also have a big impact on fly loss. Much of what we do around the brush is swing flies. For swinging, if you are tying a fly on a conventional hook, use a model of hook that might bend. Daiichi

2461 in a size 2 is a good choice for this. If you are tying flies on a shank with a trailing hook or a tube fly, often the smaller sizes of hooks will bend under stress. One of the real advantages of interchangeable hooks is if you wreck a hook, all you have to do is replace it. Spend some time experimenting—often it is the little things like hook choice that will make you more successful in the long run. Preserving your best flies will keep you in the water for more time, which will lead to more fish.

There is one timber scenario to pay careful attention to, especially if you are fishing in high water or in stretches of river that have new timber that has fallen into the water. When a large tree lands in the water, it is heavy and its roots will have a lot of mass. Over time the tree usually ends up with the roots upstream and the larger limbs facing downstream; this type of configuration commonly occurs along the edges of a river. However, after a flood takes a very large tree into the water, it may find a home in the middle of the river some distance downstream. No matter where you find a tree lying alone in a river, it is a good place to fish. A large limb facing downstream creates a perfect line on the surface. This is what we call a seam.

Seams are breaks where faster water meets slower water. Think of the fast water of a seam as the food superhighway, and the slower water as the resting place for the fish. If you are fishing in the slow-water part of the seam, which is common when you are wading, your goal is to cast square enough to the seam and to sink the fly deep enough so that it is attractive to the fish as it crosses through the seam and into the slow water. If you are fishing from the fast water into the slow water, as in the case of a boat, you will often cast square with the current, across the seam into the slower water. The fly will sink deeply, and it is a good idea to throw an upstream mend at this time. The sequence is: The fly sinks deeply in the slow side of the current and begins to swing through the seam, which is fast water. As the fly comes out of the fast side of the seam, the water below you is more moderate current. It is at this point in the presentation that the fish will strike. Often when I go to an unfamiliar stretch of river, this is something that I pay close attention to.

When you come across a good downed tree situation, your angle to the downed timber is of extreme importance. This is especially true if the run created by the tree is small. When you come to a fallen tree, the most obvious choice is to line up even with the downstream end of the tree so that you are casting perpendicular to the fallen timber, as close as you can get to it. If the water is high or the holding water is close to the tree, the fish will be sitting directly behind the tree and close to it. If you were to line up behind the tree, no matter how you cast, your fly would be past the fish before they have any opportunity to react to it.

There is a solution to this problem, especially if you are swinging flies: Line yourself up even with the timber so that you are casting at an angle, possibly a steep angle, down to the end of the timber. Your fly won't get as deep with this technique, but the fish will get a good look at it. A weighted fly and a dense sink-tip help to cut through the water quickly. I get some strange looks parking close to timber, but it accounts for a lot of fish.

Because of the size of the roots on large trees, these fallen giants will end up in 3 to 4 feet of water. This is a perfect depth for catching most predatory species. When you come to a location like this one, try to cast as closely as possible to the back of the timber. You will lose flies, but you will likely come across a great fish at some point.

REMEMBER, FOAM IS HOME

This brings up an important point. If you are fishing for steelhead in any type of stationary structure, be it a boulder or a piece of wood, remember the basic rule of fishing in moving water: "Foam is home." In a nutshell, stationary structure creates a break in the current, often between slower water on the shore side of the structure and faster water on the opposite side. The resulting seam creates a string of bubbles on the surface; i.e., foam. This creates a great feeding lane for any type of fish.

Because of the nature of water and how it carries oxygen, we often find predatory fish close to the seam when the water is comfortable for fish. However, when the water is very cold, they may sit in the very slowest water beside the seam. This is because cold water holds more oxygen for the fish. Furthermore, the metabolism of the fish is

When we talk about gravel bars, you may think of spawning fish. Gravel is so much more than just spawners, however. Gravel bars by their nature form a break in the current. For this reason, deep gravel holds migratory fish year-round, especially in moderate currents. Some of the food sources are smaller in these places, and this colorful buck fell for a darter pattern.

slower in colder water, so there is no biological need to live in fast places. Conversely, if the water temperature is uncomfortably warm for the species you are targeting, the fish will use the water with the most oxygen possible, which will be the fastest water present. There are specific ways to deal with seams that we will cover in the techniques chapter of this book.

GRAVEL BARS

When I mention gravel bars, it probably conjures up an image of spawning fish in shallow water. Though these areas hold large numbers of migratory fish in the spring and fall, they are not the type of gravel bars that I am referring to. Those types of bars are avoided when fishing baitfish patterns.

In many river systems, gravel bars draw the attention of steelhead as soon as they enter the river. Steelhead frequently enter our river systems in September and October. In parts of the Great Lakes region, king and coho salmon are spawning at this time, and lake-run browns will also start to spawn in this time frame. Steelhead will approach the salmon bedding areas to gorge on salmon eggs. Some steelhead will move upriver quite a bit at these times; however, the majority of the early steelhead will find the farthest spawning areas downstream and congregate there.

Early steelhead are often very aggressive, supercharged fish. Fresh from the lake, these fish willingly accept a variety of swung flies. Among the best of these swung flies are Egg-Sucking Leech patterns. Egg patterns can also be swung with traditional swung-fly methods with good results. You don't think of an egg pattern as a swung fly, but because of the frenzied atmosphere of fish gorging on eggs, they will become less wary of a natural presentation and will eat eggs on the swing.

The mere presence of eggs can congregate several steelhead and trout if they happen to be migrating past the area. In the fall these fish are supercharged, dumb, and aggressive. In such a place, the feeding fish will jockey for position, with the largest fish often doing most of the feeding. While behind gravelly areas, these feeding fish are often attacked by the spawning fish. This makes them even more aggressive.

You will have a couple of options when fishing a streamer behind these fish. A big sculpin pattern will work well behind spawning fish, and fish hit them aggressively. However, they can be really hard to sink. An interesting side note is that salmon will often become aggravated by a sculpin pattern, and you will have your hands full if you get one of those on your line.

A second option is to fish a more natural fly. Fish feeding behind gravel will expect eggs to come their way. They will also expect the large spawning fish to knock other food sources their way from up on the gravel. These include large nymphs and small baitfish such as darters.

If you choose to incorporate an egg into your presentation, there are other considerations. Whether you are swinging an egg fly or an Egg-Sucking Leech, pay attention to the color of the natural eggs. Usually on darker patterns such as an Egg-Sucking Leech, the egg is located at the front of a fly. However, it is not a bad idea to tie some patterns with an egg on the rear or near the bend of the fly. Fish will hit a fly differently on different days. Changing the location of the hot spot, or egg, on a fly pattern may give the fish a different target if you are getting strikes and having a hard time with the connection.

Frequently the most challenging part of getting a fall fish to bite is simply locating a steelhead in the midst of swarms of spawning salmon. When using a boat on the Muskegon, I will often cover miles of river to find a steelhead. If I see one, I will turn the boat around and position at a steep angle to the fish, allowing the fly to reach its deepest point as it approaches the fish. You may ask, "Of all these fish, how do I know which fish is a steelhead?" After all, a fresh salmon looks a lot like a fresh steelhead or lake-run brown. As we mentioned earlier, the answer is in the tail: A steelhead or brown trout will have a square-shaped tail, whereas a salmon's tail is always deeply forked. Salmon also become a dark color over the course of time.

If I am going downriver and see a square tail, good things are on the horizon. Often you will find a pod of salmon huddled closely together, only to see one different tail shape sticking out of the back of the bunch. This is especially common early in the morning before any fishing pressure. If you see such a scenario, there is a good chance you will hook a chrome fish!

When steelhead are spawning in the spring, drop-back or spent steelhead can often be caught in the dark areas surrounding the spawning fish. Often the same egg and leech patterns will produce at this time of the year. The downside to swinging flies in these areas is that swung-fly methods are at their best when you are fishing to undisturbed areas where you have the room to present your fly. Spawning areas are seldom left alone and are often heavily fished. If you are fishing in any scenario around spawning fish, don't spend too much time there. With each cast, you are more likely to snag or disturb the spawning activities.

Fishing pressure will drive a lot of fish to avoid the gravel. They will move deep and feed there during the most heavily fished times of the day. If it is a bright day, they may seek the deepest, darkest run in the area and be difficult to approach for streamer purposes. However, at other times, migratory fish simply look for the closest comfortable water, such as around rocks or fallen timber.

Gravel bars represent more than just a place to eat eggs, however. Fish will utilize them at all times of the year. Many of our larger rivers, particularly the tailwaters, have barchans of gravel. Barchans are large tracts of gravel that were historically moved around by large releases of water. These deeper, submerged gravel bars are one form of structure that is often overlooked.

Gravel bars represent a break in the current of the river. Furthermore, they are often excellent feeding areas on a year-round basis. Insects, minnows, and other sources of food proliferate in these areas. If you were to seine some of these deeper gravel bars, you would find numerous food sources large and small, notably darters, crayfish, caddis larvae, and mayfly nymphs. These deeper bars are affected by flooding and will move around more than other forms of structure on a year-to-year basis.

The trick to fishing these deeper bars is to find the one that the fish favor at a given water level. It may seem obvious but may be more tricky than you think. At normal water levels, the fish might choose the deepest pocket available, but as the river rises, they may spread out and choose pockets that were previously less desirable. The best advice to fishing such areas is to be willing to change your typical position if water conditions change.

Some of the very best winter steelhead areas that I know of are deep, submerged gravel areas that see little fishing pressure. They are ideal for covering with a streamer, but as they lack any fixed seam, they are unappealing to other types of anglers. A great combination is a medium-depth gravel area with a slow to moderate current and access to boulders or other structure. In such a place, steelhead lurk and feed. In these areas, fish natural patterns for best results.

During the spring, many fish utilize spawning areas. In my local rivers it is most common to find resident trout feeding around the shallower areas where the fish are spawning. Often you can catch these resident trout with nymphs, eggs, etc.

When it comes to catching large fish around gravel during the daytime, you should look at a gravelly area as a whole, and look for the deepest bars. In most scenarios, you have shallow gravel areas at the upstream end of a gravel stretch. As you move farther and farther downstream, the gravel bars get deeper and deeper. With few exceptions, the easiest fish to get to bite will be at these final deep gravel bars. As eggs, insects, and small fish are wiped off a gravel bar, they are washed downstream. With each passing gravel bar, more food is washed downriver. As you get to the downstream end of the gravel area, the final deep bars have the maximum amount of food. Not only that, but they also have depth, which is something that a large predator needs, especially in broad daylight. Furthermore, any fish migrating upriver will stop where a gravel bar begins, fearing moving upriver exposed in shallow water. All of these factors combined make the final gravel bars a great place to catch something big.

As you can see, reading the water and fishing to structure are vital components of fishing for migratory fish. In the coming chapters, we will cover the techniques, equipment, and flies used to catch steelhead and lake-run brown trout.

CHAPTER 4

Techniques

I am going to cover several techniques, and each has its own time and place in our river systems. Each of these methods has its virtues; you may want to keep all in your arsenal. Fly fishing appeals to different people in different ways and has something for everybody. It may be that just one or two of these techniques are what you are willing to do. Some of the things that really influence what technique you are going to use are water velocity, temperature, and clarity. After we have discussed these factors, you can make a good decision on when to use a particular technique.

The choice of presentations has a lot to do with one very important aspect of fishing for migratory fish: water temperature. Water temperature affects the size of the column of water, or "window," that the fish are willing to move through to get your fly. All of these techniques, and all the fly lines and equipment, boil down to finding ways to keep the fly in this window, this strike zone, for as long as necessary to catch a fish. As we talk about this window, keep in mind that the size of the window might generally be better when the water is warm, but you might still have a day when the window is small due to inactivity of the fish. By the same token, you may have the rare day when the water is icy cold but the fish are extremely active.

Each year, I strive to get at least one day where we catch 10 fish swinging flies. This is a difficult feat, and some years it doesn't happen at all. A couple of years ago, the best day I had swinging flies was in mid-March when the water was 35 degrees. We hooked over 20 fish on that day and landed 14. I am not a numbers guy, but this just illustrates what is possible if things go well in tough conditions. What this means for fishing is that each of these techniques has its value at any

Early in the fall, floating lines with light sink-tips can be employed with great success. This is a relaxed and rewarding time of the year to fish. During the warm-water periods, migratory fish are supercharged and will take a fly that is higher in the water column. They are frequently less selective about fly choice during these times.

time, and they are all good to have in your pocket when plan A is not working.

In the warm water of fall, the window that a fish will move through to get your fly can be extremely large. I have seen fish move like a missile across a lot of water in the fall to kill a gaudy fly. When water temperatures are in the mid 40s to low 50s, you are most likely to have this large-window situation. In the fall the numbers of fish might not be that great, so it makes sense to present a fly higher in the water column. It is important to note that a fish will not only move laterally across the water farther when the window is large, but also move up and down in the water column vertically. This means that your fly does not have to be as deep.

This has a lot of implications for how you might catch a fish. For example, if you want to catch a steelhead on your bamboo Spey rod with a floating line and minimal sink-tip, you would want to fish at a time of year when the window of predation is large. It also has implications for the flies that you use, as a Spey fly on a light wire hook with a short sink-tip could be very effective. Early fall is the time of year when you can catch fish on a lot of different flies. With the big window, the fish are less selective about the streamer flies that you fish and the baitfish that you imitate.

As we talk about this window, it is important to note something about water temperature. When the temperatures initially drop into the mid to low 30s, you may still have an active bite. The effects of cold water are not usually immediate. However, if you have an extended period of time with consistently cold temperatures, this is when the window really shrinks and you are relegated to winter fishing tactics.

Thus, as water temperatures cool, the window slowly but surely shrinks. By winter the fish often won't move very far or very quickly on a consistent basis. They especially won't move far in fast water. In this way, your techniques and the way you read the water are changed in the winter months. Thus, you have to choose water and techniques that get the fly deep and keep it there for a prolonged period of time. On the bright side, by early winter most rivers have a pretty good number of fish loaded into them. For this reason, if you do present your fly deeply enough, you can have great fishing with active fishing techniques. As the days get very short in January and early February, you will have the hardest time getting a fish to move to take a fly. At this time the most medieval and methodical techniques will get the bite.

Coupled with the smaller window, the migratory fish tend to be more selective about what they eat. Early in the fall, in warmer water, I would not discourage my clients from using their floating lines and crazy flies—we can make that work. However, to be successful with swung flies in the winter, I would insist on using the right line and proven flies. In most rivers, the fish have seen quite a few baits by the time cold-water periods arrive. Also, many of them have adapted to the river and are now acting more like large predatory resident trout.

These comments about the window of the fish apply broadly to both steelhead and lake-run brown trout up until this point. By early spring, in most rivers we are talking primarily about steelhead.

By late February and March, prior to the spawn, there is a nice expansion in the window, as the fish become active due to increased biological activity in the river. This activity was highlighted in the baitfish chapter of this book. Soon thereafter, the steelhead begin to spawn. Depending on the river, and how compressed the seasons are, this is not a great time to catch fish on active techniques, despite a lot of fish being in the rivers.

As the steelhead leave the river, the water warms and the fish are post-spawn, so the window is huge once again. In fact, post-spawn fish may have the largest window of them all. These ravenous predators abandon any sense of caution and attack large baitfish patterns with gusto on any number of techniques.

In the coming pages, we will discuss a handful of techniques that work very well with migratory fish. With each technique, we will cover what size of window that it works well with. We will start with my favorite for catching fish with a jarring strike, the classic swung-fly method.

The Classic Swung Fly

The classic swung-fly method is at its best when the window of the fish is large to medium sized.

However, with some skill and the ability to cover water, it can be effective at any time migratory fish are present.

As a preface, nothing conjures up the image of the quintessential fly fisher like someone standing in knee-deep water, casting a long Spey rod as a majestic D-loop unfolds a floating line with a classic fly pattern. Though that works in Midwest waters, this book takes a different approach.

My experience with steelhead and baitfish flies started with the summer steelhead on the Rogue River mentioned earlier in this book. After that fish, I thought, "I wonder if a fall steelhead might eat this?" So, I parked my drift boat near the top of a run and cast the fly out on a 300-grain sink-tip with a single-handed rod. The fly swung through the water column, and as it tailed out, a massive strike followed. For several years, the fish that was on my line was the biggest I had ever hooked, a 15-pound chrome male steelhead. After a furious battle, I goat-roped it into my net. These two fish cemented my love for the swung-fly method and confidence in using baitfish patterns for steelhead. There are some things about this method that are very simple, and other things that are very complex.

At the time that I caught the steelhead in the story, the fly-line technology that was available for swinging flies was in its infancy, especially as it pertains to the Midwest. Much of the guiding I did with swung flies was with single-handed rods and shooting-head-type lines. Some of the shooting heads used were pretty crude. But, since we are from the Midwest and we often use weight on the line and nymphing techniques, it was pretty elegant in the context of the alternatives. We also did a lot of swung-fly fishing with single-handed rods and Teeny-type fly lines. These are well suited for presenting the fly but can be a lot of work to use over the course of the day.

This evolved into using two-handed rods, initially also with shooting heads. Over the course of many years, the fly-line technology as it pertains to the Great Lakes region has dramatically improved. Since there was no conventional or common swung-fly rig in the Great Lakes in the early days, we tried a lot of different things. Some of these lines worked well, and some not so much. Sometimes I would have a client show up with the perfect fly line for the situation. Other times we would have lines in the boat that were wholly inadequate. Yet, even with mismatched fly lines, success would come by means of finding a way to overcome the shortcomings of the equipment. At the end of the day, our current lines are much better than the old ones. However, in the right hands many sketchy fly lines can be used to swing flies successfully.

What I have learned is that almost every fly rod and line can be used for steelhead under normal fishing conditions. By modifying the fly line and the rig, and placing yourself at the proper angle to where you suspect the fish are hiding, you can overcome most deficiencies in gear. In short, usually if you are swinging flies and not catching fish, the problem lies in reading the water or simply getting the fly down to the fish.

If you watch people Spey cast, it would be really easy to be intimidated by this method. The internet is plastered with anglers casting a country mile, catching fish on the other side of the river. Yet fishing the Midwest is inherently heavy-duty, and casting great distances is of little value most of the time. If you are fishing from a boat, and you know where the fish are, it is actually better to move closer to the fish than to cast farther.

There are a couple of good reasons for this. For one thing, each cast takes time. Think of it as an rpm. If you are making a long cast, it takes more time to physically complete the swing. Ultimately, this leads to fewer casts over the course of the day. If you are fishing an area where the fish are concentrated near your position, it makes no sense to cast a long way, other than to look cool.

Casting long does have its place in certain situations, however. Longer casts do have an advantage when you are fishing broad areas that have fish scattered throughout your swing. In such a place, the long cast will cover more fish. Long casts will also help you find fish if you are fishing an area that you are unfamiliar with. By casting long and determining where the bite comes in the drift, you can pinpoint the location of the fish. In subsequent visits to the same water, you may have more precision with your approach to the fish.

Without a doubt, longer casts lose line control. This is the Achilles' heel of fishing in a casting-centric way. A loss of line control is fine if you are fishing on a day when the water is warm and the fish are biting. However, if the water is cold, you should be trying really hard to keep the fly in front of a fish. This is only accomplished if you can slow things down with a moderate cast.

With a classic swung-fly presentation, the cast is anywhere from 90 degrees from your position to slightly downstream. Depending on the line you choose and the length of the sink-tip, you will very seldom be casting upstream. Because the fly never touches the bottom with this presentation, you won't have a lot of control over the speed of the fly. If you want to get the fly deeper, you would add a heavier sink-tip rather than trying to control the line. This is especially true if using an intermediate or sinking Spey line, less so if using a floating line.

No matter how far we are casting, I try to imagine where the fish are sitting and put that spot halfway across the swing. Where your fly lands on the water is not where you expect the fish to be. Rather, when you cast a fly line perpendicular to the current or slightly downstream, the fly swings deeply until the middle of your swing, when it is at its deepest point. The pressure of the current then accelerates your fly and lifts it in the current, and it gains speed until the end of your swing. This deepest point in the swing is where you want your fly to pass the fish.

Once your fly passes the fish, you still would like your fly to stay as deep as possible for as long as possible. In rivers with some flow, this can be a tricky proposition. One thing that has really helped in recent years is the arrival of castable intermediate Spey lines. In high-water situations, a full sinking head may be another option.

Setting yourself up with the fish at the midpoint of your swing is a good starting point. This applies whether you are wading or are fishing from a boat. The goal of swinging flies is not to just cover the fish, but to cover them deeply. Once your fly is down there, you want to keep it there for the maximum amount of time.

I have known anglers that have caught a big fish on a swung fly within five minutes of rigging their first fly and making their first cast. In some ways,

Swinging flies deep and slow produces a variety of great fish. Winter lake-run browns are commonly taken with sculpins using this method. Sculpins work well in slow, rocky water. Because sculpins have a big head, it is easier to use these patterns in areas with less current.

it is the simplest way to catch a steelhead. All that you need to do is cast a fly out square or somewhat downstream from where you are positioned and voilà! You have yourself a steelhead. It sounds really easy, doesn't it?

On the other end of the spectrum, I have also known anglers who have fished over 500 hours and never landed a steelhead. These were good and avid anglers, who unfortunately lacked one critical element: blind luck. They just didn't run into that one fish that would eat the fly no matter what. In reality, they were probably making a small mistake in presenting the fly. This small mistake cost them their success. The truth is, there is a lot to being consistently successful at swinging flies. One of the most critical elements of successfully catching fish on a swung baitfish pattern or any swung fly is how you position yourself in the current.

Your position is critical to giving you a good chance at a fish, especially as water temperatures drop as we head into winter. When you fish in the fall, the fish are very active. At the end of your swing, the current will add pressure to your fly line and lift your fly in the water. If the water is warm, this is a nothing-burger. However, if the water is cold, you need to position yourself so that the pressure is minimized on your fly line. If there is little pressure on the fly line, it can continue to stay deep, and you can catch more fish. This will also allow the fly to stay slower, which might give a fish that is not reacting quickly in cold water a chance to catch up to your fly.

Often you have the choice of either adding a longer sink-tip to your rig, which takes time, or simply moving yourself off the current in order to keep the fly deep. Moving off the current would be my first choice. When the water gets really cold, you can count on the next method to help you be successful.

The Deep and Dirty Swing

In a perfect world, all that you would need to do to be successful is use the classic swing approach described above. To some degree, that method does work all of the time, provided that you have clear water and a lot of water to choose from. If you want to open up a lot more water to potential success in adverse conditions, we should discuss the deep and dirty swing method. This deep and dirty swing is an adaptation of swinging flies that works best when the window of the fish is small and some adaptation is necessary to keep the fly in the strike zone.

As previously mentioned, we have a unique issue in the Great Lakes region: Our winter fishing fringes on extreme winter fishing. During any normal Midwest winter, our water temperatures hover around 32 degrees for months on end. During this time frame, some rivers might ice over completely and become unfishable. Others remain open and there is always somewhere to fish. It is during that time that many anglers prefer to nymph fish, which will work at even the coldest of times. For me, the best part of steelhead fishing is the strike that you receive. I am not big into casting—I am into the strike. I don't really care how many fish I catch as long as I get an occasional violent tug. That is where this method really shines. This method won't appeal to anglers who are concerned with the perfect cast. It is crude but brings out the winter animal in the fish.

This type of swinging presentation also has some applications when the water is warm. There are some places that hold steelhead and browns in the fall that are just too fast to present a fly on a typical sink-tip rig with any hope of a fish seizing the fly. In such places, this deep swing method helps a lot. When swinging flies in very fast water, the fly races across the river too quickly for even the most supercharged fish to respond well to. By allowing the fly to get to the bottom and slowing the retrieve, this method gives you a fighting chance. In most cases, the water on the bottom of the river is slower than on the surface, and many spots that appear too fast for a migratory to hold in are deceptively good. This method has a role when presenting flies in such places.

The method we are discussing really is at its best with fish that have settled into an area and are accustomed to feeding on the native baitfish and other food sources. Most commonly it is associated with pools and holes that are in proximity to the spawning areas where the fish are staging. This method works well with steelhead but also with big browns and resident trout species. Though the

water is cold, these fish have adjusted to river conditions and will take a swung fly.

The casts associated with this method are generally short to midrange, and a lot comes down to line control. The basic idea with this method is

this: You want to get your fly to literally touch the bottom of the river at least once. What this does is add another element to the swing: friction. As the water cools, the initial reaction time of the steelhead slows; I believe many times the fish still try to

Left: When you wade and swing flies, you want the water directly downstream from you to be a comfortable depth for the fish to come and eat your fly. Often this means that you are standing about waist-deep. If you are swinging flies and your fly is bumping bottom at the end of your swing, you are in too shallow of water.

bottom. This is especially true when fishing flies that imitate food sources that dart along the bottom, as fish are programmed to eat food sources that are breaking free from the bottom. I believe this is because a healthy minnow would always remain near cover, but a wounded one would come off the bottom. This injured minnow imitation triggers a strike in fish that are looking for this behavior.

Less frequently the fish will take at the end of the swing. Either way, the result is the same: You get a powerful tug, just as in the classic swing. The only difference is that the presentation itself is a lot cruder. Soon after the initial tug, there may be a pause in the fight. Often winter fish will feel like deadweight until it occurs to them that there is a hook in their mouth. At that point, it is game on. The slow head shake becomes more violent as the fish realizes its mistake.

The crude element of this presentation is simple to explain: If you are going to get your fly to the bottom, and you want it to graze before the line hits the bottom, it needs to be weighted. There are a couple of ways to accomplish this: You can add weight to the fly, or you can add some weight to the fly right above the leader. Both of these options are available in the form of tungsten. Tungsten has a real advantage in that it is not bad for the wildlife that surrounds the river, and it also sinks better than comparably sized lead. However, tungsten can crack or break when it is configured as a barbell eye, and it is also an expensive option and will likely remain so in the near future. Conversely, lead eyes tend to be more durable, plus lead is cheap.

If you choose to use a weighted fly, tungsten beads or a set of weighted eyes are a great way to go. If you are fishing a snaggy area, the weighted eyes are the best option, as they may allow your fly to ride point up, reducing fly loss. I find tungsten beads are really nice to use if I am imitating

follow your fly but just simply don't react in time. When your fly grazes the bottom, it is momentarily slowed to a stop and then accelerates to a normal swing speed when the line gets tight. Often the fish will eat the fly right as it breaks free from the a narrow baitfish pattern, such as a shiner or a fry. Fry in particular have very rounded heads so a tungsten bead is a good match. However, with anything that has any bulk, I find myself reaching for the barbell eyes. The disadvantage to using a weighted fly is that you are locked into the weight built into the fly. Furthermore, the weight inevitably robs action from the fly itself.

Many of the baitfish patterns that we use are small, but these flies simply don't fish as well when weighted. In these situations, weight can be added in front of the fly in order to get the fly to sink while still maintaining the action of the fly. It works best to place this weight a couple of feet above the fly to allow the fly the best action while still keeping it in the strike zone. Keep in mind that adding weight to the line adds another element to your rig that can snag up. If you are fishing around wood, you will lose more flies with weight on your leader. Keeping the fly in the strike zone also requires using specialized equipment that allows line control.

Sometimes you may also want to get a big fly to the bottom while still maintaining its action. This is usually only practical in short-casting, slow-water scenarios. In these places the fly is fished very slowly, so you need to maintain the action of the fly. Adding weight in front of the fly on the leader is the answer to this. Casting a big fly with added weight on the line is not for the weak of heart and is some of the heaviest-duty fishing. Wherever possible, small to medium-sized flies are a better choice.

When fishing the classic swing in heavy water, a lot of the time we are using an intermediate line with a sink-tip attached. However, these lines just can't be manipulated as well when you are trying to get a line to sink. The most controllable lines are floating lines, and that is what we rely on when using this method. With the classic swing, we are trying to get a sink-tip close to the bottom; with the deep and dirty method, we are trying to get the fly to strike the bottom, so that changes the formula we might use for our sink-tip and leader.

On a small river or in low flows, you might not need a sink-tip at all with this method. Rather, the weight on your line might suffice. However, in larger rivers I will cut a piece of sink-tip

approximately two-thirds the depth of the water I am fishing. After that, I will use a longer-than-usual leader (compared to a basic swing method leader) that is tapered and is typically 6 to 7 feet long. This is followed by the weighted fly. The reason we keep the sink-tip shorter than the depth of the water is that we want the fly, and not the fly line, to touch the bottom. This system will present much better in this way.

Once all of these elements come together, we begin a bit more technical presentation than the classic swing. Often we are looking for slow water on the inside of a seam to present to. What you do is cast your line perpendicular to your position, or in certain situations actually cast your line upstream. Using a series of stack mends, you manipulate your fly until it hits the bottom. At this moment the line is allowed to go tight and swing. With any luck you are successful and a fish murders your fly. The net result is a swung-fly strike just like you get with the classic swing.

Sometimes you are confronted with a different situation and want to swing a fly through some really slow water. In this instance, your rig is the same, but you are using a thick floating line to tow your fly along. A downstream mend with a floating fly line induces an artificial swing, making a fly appealing to fish by giving it life. This is especially useful when you are casting from current in the middle of a river into a slow side of the river. Another situation is casting behind a downed tree where you have slack water that is much slower than the main current. In such a place, you have current to work with in proximity to you, and this is what pulls your fly along in a swing.

Fishing Position When Swinging Flies

With either of the swung-fly techniques previously described, your position on the water is of paramount importance to your success as an angler. Your ability to catch fish depends as much on where you are standing or where your boat is anchored as it does on how well you cast. Your position when you fish is crucial to your success. However, it is an abstract concept to many anglers, so it is often not addressed.

Most anglers who don't catch fish swinging flies are unsuccessful because they simply don't position themselves correctly in relation to the fish. Usually the other factors are covered: They have the right fly, rod, reel, line, etc. We will cover how to position in a boat and how to position when you are wading; the idea is to get the fly deep and keep it deep for as long as possible, even at the end of your swing.

The Midwest is unique for a lot of reasons. When it comes to swinging flies, our water temperatures are on average much colder than other places. Warm water for swinging flies in our region would be anything over 36 degrees, and it is not uncommon for the winter months to have water temperatures that seldom creep much above the freezing mark. This is a big part of the reason why we use sinking lines to get our flies deep and keep them deep. It is also a large part of the reason why a boat makes such a great instrument for swinging flies on our large rivers.

If you read a typical western fly-fishing book, you won't find a whole lot about fishing from a boat for migratory fish. This is largely because in some states it is not legal to fish from a boat while it is anchored in a river. For this reason, the tradition of swinging flies has evolved around wading. This has to do with who owns the riverbed; in Midwest states like Michigan, navigable rivers are considered state property, so our steelhead fishing has evolved to incorporate fishing from a boat. If you couple a stable boat with an electric anchor system, it becomes an efficient tool for stepping through a run. There are other places, even in the Midwest, where landowners own the riverbed. In these places, fishing is restricted to the wading angler. In many ways, Midwest steelhead fishing has plotted a course that is considerably different than the fishing out West, and in this regard it is a good thing.

In most instances, the idea when swinging flies from a boat is to cast the fly square or slightly downstream in water that is 3 to 6 feet in depth and holding steelhead. This depth range is considered ideal no matter where you swing flies. As the fly swings around and the line tightens, you want to be positioned in slow or shallow enough water that the fly is not lifted all the way to the surface at the end of the swing (in a perfect world it would remain within a foot of the riverbed). This becomes more and more crucial as the water gets colder. If you are fishing an area where you feel that the fly is swinging too high at the end of your swing, you should consider positioning yourself a little shallower or using a heavier fly and sink-tip.

One of the principles of either of the swung-fly methods is called "stepping through a run." The idea is that after each cast, you move your feet if you were wading a little bit, or in the case of a boat, you would lift the anchor and move a few feet. In your typical run, you would move straight downstream with each step.

The steps you would take with a boat are larger than the steps you would take when wading. If you find that your boat is taking huge steps, a good work-around is to make casts of different lengths before taking the next step. Taking huge steps is a common problem when anglers are using a lightweight anchor on their boat. It may also be caused by an imbalanced boat, when the motor end of the boat is so heavy that it makes it difficult for an anchor to stay on the riverbed. Carefully balancing the weight in your boat can make it a lot easier to walk through a run. A boat has a huge advantage of being able to cover water quickly. A consideration when Spey casting from a boat is that fishing above the water in a boat effectively makes your rod at least 2 feet longer. If you are accustomed to wading, you will need to make adjustments to how you anchor the cast when you start swinging from a boat.

A boat is an asset for covering water. However, it is impossible to exactly control how large of a step you take through a run in a boat—to some degree you are at the mercy of the river for this. You will lack the precision from a boat that you would get from wading. If you want to be thorough, nothing is better than wading and actually stepping through a likely spot. The downside to wading is that in its thoroughness, it takes a lot of time to fish through each run. There are other considerations as well: If the weather is very cold, you will find it much easier to stay warm while in a boat, without the pressure of cold water on your legs. Even if you are a wading angler, a boat is a great asset to get from spot to spot to swing flies. This can be done on any river but is especially common on drift-boat rivers such as Michigan's Pere Marquette.

Wading anglers have an advantage in precision over boat anglers. After all, when you step through a run, you are in precise control of your presentation. Furthermore, the modern two-handed rods were built with the wading angler in mind. Positioning as a wading angler can be a lot more tricky. As a wading angler, you have to keep your own safety in mind, and you might not be able to get the perfect swing due to the physical qualities of the run. You may be forced to stand in water that makes your fly bottom out at the end of the swing, for example. This would be true in the case of a steep drop-off in depth or a sudden increase in current as you move from shore.

On the bright side, you are typically wading the edges of a pool or run. In these places the current is a bit slower, so you can cast your fly out into the current and swing it back below you. Usually the depth that you are standing in is shallow enough to get the fly near the bottom. Unlike fishing from a boat, the problem isn't getting the fly to remain close enough to the bottom at the end of the swing—it's your fly swinging around and clobbering the bottom at the end of the swing.

For this reason, when you wade, line control is a fundamental requirement. Often for casting reasons you would be using lighter sink-tips and flies when wading, so short and controlled casts will compensate and help you to fish a fly deeply through the drift. Stack mending and upstream mends will help to sink a lighter fly. Wading is more technical than boat fishing, but boat fishing has the advantage of coverage.

Whether you are fishing from a boat or wading, you may wonder how big the steps should be when swinging a fly. When wading, a step is usually exactly what it sounds like. You would make a cast, and after the swing is complete, you would take a step. In this way, you would work your way down through a run. Much of the time, you won't have to give too much thought to how you step through the river, as your typical walking stride might be just fine.

There are some instances where you might consider taking bigger steps. For example, if the bite is extremely good and the fish are hot, you might want to take bigger steps. When the fish are taking the swing well, covering the maximum amount of water will result in more fish. Thus, if you are taking the largest steps possible on a day with a great bite, it makes sense that you would catch more fish in this way. These crazy-good bite days are often in the fall, when the water temperature is at its warmest. The perfect storm for a big day of fishing is good numbers of fish with reasonably warm water. This combination of factors most likely will occur late in the fall. Often we have a large push of fish just before winter. In combination with warm water temps, this is the formula for the most successful fishing trips.

The most common scenario on a guide trip is that we start working through a run taking normal-sized steps. Steelhead give themselves away by pulling or tapping on the line, even if they are not fully committing. If there is a lot of this type of action, we start taking larger steps, and the fishing takes on a quicker pace. The frequent bites mean that the fish are active and their window is very large. Using larger steps goes hand in hand with fish being able to see your fly from a greater distance. To make it easier to see from a distance, you would move the fly up the water column. An easy way to do this is to use a lighter sink-tip and fly.

Big steps, by nature, consume water really quickly. If you have a whole day to fish and have unlimited water to work with, big steps will maximize the amount of water you can cover in a day. On a day guiding with big steps, I might cover 10 miles or more from a boat over the course of a day. Using big steps is a glancing way to fish that puts your fly over a lot of fish in short order but does not cover them thoroughly.

Conversely, there are times when smaller steps can make for a successful day. This is usually the case when you are trying to make lemonade out of lemons. One obvious time that smaller steps are best is when the fishing is not so good or if you are fishing in cold water. The smaller your steps are going through a run, the more likely your fly is going deep and hopefully swinging in front of the eyes of a fish. In this case, taking small steps would be used in conjunction with a heavy fly or heavy sink-tip. Getting a sullen fish to strike often involves keeping the fly in the strike zone.

Another instance when you would use small steps is in high or dirty water. This is something that is often associated with late winter. At this time the water is cold, but the fish concentrations are good. Because fish concentrations are good, there is no reason not to work slowly and methodically to marshal a strike.

Using small steps in a run is time-consuming and cuts the amount of water you fish in a day. However, there are practical reasons why you might take small steps through a run. One reason is that you might be restricted to the amount of water that you can fish in a day. In such a case, using tiny steps maximizes the amount of water fished.

Often while fishing through a run, you will be working at a normal pace or with large steps. Suddenly, you get a violent pull on the line but no connection results. In this instance, using very small steps really shines. Small steps will ensure that your fly ends up in front of an aggressive fish. Many times, slowing down to small steps after a bite has produced a great fish! Remember that fish are living in current that is constantly pushing against them. If a fish chases and bites your fly, the current will make it more work for him to return to his original spot. If there are resting places downstream, he will simply drop into those. This is a good thing for an angler stepping downstream through a run! If you have not pricked the fish, he will take your fly again provided that you are careful to cover the water with these small steps.

If being thorough is a great concern, if you know that you are going by a large number of fish, or if the water clarity is poor, there is no reason not to throw multiple casts per step to maximize the amount of times your fly goes past a fish. In most scenarios the fish takes the fly on the first pass through, but this is not always the case. I find that every river has certain areas where the fish concentrate while migrating. If you happen to find one of these areas, you would be well advised to take several casts per step, as a new fish might be seeing your fly at any time.

As you work down through a run, be it while wading or from a boat, there is something to be said about the timing of your cast. The very best thing that you can do is allow your fly to swing around completely before initiating your next cast. In the best-case scenario, your fly is dangling below your position as you make the step. The reason for this is simple: Many of the bites that you will get will be at the end of the swing or on the dangle.

As your fly whips across the current, it is often garnering the attention of a migratory fish from some distance away. The fish breaks free from the bottom, streaking after your fly. If that fish has come from some distance, it may take him a little while to catch up with your fly. Allowing for a dangle while you step buys the fish some time.

I have had many comical encounters with fish over the years after a long dangle. I remember guiding a man once when I was just starting to guide swung-fly trips. At the time, everyone either chuck-and-ducked or indicator fished for steelhead. As I was newish to guiding, my client raised an eyebrow and I could tell that he was humoring me as we fished large sculpin patterns on sink-tip lines. I am pretty sure that he thought he was paying some trout bum kid for a scenic boat ride. A few hours into the day, he made a cast and turned around to talk to me. The fly hung in the water for a long time as he was talking my ear off. With the line over his shoulder, a fish smashed his fly and pulled the rod out of his hand. His facial expression was priceless as he spun around and struggled to pick up the rod as it was bouncing toward the front of the boat. I looked downstream only to see a massive buck steelhead dancing on the water, and then breaking the line. For the rest of the day, that client grabbed the rod so tightly his knuckles were white. The moral of this story is always let your fly dangle at the end of any swung-fly presentation.

In other cases, a fish will chase your fly all the way across the river but will then sit behind the fly. If you step toward the fish with the fly dangling, this will get into the space of the fish and trigger an aggressive take.

As a side note to all of this, many of us who swing flies from a boat use an electric anchor. It is uncanny the amount of fish we catch over the course of the year while the boat is dropping back toward the fish after hanging in the water for a long period of time.

On the flip side of this, one of the most frustrating things in all of guiding is having anglers who begin to retrieve the fly too quickly before it has reached the end of the swing. Resist the urge to do this! Always allow your fly to swing until it is directly downstream from you. Ideally, don't cast again until after your step is completed. If you are having trouble catching fish on the swing, pay attention to the end of the drift. More often than not, this is where the problem lies.

If you swing flies from a boat, controlling the size of your steps is an art in itself. The real key is to lift the boat anchor only until it is slightly off the bottom of the river before dropping it again. If you lift the anchor too high, you will take enormous steps and that won't be good in most circumstances. In this case, your boat anchor should be very heavy, as a heavy anchor will help stop the boat immediately. If your anchor is too light, your boat will not stop quickly or dependably and this will ruin your presentation.

Many of us who use boats to swing flies use a chain anchor made from scrap chain. There is a good reason for this: When you are swinging flies, you can hear the chain as it is just barely touching the riverbed. This allows for quick and precise stops of the boat, and also allows for tiny steps as you move the boat. A chain anchor has other advantages as well. Chain does not snag on the bottom, so you will very seldom lose an anchor. Lifting an anchor numerous times during the day can put a strain on your anchor system. These systems are rugged, but because the chain does not snag when you lift it, it does not cause wear and tear like other anchors, such as a lead pyramid anchor. If you are going to step through a run in a boat, chain is the way to go.

If you own a boat and it is difficult to pull anchor on that vessel, you may not want to constantly move to approach the fish. In these situations, you can still fish successfully. This is one occasion where you would want to take multiple casts from

A drift boat is a great asset for stripping flies for migratory fish. Drift boats are easier to slow to a good speed. They are also physically easier to row and are less susceptible to wind. Photo credit: Jon Ray.

each step. The idea would be to place the anchor of your boat and then make a short swing. Follow this with three or four progressively longer casts until you have exhausted your range. After this is complete, move your boat a step. This is a good way to fish if you are lifting an anchor manually and want to last through a day of fishing.

The Stripping Retrieve

The stripping retrieve is one of the most common and effective presentations for brown trout. The Midwest has churned out some great streamer anglers over the years. Kelly Galloup, who now resides in Montana, is still renowned in this area for his early work streamer fishing. When you look at our resident trout fisheries, the numbers of fish that we have don't rival the numbers per acre in your typical western stream. However, due in part to our baitfish populations, the fertile latitude of the region, and the countless miles of river available, our streams can grow some mighty big brown trout. Trout streams that are connected to the Great Lakes have migratory fish as well, so there is a lot of crossover and migratory fish are often caught as the ultimate bonus while stripping flies for resident fish.

When I first started guiding, most of the fall and winter trips that I ran were stripping flies for trout. At the time, Teeny fly lines were considered the pinnacle of fly line technology for catching fish with this method. While stripping sculpin patterns with these lines, we would catch resident and lake-run brown trout. As I curried favor with the customer by catching trout, we would use the exact same Teeny lines to swing flies for steelhead. Back then, most people considered fishing a bulky sculpin for steelhead a crazy thing, and it was necessary to mix methods. In the late '80s and '90s, the state of Michigan had a lot of money and a large percentage of sportsmen. As a result, a lot of fish were being planted and we had lots of lake-run browns.

As things progressed, on the years that steelhead were abundant, I would do more swinging of flies, mostly with single-handed rods. We would catch the occasional lake-run brown, but swinging typically took more steelhead. There were other years when lake-run browns were more prevalent and we would strip flies, catching lake-runs with the odd steelhead.

From the perspective of a large river, I view stripping flies as the primary streamer technique for brown trout and a secondary technique for steelhead. Unlike the swung-fly method, which is an amazing strike that you feel, stripping a fly is an exciting visual take. It is a method that is gaining popularity for other migratories such as steelhead, especially on smaller waterways. Also, if you want a chance at a king or coho salmon on a streamer, stripping a fly is how you would get this done.

Stripping big flies for big fish is a hallmark of the Great Lakes region. It is a great way to take lake-run browns that enter our streams in the fall to spawn and feed ravenously while hanging out prior to returning to the lake. Even if you prefer to swing a fly, there are a lot of circumstances where you may want to pack a single-handed rod to try for migratory fish.

The technique is very basic and involves casting your fly out with a full-sinking or sink-tip line and retrieving it toward your position in erratic strips. The rod can be used to add action, and you can place the rod under your armpit to give the fly some reel speed. Typically the fly is casted square from your position and retrieved in a jerky, spastic action. This is a great way to imitate those baitfish that lack a swim bladder and swim in spurts, such as sculpins, gobies, and darters.

The stripping technique can be effectively employed when wading; however, it is at its best from a boat that is being rowed along with the current. Many streamers get deeper and perform better when fished from a boat that is being rowed downstream. Furthermore, as you are typically casting a single-handed rod with a sink-tip, it helps to have room to backcast, and a boat makes this process easier and less costly, as you don't hook as many trees on your backcast. Furthermore, by nature you are covering a lot of water when rowing a boat, and this lends itself very well to stripping flies. When you use this streamer method, a fish is going to either bite your fly on the first pass or ignore it. Thus, it is pointless to make numerous casts to the same spot. By fishing from a moving boat you are constantly covering new water. This coverage of water makes the best use of time.

There are a couple of important things to remember about stripping flies. For one, this is a manual operation of adding action to your bait. As such, if you look at your fly when you are retrieving it and it is not moving much, it is time to change your retrieve or change your fly to one with more action. If you are lazy with your retrieve, the fly will simply not move much and the fish will be unlikely to eat it.

As a guide, there are some things that I can do to compensate for poor presentation. One of the very best things that can be done in this situation is to use realistic flies that imitate specific baitfish. Experienced anglers can elicit strikes from attractor flies on the strip. However, when presentations are poor, a natural pattern can help compensate to a degree. This is because fish (really any gamefish) will be more forgiving of an accurate imitation than they will be of an inaccurate pattern on the strip. If your fly stops moving, it still looks like food to the fish, and that might be just good enough to get the job done.

Also, be cognizant of where your rod tip is. In most cases, keeping the rod low is the best bet for a good retrieve that keeps the fly deep. More importantly, the low rod position makes it possible to strike a large fish when it attacks.

Sometimes, especially in the winter, you are presenting flies to fish in very slow water. Without stripping your fly, you would not be able to fish these areas and the fly would be dead in the water. Winter brown trout, including the lake run variety, will often move into brush on the very slow edges of the river. These areas will have sufficient oxygen in the winter months, and this is where baitfish will be congregated for them to eat. Inside bends of rivers are another great example of a place where a stripped fly would be best.

Another migratory fish scenario is when you are fishing broad and slow areas of the river. This is common in the lowest reaches of many streams. In these places the broad river makes the water generic and structure undefined. You could spend weeks trying to anywise such a piece of water with other techniques, but stripping a fly reveals good holding areas. If you have a fish chase or strike, it will be worth a more careful look. That is where other techniques come in. Furthermore, if the area is unprotected, any breeze would create chop on the water, making a swung-fly presentation unattractive to the fish and unpleasant for the angler. In these same waters, an animated fly will take the fish that other methods just will not.

At certain points in their tenure in the river, steelhead are especially susceptible to taking a stripped fly. One of those times is when the fish first enter the river and the water temperatures are at their warmest. These fish are coming in from the big lake, so they are accustomed to eating baitfish. Another time when steelhead and lake-run brown trout respond well to a stripped fly is immediately after they spawn. At this point they need to pack on calories lost in the spawning process. A big meal is very appealing when stripped broadside to the current. Sculpins and big shiner patterns are very good bets when this is going on. Drop-back steelhead are a springtime phenomenon, so they are a common bonus fish while stripping flies for trout.

Steelhead are steelhead, and they require a precise presentation during the cold-water periods. With a swung fly, the colder the water, the deeper you must present the fly. Furthermore, the colder the water, the more likely you will be using natural baitfish colors. The same is true for any of these methods, including stripping flies. Fishing from a boat is helpful, as your streamer will get deeper as your boat takes the tension off your line by slowly moving downstream with the current. This same rowing action can help to combine the stripping and swinging presentations—the fly will swing as you pause on the strip. This can be too much for a steelhead to handle, and they may slaughter a fly.

Many of our larger rivers split into a delta (braids) as they approach their inlet into the lake. These areas are very tight, and swinging a fly is of limited value. Often there is brush that the fly has to be maneuvered around, and the stripping retrieve allows for this. A stripped fly can be stripped just about anywhere, and this is one place where stripping a fly is of value.

Fishing pier heads and river inlets also requires a stripped fly. In the majority of these places, there is little current and high winds are often a problem. In any still-water situation, stripping a fly is your only real choice of presenting baitfish patterns with a fly rod. There is no current to swing a fly through, and a nymph would likewise appear dead in the water. Stripping a goby pattern along the rocks and cement often found at river mouths can produce a wide array of predator fishes, including the ones that are the focus of this book.

If you are specifically fishing for lake-run brown trout, these fish are not as restricted to depth as steelhead are. You may be fishing water that is shallower than your typical steelhead water, and this too would require a stripped fly. Lake-run browns follow the food, and if the big baitfish are in shallow water, that is where they will be.

There are two schools of thought with this style of fishing, and both have their strengths and appeal to different types of anglers. These schools really revolve around the size of the flies that you like to fish.

Fishing very large flies is the style of the youthful, up-and-coming crowd. Many of the guides that are around are either in that crowd or were in it at one point. There is good reason for this. Casting very large baits requires physical stamina and consistent casting accuracy at the same time. Getting a big fish to chase a large streamer is an adrenaline rush, to say the least. There is no dispute that large fish eat large flies, and there are large food sources that fit very well into this category. Some baitfish that are commonly imitated are smaller trout, sculpins, gobies, large shiner species, and juvenile suckers, to name just a few. Shiners are of particular importance in the winter months, as they lose their hiding places in the weed beds. If you are fishing near the mouth of a river, stripping shad and alewife imitations is also a safe bet, as these Great Lakes forage species move in and out of our rivers.

Smaller trout can be of particular interest in Michigan, especially in the spring, when these fish are often planted. These naive fish are very vulnerable to predation, and brown trout and steelhead will readily prey upon them.

Over the past 25 years, I have launched a boat thousands of times, so I have spent a lot of time around boat launches. Often I would get to the boat launch early, or my clients would be running late. This has led to a lot of cumulative time watching the world go by. Over those years, I have seen some crazy large trout feeding on juvenile trout,

the "planters," in front of the boat launches. Stripping big flies in the vicinity of these areas catches big things. This is a common place to find a drop-back steelhead, as small trout are often planted around the time that steelhead spawn. Unwary, pellet-fed trout are a favorite snack for drop-back steelhead. Other native fish, such as walleye, can also be caught while stripping flies around planting areas. An interesting footnote is that in the spring, walleye themselves have completed spawning and are also drop back fish. They are a neat bonus fish but can be targeted with swung flies and stripped flies using many of the same baitfish patterns.

Yet it is not always necessary to cast such large flies while using the stripping method. The second school of thought is casting smaller patterns. These smaller patterns typically are pretty close imitations of some of the food sources discussed earlier in this book. Most brown trout, big or small, are not eating huge things all the time. The majority of the food sources in a river are usually lower on the food chain and are smaller. If small food sources are very abundant, even the largest of fish will take them. Not only will they eat them, but they will eat lots of them. Darters, shiners, crayfish, hellgramites, etc., which are all commonly imitated with streamers, are typically 1 to 4 inches in length. Fry, hugging the inside bends and slow areas of the river, also fall into this category. Food sources large and small can be imitated with a stripping retrieve.

Because of the smaller size of these food sources, it is often a good idea to fish two at a time. This way, you can imitate a schooling type of baitfish or imitate two different fish simultaneously. During the late spring, we use this method all of the time. At that time it will catch drop-back steelhead, resident trout, and the occasional lake brown. A common combination for me is a sparkly minnow pattern that incorporates a lot of flash (often copper); I follow this fly with a fry pattern or a sculpin pattern. The Queen of the Muddy Waters, which is detailed in the fly tying section, is a common lead fly for this. Conversely, the second fly is usually an accurate imitation of a food source. A fish might take either one of these patterns at any time but often will streak after the flashy fly, only to turn and eat the natural as it approaches your location.

Right: Twitching a fry pattern with a light switch rod is a great way to catch steelhead, both in the middle of winter and in the spring. This is a drop-back fish that was caught with this technique at the end of a run in early June. Often the ultra-prime spots where you catch a steelhead at the beginning of the season in the fall will hold the last fish of the season. This was the last steelhead I caught the spring this image was taken.

As a guide, smaller patterns have the obvious advantage of being easy to cast. Not every client is capable of casting a huge fly in a way that would catch fish. Yet the smaller flies can be just as deadly, as long as you find a way to match the hatch. By using flash and other synthetic materials, smaller flies can be given a presence that is very appealing, even to the largest fish.

The Switch with a Twitch

This is a technique that we use both in the dead of winter and again in the spring, when targeting large brown trout and steelhead. It is a combination of the previous methods and works any time fish are concentrated on the slow edge of the river, often in the slack water on the shore side of a fast seam. This is a style of fishing that works well when you want to draw the strike of a baitfish-eating predator but stripping might not be as ideal or as thorough.

In the dead of winter, trout and baitfish accumulate on the slow edges of our rivers. Cold water holds more oxygen than warm water does, and this allows predator fish to move into ultraslow water to feed and grow large on any number of food sources. This often includes tiny food sources such as midges, but it also includes any minnows that are present in the area. Small and natural shiner patterns work great for this, as do smaller bottom-dwelling minnow patterns such as darters. Large flies are not best suited to this style of fishing. In the dead of winter, you need a fly to get down quickly, and bulky flies are not good in this regard. If you want to catch a steelhead or nice trout in this situation, your options are to either fish tiny nymphs under an indicator or fish a tight-line swing method such as this one.

Months go by until spring, when again this technique works great. However, though the method is the same, the reason the fish are on the edges is different: In the spring, salmon, steelhead, and sucker fry are concentrated along the edges, unable to fight the strong currents in the middle of the stream. This makes it necessary to cast into that

slow water once again and to allow the fly to swing out. These fry can take a variety of forms, but when targeting steelhead and brown trout in this area, we are most commonly imitating king salmon fry. After the migratory fish leave, you can continue to use this method for resident trout or even smallmouth bass when imitating sucker fry or steelhead fry.

This method breaks from the other swing methods in that it helps a lot to add action to the fly as it comes into the current. Typically your fly will have some weight incorporated into it, and after it hits the bottom, you will stack some mends to allow it to graze the bottom. As soon as it begins to swing, you will add twitches to the fly to activate it. These twitches can be applied by stripping and releasing or raising and lowering the fly line. Regardless of how you do it, the action you impart is not constant: You will twitch a couple of times and then pause, and repeat. Because the water is slow, adding action to the fly will not bring it too far off the bottom. Often with this method the fish will attack as soon as the fly comes mid-swing or approaches the faster water.

As a side note, many anglers who fish wet flies for resident trout add no action to their presentations. If you fish a fly that represents a minnow for trout, such as a tiny fry pattern, the more twitching you add, the better. I have a good client who loves to fish dry and wet flies for trout. When I take him wet-fly fishing, he spends the day doing his patented "spastic twitch," in which he twitches more than anyone I have ever seen. He catches some very nice fish, year after year, with this presentation.

Getting back to migratory fish, in ideal circumstances, you will be casting from deeper, faster water into slower and shallower water. For this reason, this style of fishing is often best performed from a boat if you are fishing a large body of water. This is especially true in the winter. If you are wading, this is still a great tactic, but you will have to either back away from the slower water and avoid the seam altogether, or use a heavier fly to cast into the fast side of the seam and cast past it from the slow side to get the fly down. This is often a more technical form of swinging in the winter, and using upstream mends, reach casts, or stack mends can help your fly get deep. If you fish this way at warm-water times of the year, it can be just as deadly while wading.

When fishing this way, you can really cover slow-moving water thoroughly. Typically you would make a cast and then move a little bit, in small increments. You would be stepping through

In many Midwest rivers, this twitching method is used to imitate some type of fry. Pictured are some king salmon fry; this is how these minnows look as the steelhead leave the rivers in the spring. King salmon are one of the most successful migratory fish at reproducing. Their young leave rivers before the water gets too warm, giving them a better chance of survival.

Nymphing is always a great fallback style of fishing that is good for catching numbers of fish. Pictured are Ed McCoy and Jon Ray on their home waters of the Manistee River system. In large rivers with high currents, a sizable indicator supporting some weight is necessary to get the fly to the proper depth and keep it there.

the run in small steps, especially in the winter-time. This would allow you to cover a concentration of fish.

Nymph-Fishing Methods with Baitfish Patterns

This book is specifically meant to teach how to catch migratory fish with baitfish patterns and is largely focused on streamer fishing. Though the book is really geared toward sink-tip methods, such as the swung fly or the streamer, at its core it is really about any method that will help you catch fish with a baitfish pattern.

There are really two different ways of nymph fishing that are distinct from one another and will present a baitfish imitation well. One involves fishing a strike indicator, the other does not.

When you fish with an indicator, you are trying to manipulate the floating fly line in such a way that the fly fishes in a straight line as it moves down the river. This is perfect for fishing such imitations as small insects. However, many baitfish are a different sort of animal entirely and attract predators when they swim erratically, not in a straight line at all.

A good way to nymph fish with an indicator is to use two flies, one that imitates a nymph or an egg and one that imitates a small baitfish (salmon fry patterns are a prime example of this). Use a little more weight than normal, and as the presentation starts to drag, allow the fly to swing out. On the straight part of the drift, the fish may bite the nymph pattern. However, the swing part may coax a strike from a fish that otherwise would be overlooked.

Sometimes, you can get rid of the external weight altogether. Rather than using two flies and a sinker, use one weighted fly at the bottom of the rig and a more conventional nymph above it, and proceed to dead-drift it. The fly can be a sculpin, goby, or crayfish imitation; ideally you would use a very realistic imitation, as it will only be moved by the current. If you do this, always let it swing at the end of the drift, and expect a violent strike. The flies can be weighted in a conventional way or tied on jig heads when used as the weight in a nymphing rig. If you tie such a fly on a jig head, tungsten bead heads will be the most efficient delivery system.

This is a technique we use in the dead of winter, and it is good for steelhead and resident trout. If you want to get the most out of your swing while using an indicator, make your fly or weight extra heavy. This will give you a longer finishing swing on your presentation.

There is one final method that we should discuss when covering fishing baitfishes. It is the often maligned method of deep nymphing, often called "chucking and ducking." When people ask about this method, I describe it as being crude but effective.

Chucking and ducking does have one real strength that fits in very well with the theme of this book: It presents baitfish patterns really well. Essentially, a chuck-and-duck rig gets a fly very deep with an extremely short sink-tip—well, I call it a "sink-tip" with a smile on my face, as it is really just a big sinker. The fly is bounced along the bottom until contact is lost. At this point, many anglers bring it in.

I only mention this style of fishing because it is an effective way to present baitfish patterns deeply, especially in adverse conditions. Toward the end of winter, the water in many Midwest rivers is high and cold. There is a wall of heavy current between you and the fish and limited visibility, and since the water is so cold, they won't react quickly enough to the fly to eat in on a streamer presentation. As a guide on a big river, we are often presented with a scenario where we can get a lot of fish to bite a baitfish pattern, but we have to go medieval to do so. And so, we bounce a fly through a run. To present a baitfish pattern in this scenario, at the end of the drift, when contact is lost with the bottom, the fly is allowed to swing out. One of the prime flies that we use at this time of the year is a salmon parr imitation; since it is a baitfish pattern, you can see how it would work well to allow the fly to swing out at the end of the drift.

You may wonder, with the availability of indicators, why you would ever use a tight-line-style of nymph fishing. There is another benefit to using this technique versus an indicator rig: The bottom-bouncing technique does not incorporate a floating fly line or a float into the equation. This does not affect the first part of your nymphing presentation, but as your fly swings out, it will swing much deeper without a thick floating line and a float.

Think of it this way: When you fish a caddis larva, a stonefly, or an egg, floats and indicators will be more effective because they give you a drift that is perfectly in line with the current. These types of foods don't swim much, and thus they are a great way to get things done. However, baitfish swim erratically and seldom move perfectly in the current. A tight-line presentation will not move in a straight line with the current, as there is pressure on your line from the current. This will cause your fly to naturally swing at the end of your drift, and this is very appealing when throwing any type of minnow pattern.

In the spring on large rivers, deep nymph fishing may be the best option for putting a bend in the rod. It can also be used in situations where the conditions are extremely windy and Spey casting or casting a heavy sink-tip overhead is not practical.

A Couple Obscure Things You Could Try

There are a couple of other techniques that take some really nice trout from year to year. One of these tactics was designed for smallmouth bass. I guide on a river that has trout, smallmouth bass, and migratory fish all in the same water. While using this tactic for trout, we found that we also caught some of the cool-water fish. After tweaking the fly patterns, it can be an effective tool for any number of species and works great when presenting flies deep and slow.

This method is often called the "Holschlag hop." It is named after a well-respected smallmouth guide who is from Minnesota, Tim Holschlag. The principle behind this method is simple. It incorporates a floating fly line, with a large front taper. Place a small cork or strike indicator (I use one called the Lil' Corky) at the end of your leader. The leader itself should be twice the depth of the water. At the end of the leader, place your fly selection. This would usually be a weighted crayfish, goby, or sculpin imitation.

Cast this outfit upstream at a 45-degree angle. Unlike the previous nymphing method, we are not trying to create a perfect dead drift. The intention is to cast upriver with this small indicator to get the fly to sink. Mend approximately half of the line on the water, so that it forms an S. At this point, give the fly a twitch, and then a pause. In so doing, you may get any type of predator to bite. This works well from a stationary standpoint, and can work even better on a large river in a boat, where you

can cast and effectively fish a great distance while the boat is moving. This is just another weapon in the arsenal and a neat trick to pull out when nothing else is working.

Typically the fly selection for migratory fish is a lot more natural than what we would use for smallmouth with this method. Salmonids tend to like small crayfish patterns, and also like goby patterns when fished under a float. This hopping method can be adapted to most gamefish in our rivers and is definitely something worth a try when you are striking out with other tactics.

Another method that sometimes produces is to cast a sculpin or goby pattern upriver with a single-handed rod and sink-tip line. This can take brown trout and steelhead in deep and slow areas. Throw the same S type of a mend, and as the line tightens up and passes your body, start jigging the fly. At the end of the drift, the fly is reasonably deep, and you can allow it to swing out to take a pursuing fish.

Often side pressure is misunderstood or badly applied. When maneuvering a big fish upstream, you would lean toward your upstream shoulder. To move a fish across the current, you would use your downstream shoulder. Whatever you do, change shoulders with your rod slowly. Herky-jerky movements are the most common source of lost fish. Migratory fish have soft mouths, and constant pressure is mandatory.

Guide Drew Rosema is pictured landing a great steelhead with some clients. That rubber-lined landing net will be easy on the fish. Quick and careful handling of a fish is always the best way to ensure the survival of a gamefish.

These are just a couple of oddball techniques that can never hurt to try. There are times of the year, however, when I am pretty fixed on a particular method. For example, during the fall and winter, the swung fly is king, and I have a real passion for it. Conditions would have to be pretty hideous if you didn't find me swinging flies in the fall and winter. However, as we head into spring, a diverse spectrum of all these techniques will add to your success. Changing things up also makes fishing more interesting. No matter how the fly is presented, baitfish patterns are always in the boat and almost always on the line.

Fighting a Big Fish

When everything comes together and you finally hook a big fish, you want to capitalize on the opportunity and land it. When you first hook a big migratory fish, your enemy is slack in the line. Steelhead and brown trout both have a relatively soft mouth, and they will easily throw a hook if given the opportunity. When you initially hook a fish, it is always more important that the rod stays bent than getting the line onto the reel. Thus, you may find yourself stripping line in the chaos until the fish pulls enough of the line for it to be tight.

There are good ways to steer a fish. A neutral fight will involve keeping the rod high and bent. This style of fighting a fish is appropriate in a boat, and usually you will land a fish this way. The boat can be maneuvered, which gives you a big advantage. To speed the landing of the fish, use the vector of your pull to get it to (hopefully) do what you want. If you want a fish to come upstream toward your position, lean hard and low to your upstream shoulder. If, however, the fish is perpendicular to where you are standing or somewhat upstream, lean to your downstream shoulder. Understanding these basic principles will aid in landing fish.

Handling the Fish

Let's face it, many of us practice catch-and-release fishing, and this book deals with catching some pretty good fish. Inevitably, you will want to take a picture with a fish. If you are fishing in a wading scenario, it is really easy to take care of the fish.

Ideally the angler keeps the fish near or partially in the water, you get the grip-and-grin, and the fish is back in the river, little worse for wear. In this situation, all that you have to be careful of is that you don't grip the fish too hard, especially toward the front, as that is where their heart is. A death grip on a fish's vital organs is exactly that. With some care, releasing fish caught while wade fishing is usually pretty low stress for the fish.

Many of us guide and fish from boats, and it is simply not practical to hold a fish in the water when taking a shot of a client with a fish. If you are fishing in a big river, such an attempt would mean moving the boat to shore, getting the angler safely out of the boat, and then taking a shot. The photo would look impressive, but it would take a lot of time, and time in a net in a moving boat is not a good thing for a fish.

At the same time, the very last thing that you want to do is drop a fish on its head in the boat if you are planning on releasing it. I used to handle fish without any tools, and some clients could hold a fish and others could not. When handling a fish without tools in a boat, try to stay low in the boat with the fish while kneeling, as the fish will only have a short distance to fall if you do drop it. I use a rubber net and try to keep it under the fish for any fish shots. The net is wet and protects the slime on the fish should something go wrong.

Though they are not perfect solutions, a couple pieces of equipment can really help in handing fish. One less-desirable tool is a landing glove that allows you to grip the tail of a fish more easily. This type of fish-handling tool is frowned upon, especially if you look at the internet, but many anglers who never fish from boats don't realize the choices that you must make when handling fish in a boat. Fish-handling gloves are readily available at shops and are typically made of some form of mesh. The main drawback of the mesh glove is that it may remove slime and scales from the fish. Compared to dropping a fish on its head, however, this is a lesser evil. A much better option for handling fish is the use of a gripping tool.

Gripping tools are not pretty, but they are a very reliable way of safely handling fish. With good technique, they minimize stress on the fish and are really the best option for quick handling and documenting a big fish. The best of these tools is the BogaGrip. With the gripping tool, you grab the lip of the fish. If you want to do minimum damage to the fish, you will always support the weight of the fish with your other hand, from the moment it leaves the net all the way until the time the picture is taken. Usually you support the fish in its midsection to prevent hurting its vital organs. In this way, there is a little stress put on the face and head of the fish.

These tools often have a built-in scale for the fish. Usually I will only weigh extremely exceptional fish, as lifting a fish by the mouth with one of these tools is very hard on the fish and could easily hurt them. A grip also really shines for reviving fish, as they can be held in the current with little stress and simply unclipped when the fish is ready to go. If a fish is not properly revived, it has less chance of survival, so this is an important step in my mind.

From a boat, anglers often hold a fish on a grip before releasing it by using a tether. If the tether is stretchy like a bungee cord, this can make it easier on the fish and allows for a good recovery. One of the biggest mistakes I see all the time is people with fish on a tether with the fish sticking its head out of the water. If you are attempting to revive a fish, do not ignore it while it is hanging over the side of your boat. The fish will die, and you will look bad to any passing boat.

Remember as you read this that most of our fishing is from a boat. If a client catches an exceptional fish, I think that they should be allowed a picture of it. I also believe that the fish should be stressed minimally in the process. Migratory fish are generally pretty tough; water temperatures are favorable for their survival, and they are built for a long migration. As water temperatures become unfavorable for the fish, such as stream trout in

It's always a treat to see a skilled angler with a great fish. Here Jeff Liskay holds a perfect specimen in the water for the shot. In a perfect world, all fish pictures would be taken with the fish in the water. However, the constraints of fishing in a boat don't always make this possible. You can take steps to protect any fish before release.

the summer, we avoid handling them at all. The main goal of any fish-handling apparatus such as a glove or a gripping tool is to avoid having a fish dropped on its head. This should be avoided at all costs. The other goal is a speedy return to the water for the fish.

If you are fishing from a boat and using a net, some nets are a lot better for fish than others. Look for nets that are designed to be easy on the fish but that also don't tangle your fly line. My preferred nets have rubber mesh, and are very easy on the fish and never tangle your fly.

We advocate for catch-and-release of these great gamefish. A nice steelhead or brown trout is a great fish that can be caught by several anglers over the course of its stay in the river. We are increasingly sharing our rivers with many other anglers, and this can only help keep the fishing good for all of them.

One unpleasant subject is that of fish mortality. Catch-and-release should not be used at all costs. On very rare occasions, a migratory fish will get hooked in the tongue. This is usually caused when you step through a run and at the end of the swing, take a step. The fish is eating your fly while the fly is essentially dropping down its throat. When the hook is removed in these cases, the fish bleeds heavily, and this is a mortal wound. If you see this immediately upon landing, you can preempt mortality by cutting the hook in the middle of the bend with diagonal pliers. This allows the fish to rid itself of the remnant of the hook. If you do pull such a hook out, the fish will bleed profusely. In this regrettable situation, you best honor the fish and our sport when you keep the fish. There is nothing worse than releasing a noble fish only to see it float to the surface or sink to the bottom yards downriver.

Catch-and-release is a fantastic way to maintain our fisheries, but it should not be done just for the sake of releasing a fish. Honor the fish.

Left: The goal after landing a great fish is to make sure it goes home safely. We shall meet again

CHAPTER 5

Equipment

This book is written from a fishing guide's perspective with the goal of improving angling versus casting. A primary goal is to help you read water and learn to fish various baitfish species. There is an underlying thread when we discuss equipment: Most of the stuff discussed in this book involves casting either a weighted fly or a sink-tip line. In big rivers, sink-tip fishing is a bread-and-butter approach to catching big fish. I feel obligated to write a section on this, as without some rudimentary knowledge about casting heavy-duty rigs, bad things can happen. This is one example:

When I first started to guide swung-fly trips for steelhead many years ago, we didn't have very good technology in fly lines, and many of the lines at the time were just plain hard to cast. Because it was necessary to get deep, I would use single-handed lines with my clients. The very best of these were the Teeny lines that continue to be available to this day.

One brisk, windy fall day, I had a typical day trip with a client. I had guided him before, and knew him to be a good caster. I rigged a sink-tip and a 300-grain line, coupled with a big sculpin pattern. At the time, all I had confidence in were these big wind-resistant patterns. I preface the rest of the story by telling you that this particular client had a particularly large forehead. When he picked up the sink-tip to cast, he aerialized it like a floating line and made far too many false casts. This is the kiss of death with single-handed sinking lines, as they become uncontrollable with too much line out. Inevitably, he lost control of the line on a backcast, and the fly came back and struck him. Much to my chagrin, the fly had stuck in his flesh, dead center in the middle of his oblong forehead. As a young guide, I didn't show my maturity very well. He looked so ridiculous that I started to laugh—I

The right equipment makes fishing practical and fun! Streamer fishing for migratory fish is a lot of work, but is rewarding. You do not want to be under-gunned, and if you are new to migratory fish, you should lean toward the heavy side with equipment. If you do hook a big fish, you want equipment that is up to the task.

just couldn't help it. I could tell my client was mortified by this, and I tried to recover and helped pry the fly out of his mighty head.

What followed was an awkward silence in the boat. We continued to fish to no avail, but later hooked a nice steelhead. Toward the end of the day, as my client was getting tired, he made another errant cast. This one struck me in the middle of the head. I heard him chuckle, and with his back turned, I could just hear him say "Touché" under his breath.

Fishing with sinking fly lines is challenging. Going forward, I feel obligated to provide you with some information about the right equipment and fishing sink-tips.

Fly Rods

The overwhelming trend in the last decade has been toward two-handed rods for swinging flies, especially on big rivers. These two-handed rods are used to cast and dead-swing a fly, and they are very good at that job. However, if you want to strip a streamer or cast a wet fly with an active twitch, single-handed rods are indispensable.

I take a lot of people on trips involving streamer fishing with single-handed rods, and it can be downright dangerous to teach beginners how to cast a sink-tip in a boat. The best advice I can give is to think of a sink-tip line as a different animal than a floating line. Think of the sinking part of the line as an actual sinker.

False casting should be kept to a minimum; one false cast is the best number, but if you must use two, this is how you should consider doing it: With the initial short forward cast, allow the line to graze the water in front of you. Proceed to make one more false cast, and shoot the line in front of you. This will ensure a good and powerful cast, and if you are fishing with a friend, it will keep them safe. If you are fishing a fly with heavy eyes, this will also prevent you from getting hit in the head when the fly comes forward. This is a simple tip that helps so much.

If you are swinging flies with a single-handed rod and wading, learning single-handed Spey casts is a real asset. These casts can help you launch a sink-tip, but can also help you throw a roll cast

with enough energy to carry a weighted fly. Getting a fly some distance without a backcast is a huge asset when you are wading a river and there are a lot of trees behind you—something that is very common in the Midwest. One of the casts that is very useful is the snap T. Adding a haul to a snap T is a great way to cast a sink-tip line on a single-handed rod in close quarters. This is a technique perfected by one of the greats in the fly-fishing business, Simon Gawesworth.

As a general standard with single-handed rods, we use 7- to 9-weight rods for all types of migratory fish as well as larger resident fish. Typically, shorter rods do well in the wind and punch a fly very well; however, they lack line control. Thus, any single-handed rod in this category less than 9 feet in length is made specifically to strip flies. As single-handed rods get longer, they become better for line control and are often specifically made for migratory fish. Rods that are 9½ to 10 feet in length can roll cast and make easy work of single-handed Spey casts. Longer rods are heavier and more fatiguing over a long day on the water. They are also more forgiving when playing larger fish. However, they don't cast quite as well in windy conditions. As you get into the territory of rods longer than 10 feet, you enter the realm of the switch rod.

When you strip flies, a single-handed rod is the way to go—there is nothing better. However, a single-handed rod has a couple of things that work against it in the swung-fly department. First of all, if you are wading and are throwing a heavy-duty sink-tip, you probably won't be able to get away with roll casting it all of the time. As a result, you will always need room behind you for a backcast. Some of the single-handed Spey lines have alleviated this problem, but you still will be limited. My advice is to under-line the rod if you are going to add a heavy sink-tip. The combined grains of the line are the bottom-line number to concern yourself with when considering the line for your stick.

A short, single-handed Skagit-type line will fish very well if you need to interchange tips. However, if you are overhead casting, you will likely experience some hinging as you try to cast long distances, unless you are an extraordinary caster. This is OK—just fish within the limitations of the line. Again, casting long distance is not really the best approach to success with swung flies in my mind.

Fatigue is a second issue with a single-handed rod. Over a full day of fishing, you will use a lot more energy casting a heavy tip with a single-handed rod than you would if you were an adequate two-handed rod caster. Two-handed rods or switch rods have a further advantage in that they are better at fighting fish. I have found over the years that mathematically we simply land more fish with a two-handed rod.

As we head into winter and line control is more of an issue, the more rod length that you have, the better. This will allow you to reach mend and drive a fly to the bottom of the river. It will allow you to do what is needed to cast a heavy fly and control its descent to the bottom.

One last advantage a longer rod has over a single-handed rod is in the department of what they can handle. When paired with a weighted fly, you are able to cast a longer head with a longer rod. This will come into play whenever there is high water.

It would seem as though single-handed rods have a lot of disadvantages for swinging flies, but they are effective tools and very fun. Though they are not always easy to use when wading, in a boat there are tight places that you fish that are a lot easier to cover with a single-handed rod. When I fish some of the gnarly areas with an overhead canopy of trees, it is good to have a single-handed rod along to complete the cast. Single hand rods will always have a place as a primary tool of streamer fishermen. Switch rods and full spey rods also have their place.

In recent years, switch rods have entered the market. For the first few years after their entrance into the world of fly fishing, these rods were a bit of an enigma, as there was some confusion about how to line them. It took a while for the fly-line industry to produce lines that work really well for what we do. The popularity of switch rods has grown a lot, and in response the fly-line manufacturers have produced some great products that make them very useful tools for river anglers. Most commonly these fly lines are Skagit-type lines that

can punch a light sink-tip moderate distances with ease.

As with single-handed rods, an important thing to note with switch rods is that you have to keep the weight of the sink-tip you are going to use in mind when purchasing a line. If you are going to use a heavier sink-tip, you will want to use a lighter belly. If you use a total of too many grains, the rod will over-line and will be a real dog to cast. This is true with all fly rods, but it is especially true with lighter rods. For example, if you are using a 15-foot 9-weight Spey rod, a 120-grain tip will be a proportionally small amount of the overall grains of your fly line. If you are using a 580-grain line, for a total of 700 grains, the rod will be slightly over-lined. However, if you add that same 120-grain sink-tip to a 4-weight switch rod's 280-grain line, the tip would massively over-line the rod. In the Midwest we are usually using heavier and denser sink-tips than in other parts of the country. If you buy a fly rod for swinging flies and find that it is incredibly difficult to cast, it may not be the rod's problem but rather the line/sink-tip combination that you have added to it. You may be using too many grains.

Getting back to our discussion on switch rods, they have come a long way and are mostly used as a swung-fly rod. They are at their best with a classic swing but also work very well with a twitching presentation. Heavier switch rods are marketed toward migratory fish, whereas lighter rods are marketed toward trout. The lighter switch rods have some interesting applications for species such as smallmouth bass in tight quarters. They are also commonly used for some indicator/nymphing techniques on large rivers with large floats.

These rods are a real asset to any wading angler in small to moderate-sized rivers. They easily get you into tight spaces that would be difficult with other rods. On a typical small river, a switch rod is the perfect length to give you the ability to Spey cast while still keeping you under the canopy of any trees. In the typical Midwest stream with hardwoods along the bank, you will struggle to cast in some places if you go longer than 12 feet in a small to medium-sized stream. If you are going to use a switch rod to fish a sink-tip,

Right: The real strength of the switch rod is in small to medium-sized rivers with a canopy of trees over top. In these places anything more than a 12-foot rod is overkill. Switch rods, which typically range from 10½ to 11½ feet, can be used for a variety of tasks in this scenario. Here Jeff Hubbard skillfully casts a switch on the Pere Marquette River.

I strongly recommend leaning toward a fast rod over a slow one, as they will give you the muscle to propel the fly.

Though switch rods are fantastic for small to medium-sized rivers, large rivers and boat fishing can present some challenges with these rods. There are limits to what a switch rod can do, and for the typical angler, their short length is going to be problematic when fishing a big river. There are two issues that you will face:

The first issue is that you will quickly hit a wall with how long a sink-tip you can use and also how heavy a fly you can use with a switch rod. For this reason, you will be limited to fishing low to moderate water conditions and will struggle to get the fly deep. The fishing will likely feel heavy and sloppy. In high flows, you will find yourself defeated with a switch rod. As the water gets cold and you need to fish deep, the switch rod will not be the right tool.

The second issue with switch rods that I see all the time on the Muskegon is that they are exhausting to cast in windy situations and force a shorter presentation. This is more of a mental block than anything that prevents fish-catching. Most people naturally want to fish farther away from themselves and cast far. A switch rod, due to its short head, will fish great in close on a big river—you just have to resign yourself to shorter presentations. This is especially true when you have any form of adverse conditions.

A final disadvantage of the switch rod comes when you are fishing from a boat. In general, I would prefer anglers to either fish a two-handed rod (full Spey) or a single-handed rod from the boat when swinging flies. The real problem lies with being able to cast over parts of the boat when you are setting up to Spey cast. Your typical boat on a large river will have some form of outboard motor on it, and casting over an outboard motor with a switch rod can be problematic. As you try to set your anchor while casting, you are forced then to go over the motor, and this is tiring and frustrating without some length. On the bow end of the boat, you have an anchor system, and casting over this can also be problematic for the same reason. If you are swinging flies from a boat, a longer two-handed rod will be the king.

With a two-handed rod, there are other considerations: A modern two-handed rod has a lot going for it, if your game is swinging flies. Some of these rods have limited applications for stripping flies, and are sometimes used in that capacity for fly fishing the surf. However, the main application of a two-handed rod is the swing, and a modern Spey rod performs that task very well.

Most Spey rods are 12 to 16 feet long. For fishing in Midwest waters, you seldom have to use anything longer than 14 feet. Two-handed rods are designed for wading and casting with a limited amount of space behind you. For large rivers during the fall, the most common rod for me is a 12- to 13-foot 7-weight rod that is on the quick end of things. This will cover a dense 8- to 12-foot

Large Midwest rivers are ideally suited for modern two-handed rods, and they are essential for presenting baitfish patterns in the winter months. For the big rivers in Michigan, a 13-foot 8-weight with a stiff action is our all-around choice.

sink-tip and can cast most fly patterns with relative ease.

As the water cools, we increasingly look for heavier gear. During this time period, a 13-foot 8-weight is ideal. For larger Midwest waters, if you had to pick one do-it-all rod, a 13-foot 8-weight would be it. If the water gets very cold, or very high, this might be the time to crack out the 14-foot 9-weight if you have one at your disposal.

There are occasionally times when I will use an even longer two-handed rod, especially a 15-foot 9-weight. Usually this is during very cold weather periods where I am only casting the length of the head. The reason for this is that in the middle of the winter, stripping line will quickly force your guides to freeze up. Using a little longer rod and fishing just the length of the head will make this

a moot point. If you are just casting the length of your head, you are not taking in any line at all, and it is just a matter of cast, swing, step, cast, swing, step . . .

A longer rod such as this 15-foot 9-weight might also have some application for the deep and dirty swing that we discussed earlier. A long rod is the ultimate in line control, and the ability to stack mend a heavy fly to the bottom is an asset that you gain with a long rod.

A two-handed rod is a real luxury when fishing from a boat. It eliminates any of the problems you might have with a switch rod. If you have a moderate amount of casting ability, casting such a rod from a boat is less fatiguing than any of the other methods discussed here. A two-handed rod makes it easy to keep the line away from the boat

A two-handed rod gives you a lot of flexibility when fishing heavy tips and wading. As a general rule, you can always cast a light-sink-rate tip with a heavy rod. However, you will find it very difficult to cast a fast-sinking long tip with a rod that is too light.

when casting, and the length of the rod gives you flexibility in where you place your anchor. This can be a real issue, as most boats on larger rivers have outboards.

One last advantage to fishing short is that it gives you the ability to keep your hands warm if you are fishing in extreme conditions. One of my favorite things to do in the bitter cold days of winter is to fish with mittens. I will not take my hands out of them unless I hook a fish. With mittens, you can only fish the head of your line, as you lack the ability to strip any line in. A side benefit to this is that you won't get ice on your guides, as little line is being brought into the rod. This will allow you to land a large fish rather than fighting iced guides when it matters most. Yet another glorious aspect of mittens is that you can cram them full of hand

warmers. With my circulation, this is the only way I can fish when it is 15 degrees out. If you decide to fish with mittens, remember that you will have to take those mittens off to physically reel in a fish. Usually when I hook a fish while wearing mittens, the first thing I do upon hooking the fish is throw those mittens to the side.

As you can see, rods from 8½ feet to 14 feet have a place in the Great Lakes fly fisher's arsenal. Again, much of our streamer fishing, regardless of technique, is with sink-tip lines. If you find that you are fishing around narrow, brushy areas, you will want a tight loop, as overhanging trees can create a lot of problems. Over the course of a season, I have clients show up with a wide array of equipment. If a client has a favorite rod, we make use of it, but a slow-action rod adds another element of challenge to an already challenging game. These rods might be slow graphite, fiberglass, or even bamboo. When casting them, a big, open loop is created, and these big loops find trees and whip the surface of the river into a frothy cappuccino. The combination of slow rods and fishing around woody structure is a recipe for catastrophic fly loss. These slower rods will also have a harder time casting heavy sink-tips. Slower rods can, however, be used well in broad, open rivers where overhanging trees and tight loops are not important. A slower rod can be a good tool in the hands of an experienced angler—they are just not recommended for beginners.

Fast rods, on the other hand, can cast tight loops and can handle the maximum amount of sink-tip. If you find a fast rod is too fast for your preference, you can over-line it to slow it down.

In recent years, fly rods have been rated not only by their line weight, but also by the amount of grains that they can safely cast. This is an improvement from years past, when there was no universal standard for Spey lines and an 8-weight from one company was similar to an 11-weight from another. When purchasing a fly line, it is common to overlook the fact that this grain weight includes the head of the line. If you are using a belly that weighs the amount of the rating and you then add a tip, your rod will be massively overweighted and you will be disappointed in its casting prowess.

As previously mentioned, this is especially true in smaller Spey rods and switch rods. For example, a 150-grain sink-tip will make less of an impact on a long, heavy two-handed rod than on a 5-weight switch rod. The 5-weight switch would be massively overloaded. If you are having any questions

At the heart of a migratory fish system is the reel. Such a reel must be large enough to hold whatever line you are going to use and should have a stout drag. There are a lot of choices when it comes to reels. Make sure you know the strengths and weaknesses of your equipment before you make a big purchase.

Disc drag reels are the gold standard for any migratory fish. They increase your chances of landing an awesome fish, like this 12-pound lake-run brown. I do not recommend dunking the fly reel as I did in this shot. After landing this fish and taking the picture, I quickly realized that the reel had frozen.

about two-handed rods, the best advice I can give is to talk to the experts at your local fly shop.

As we head toward the next section on reels, there is one golden rule for purchasing rods that you can take to the bank. If you are only going to buy one fly rod for fishing for migratory fish, be it with a swung-fly or stripping technique, purchase a rod that is on the heavy line weight side. Remember, a heavier line weight fly rod will be able to handle a light sinking tip up to a heavy fly or sink-tip. If you purchase a lighter rod, it will not be able to handle the more industrial applications that we so often face. This makes lighter fly rods more specialized and heavier rods more universal in the world of fishing for migratory fish.

Fly Reels

If you asked me about the importance of fly reels, I would say that they can be construed as extremely

important or not important at all depending on how experienced you are at fighting fish and how badly you want to land one. When we talk about catching migratory fish on streamers, it is a low-numbers, low-percentage game. There are a lot of days streamer fishing that you might have only one or two shots at a fish. As you are fishing along on a typical day, you might go hours without catching a fish, and then suddenly a large awesome fish hammers your fly. This is the most critical moment in the entire process of catching a fish. If an angler has not caught a lot of fish and gets nervous, the equipment has to make up for any mistakes made by the angler. That is why, as I guide, I feel that every piece of gear, every knot, and every hook add up to giving you a better shot at catching a fish.

If you are fishing with a single-handed rod, you are most likely going to be using a fly reel with a disc drag. Most outfitters and fly shops will steer you toward a reel with a smooth disc drag with low startup inertia, particularly for swinging flies. It is difficult to pick a bad disc drag reel these days, and the technology has evolved to where they seldom need any maintenance.

As mentioned above, with steelhead and trout, if you survive the first minute of the fight, your chances of landing the fish go up exponentially. It is important that any reel you purchase has smooth start-up inertia and does not apply too much or too little drag early in fight. Regardless of whether you are using a single-handed or two-handed rod, purchase the largest-diameter reel that you are comfortable casting with all day. The large circumference of the spool will help a lot with retrieving line and keeping up with hot fish.

If you fish in the winter, there are other things to consider. First of all, many modern reels are heavily ported, meaning they have a lot of holes cut in

their side. This saves a lot of weight on the reel, but it also allows water easy access to your drag spindle. If this water freezes, you may very well lose a fish because you are unable to pull line off the reel. In the late fall and winter, miserable weather conditions are the norm. Water has a lot of opportunity to get into your reel, and if the air temperature dips below freezing, there will be trouble ahead.

As I write this, I am reminded of a fish that exemplifies this problem. A few years ago, I was out wading with my friend Erik Rambo, who was helping me put together our first steelhead video, *Searching for Steelhead*. Erik is a great guy and a super friend; we had a lot of fun on the productions. I was very sick with a cold/flu deal on the day in question. We came to a nice run on the river after walking in quite some distance, and I groggily headed down to the water. It was extremely cold,

I have mixed feelings about click-and-pawl reels, but one thing is for sure: They make a cool noise when you hook a big fish. A good reel is a tool for fishing, and if you understand the strengths and weaknesses of your equipment, you can make it work.

and while I was sliding down the hill into the river, my heavily ported reel got some water in it. On the first few casts, I was able to get enough line out. As it was extremely cold, I was only fishing the length of the head of the fly line, and did not test the drag for some time. This almost cost me a great fish. While casting a big sculpin, I felt a heavy pull on the line. Soon after lifting the rod and feeling the weight of the fish, I realized that the reel was frozen solid. With little hope of getting any line to play off the reel, I started to run after the fish. Each time the fish would run, I would chase after it on foot, hoping that I could keep up with it. At 240 pounds, I am no ballerina. Courtesy of some heavy tippet and a lethargic fish in icy cold water, I did manage to land it. It was a really nice lake-run brown. By all rights, I should have lost that fish, but we managed to win that one.

Not only could you lose a fish, but you may also wreck the drag surface in the process of forcing line off the reel when it is frozen. This is true of a lot of reels in the middle price range. If the disc surface is made of plastic or Delrin teeth, they won't hold up if you are in icy conditions. If such a reel freezes up, only allowing it to thaw will keep the drag intact. If you pull on the line and the reel is frozen, it will strip the drag surface.

If you are using a two-handed rod, note that the weight of the reel is not much of an issue; i.e., you can use a heavy reel. In such a case, you might choose a heavy reel without porting. Some manufacturers offer un-ported reel options, and this is a good thing for Spey anglers. One company that comes to mind is Abel Reels, but there are others as well.

As you get into Spey fishing, you may get the retro idea of buying a click-and-pawl reel. These reels make a cool noise when you hook a fish. Some of the most expensive ones have pretty sophisticated, Swiss-watch-like precision drag systems that work pretty well. However, more commonly your typical midrange click-and-pawl reel has a minimal drag system that overruns when a large fish smokes out some line. If landing every fish is not so important to you or if you have a lot of experience catching large fish, then go ahead and enjoy the fight and sound of one of these reels. I own several of them, and sometimes I just feel like fishing with them, despite their drawbacks. It is nice to hear them sing.

On the other hand, if landing a fish is one of your primary concerns, a disc drag reel will without a doubt land more fish than a click-and-pawl reel. I regularly guide a great guy who insists on using click-and-pawl reels. A couple of seasons ago, the early fall fishing was pretty slow. After exploring every possible venue, we finally found a fish. The fish struck with incredible intensity and immediately headed for a brush pile. Even though we had heavy tippet, there was no way to add drag pressure with the reel. I gasped as this massive 15-pound-plus chrome steelhead jumped into the brush, never to be seen again. This was just one of many fish that may have been landed with a more consistent drag.

Every guide that I know who runs swung-fly trips will attest to the fact that click-and-pawl reels lose more fish on a day-to-day basis than do disc drag reels. When someone shows up with one of these on a guide trip, we know our odds of landing a fish have dropped considerably. This is usually OK—most people who fish click-and-pawl reels are aware of their drawbacks and are fishing on their own terms. What typically happens is that a fish strikes the fly very hard and makes the initial run. Because there is no real drag surface, the reel creates a backlash which in turn leads to uneven drag pressure. If the fish is hot, it is typically lost.

In summary, for ambience and nostalgia, go ahead and buy a click-and-pawl reel. For landing a higher percentage of fish, a quality disc drag reel will be the right investment. A good reel is just one thing in the chain of equipment that makes for a successful fishing trip.

Fly Lines

I have been streamer fishing for about 30 years now, and guiding for more than 20. I believe that we are in a golden age of fly lines, where the design and coatings of the lines are all so good and so well designed. Unfortunately, the pricing has also changed with the technology. I am not sure how streamer fishing will continue to change, but I do know that things will continue to be refined over time. To illustrate how streamer fishing has changed over the last three decades, let's take a look at how the lines have changed.

1990s: When I first started to gain faith in fishing streamers for steelhead in West Michigan, there was very little information available about it. Some good general information came out of the West Coast, but there was little to be found that applied to the Midwest. Most of the information that I gathered at the time indicated that steelhead could be taken with streamers, but only when the water was above 38 degrees.

Most of the appropriate fly lines in the Midwest market were single-handed lines, the Teeny-type lines such as the T-200 and T-300, which were the mainstay for stripping streamers and for swinging flies in the region. Most of the initial success I personally had during this time was with these types of dense sink-tips. These lines became the gold standard for any type of streamer fishing, and similar lines by various manufacturers are popular to this day. In the right hands, they will always catch fish on the swing in a pinch. At the same time, you can use them for a lot of other applications. If you fish big rivers, chances are you will carry something like these lines in your box.

I first started using Spey gear in the late 1990s. I tried some of the Spey lines that were available, but the breadth of my knowledge combined with their poor performance for the job at hand led me to fish very fast Spey rods with shooting heads. For me, this was a golden time of swinging flies. I was not married, and I was fishing a big river with lots of steelhead and lake run browns. There was little fishing pressure.

During the tremendous run of steelhead that we had in the winter of 1999/2000, it was not uncommon to catch 10 or more fish swinging flies in a day when the bite was on. The fish were very large, so it was a wonderful time to learn a lot about swinging flies. This was the time that the swung-fly business really took off for me.

It was also a golden time for lake-run brown trout, as they were heavily planted in the Great Lakes in this time frame. Early in my guide career, it was really hard to convince people to swing flies for steelhead—the typical client just had no confidence in it. As a result, I ran a lot of streamer-stripping-type trips in the fall and winter,

and learned a lot about fishing for the lake-run browns. The standard fare for those was always a large earth-tone sculpin pattern. Often we would use two flies, with the forward fly being a gaudy attractor.

During this same time frame, zebra mussels invaded a lot of our rivers. They didn't help the fisheries in many regards, but they did do one great thing for anglers at that time. Since they initially made the water ultraclear, you could often see bottom in 7 to 12 feet of moving water. This was great for observing fish and learning how they relate to cover.

2000s: During the next several years, I had a lot of success with these sink-tip-type lines and continued to use shooting-type lines. A new product, the T14, a bulk sink-tip line, had a profound impact on the fishing.

I can't understate the value of using a bulk sink-tip line. Now, I could use Spey lines and simply discard the light tips that are included with them, replacing them with custom-cut tips of T14. I am a big believer in bulk sink-tips, and I exclusively use them in various densities to this day. If you are looking to get into streamer fishing on the swung fly, there are a lot of different products on the market, to the extent that it can be very confusing. Do yourself a favor and purchase a bulk sink-tip, at least until you understand what you need to do in your local river. This will add to your success quickly.

In the 2000s Spey line manufacturers started to become more and more responsive to the Great Lakes market, and soon we had a mature streamer fishery throughout the region.

2010s: This is the time when swinging flies really took off, and the availability of fly lines that are practical for any level of caster really made a difference in our area.

One thing that you have to understand is that there are fly lines that are built for the European market that work very well for our waters. This is especially true of the intermediate and full-sinking lines that came to the market about a decade ago. Among these, the most popular was a line by the European company Guideline called the DDC. This was a very well-designed line that fished very deeply. When cut back a bit, it was an easy line

In the last 10 years, one of the best products on the market for my game on big rivers is the intermediate sinking line. These lines get the fly deep but also keep it deep with the appropriate sink-tip. This one is a Scientific Anglers line, but they are made by a variety of different manufacturers.

to cast, with a heavy sink-tip. This line was very practical, and many anglers in Michigan used it. It is a very durable line, and I have clients that still use it to this day.

Guideline eventually exited the Midwest market, and that was OK because the more prominent US brands started to make some truly great lines for our market. As a direct replacement for the intermediate heads, most of these companies released compressed intermediate heads that were similar to the Guideline heads but more supple.

Another kind of line also emerged in this same time frame, this one from the West Coast, called a Skagit head. These lines are ideal for fishing in cold water, with short, heavy sink-tips that work so well in our waters. They have made Spey casting much more practical to the masses, and most anglers can take some basic lessons and be fishing them with little frustration in short order. These lines have mainstreamed Spey fishing in the Midwest and have made it a regular part of the fly angler's

arsenal. If you would have asked your typical Midwest fly angler what kind of rod they used 10 years ago, most would have said a 5- or 6-weight single-handed rod for trout or bass and an 8-weight single-handed rod for steelhead or salmon. These days, many anglers own one of those rods as well as a two-handed rod. Angler-friendly fly lines are one of the main reasons for this development.

SKAGIT LINES

Skagit lines cram a lot of mass into a very short head. In our waters, they are generally great lines but work best when cast short to medium distances. Skagits can be purchased as floating bellies and as intermediates. Both of these lines are appropriate for our waters.

Intermediate Skagit lines are workhorse lines for big rivers and can turn over big flies. You can't control them much once they hit the water, but they will keep your fly deep throughout the swing with the appropriate sink-tip.

Floating Skagit lines have great applications both as an all-around wading line and as a wintertime deep-swing line. If you are going to buy one line for a variety of different rivers and situations, a floating Skagit is among the most versatile and can handle flies big and small.

Floating Skagit lines work well during the winter months, and they are the main lines used for the deep and dirty swing described in the previous chapter. The floating belly allows great speed and line control turns over a ton of weight. This floating section also allows you to pull your line along in areas with slow current. In order to do this, you would cast from an area or seam of quick current, and cast it into slow or stagnant water. The floating section of line will pick up the close, faster current and you can manipulate the line to pull the fly through the slower water at the speed that you want.

Floating Skagit lines are an all-purpose Spey line and are a good choice if you fish a variety of different rivers. If you are new to spey fishing, they are the easiest lines to cast. They are at their best at moderate distances, especially if you are fishing in cold-water conditions. Because of the immense thickness of their belly, they can pull your fly off the bottom when cast far. In this way, they can negate your sink-tip and fish shallower than preferred. That is why it is so critical to mitigate your casting distance and keep things reasonably close, as you can still get the fly down well over medium distances.

Floating Skagit lines are an all-purpose line, whereas the intermediates are best for deep rivers or when fishing from a boat. Floating Skagit lines have worked their way into the light switch rod market and work extremely well. It is now possible to cast a really light switch rod with a sinking leader and take the fly deep. These rods can be anything from a 4-weight up to an 8-weight. The lines of lighter rods can carry less sink-tip. However, because the lines are thinner than the lines used in full Spey rods, they don't have to work as hard to cut through the current and can often get quite deep. They have a great application, especially in the spring when fishing smaller flies and some fry patterns along the edges of the river.

If you are going to cast any distance, the right shooting line can make all the difference. Mono lines, like the one pictured, pick up less ice in bitter conditions. However, if you are wading they may be more difficult to pick up from the water, and many of them sink.

SHOOTING LINES

If you are using any type of shooting head system, you will need to purchase a shooting line (also called a running line) that follows the head. It is the part of the line that physically shoots out of your guides as you complete your cast.

Usually the heavier the head you are using, the thicker the shooting line you would want to use. Shooting lines are a vital part of your rig and should be replaced from time to time. Modern heads will last basically forever, but you may lose them in a tree or on the bottom of the river if you don't replace your shooting line every so often. Shooting lines are often rated by their breaking strength, and I seldom use ones that are less than 30 pounds test. Furthermore, if you plan on fishing heavy tippet, you should go with a thicker corresponding running line. With strong tippet any imperfection in the running line will increase the chances that you lose your line system if you get a snag.

In general terms, the larger the river you are fishing, the more important the shooting line becomes. Many smaller rivers only require short amounts of running line in practical use, and at these ranges just about any running line will work. The more line you choose to cast, the more critical your line choice becomes. There are practical considerations that come into play when selecting these lines, and they can make your fishing more pleasant or more miserable if you don't choose wisely. Shooting lines can be textured, braided, floating, intermediate, or made out of monofilament.

If you are wading, you will find a floating running line much easier to control and cast. If you choose a floating running line, keep it clean, as a higher-floating running line will be easier to lift off the water and will be less prone to tangling. Floating running lines have a shorter life cycle than some of the other types of lines. If you step on them while fishing, this can really damage them. If you fish a lot, it is a good idea to replace a floating running line on a yearly basis.

For the ultimate in line control, some of the floating running lines have a slight taper to them. These thicker sections help keep the line nearer to the surface, and this gives you more line control. This belly section does add a few more grains to your outfit, which may be a consideration when you are matching them with a head.

I can tell you from experience that some of these lines are really sensitive to the cold. As Spey fishing has progressed, I have found as a guide that more and more anglers prefer to use their own gear. I have had two anglers casting in the boat, one with an appropriate running line for cold water and the other with one best suited for warmer conditions. The client with the appropriate line will spend a lot more time fishing, whereas the other person has a more frustrating day breaking ice out of the guides. You can guess which angler typically catches the most fish. These differences in running lines have nearly ended some fishing friendships in the boat.

If you plan on fishing when it is below freezing and are going to fish more distance than just the head of the line, the material that the running line is made out of will make all the difference. If you choose a textured line or a braided line, you are in for a real nightmare as the temperature drops. These lines pick up water and as you strip them through your guides, they form ice. Some of them create lots of ice. In this situation, you might only get a cast or two before shooting any line becomes impossible. This can lead to a lot of wasted time and frustration.

One other note about some of the braided lines is that they may work well in above-freezing temperatures until you get a knot in them. These knots can be nearly impossible to repair, and more often than not the line ends up in the trash can when this happens.

If you do fish when it is really cold, you may want to consider using a thinner running line than at other times of the year. This will buy you some time as your guides freeze up, as they simply need a smaller hole to pass through.

If you are comfortable with using a monofilament running line (Rio's SlickShooter is the most common), you will find that they pick up a minimum of ice. However, they do take some getting used to. I will tell you a dirty little secret: There are a lot of dirt-cheap monofilaments that are used for spin-fishing applications that make durable, castable running lines. It may be sputton to mention this, but one of the best examples is the high-visibility 40-pound Trilene Big Game line.

In a pinch, monofilament running lines can be knotted directly to the head that you are using. This is useful if you are quickly changing heads in extreme conditions. Monofilament can be trimmed at any time, which makes it useful for guiding. When a section of line gets bad, you simply cut it back.

I typically use brand name shooting lines on my reels but always carry a spool of this Trilene in the event of line failure. If you fish from a boat in the winter, using a mono running line is by far the best solution to tough conditions. This is especially true if you want to cast any distance past the length of the head you are fishing.

One of the critical connections you will make is from the running line to the head that you are using. Floating running lines often have a loop attached to them, allowing for a loop-to-loop connection. Eventually this connection will give out, as welded small-diameter loops are not impervious to the elements. When this happens, you have a few option: you can re-weld the loop (this is difficult and time-consuming); you can fashion some other kind of loop on the end, such as a braided one (these work but will fail); or you can simply fold the running line over and put a monofilament nail knot over it, which is a great quick and easy way of doing things that does not create a large loop.

If you use a monofilament or braided shooting line, you can tie a loop knot directly into the end of the line. This will create a strong connection. If the mono you are using is not too thick, you can also knot the running line directly to the loop of the head. If I am changing lines in the boat and I want to save time, I often go down this path and there is little downside to it, other than it may cause more wear on the loop of the head. It is also clunkier going through your guides than the other methods.

Fly lines have come a long way and continue to change. If you want to strip a streamer or swing a fly anywhere in the Great Lakes region, there is a practical fly line that can help you make a great presentation to a memorable fish.

Leaders and Tippets

By now, hopefully you have a grasp of what rod, reel, and line to consider for the waters you fish. Swinging and stripping flies are heavy-duty methods of fishing, so you don't have to concern yourself with being too technical about the terminal end of your gear.

If you are fishing a sink-tip line during the warmer times of the year, your fly is swimming quickly and you are not trying to slow it down too much, so the emphasis is on covering water versus a deliberate and deep presentation. In these situations a straight section of heavy mono crosses the bridge between your fly line/sink-tip and your fly. Typically you would tie one end of a straight piece of mono directly to your line and the other end to your fly, with nothing in between. This absolutely minimizes the chance of failure. There is no dispute that the more knots you use, the more likely you are to lose a fish—I have seen it too many times.

In my opinion, 12-pound tippet is the magical number. If you fish less than 12-pound tippet, you will simply lose fish more frequently. However, 12- to 18-pound tippet will be successful at landing fish more often than not. Furthermore, heavy tippet will preserve a lot of flies that might end up decorating a tree. Many of the hooks that I use will bend when used in conjunction with 12-pound tippet. However, if I drop any lower than 12 pounds, it is hard to find a hook that will bend in a snag and yet still not bend when a big fish is hooked. If you are fishing a shank or tube fly and have tied your fly durably, you can simply remove a faulty hook after a snag, replace it with a new one, and the fly is good as new.

As a general rule of thumb, I start a day swung-fly fishing with 12-pound tippet (the brand I use is Maxima, but whatever works for you). If the bite is very strong, I will upgrade this to 14- or 15-pound, as I feel it preserves flies. The days are short in the fall and into the winter, and every second that the fly remains in the water counts toward more swings over the fish. Thus, if you can prevent fly loss, you are fishing more. Heavy tippet makes sense.

Heading into winter, you may find yourself with a more technical presentation, where you are mending your fly line to get the fly to the bottom of the river. In these scenarios you will use a longer leader and a weighted fly to get the fly to the bottom as described in the techniques chapter of this book. You can approach this a couple of different ways. An easy solution would be to purchase a short and heavy leader from your local fly shop. You can easily manufacture a leader, and it need not be anything fancy. A typical leader for me would be about 6 or 7 feet. It would start with 30-pound and progress to 20-pound, 15-pound, and then the tippet.

Of course, by knotting your own leader, you introduce possible failure points, and that must be a consideration if you are not real confident in your knots. The final knot between your leader and your tippet is always the most likely failure point. One trick I employ a lot is to use a very small swivel at this point and attach the tippet from there. Because your tippet with these slower presentations may be lighter than at other times of the year, this small swivel will strengthen your rig and will help you confidently land big fish.

As I side note, it should be mentioned that heavier tippet has become a necessity in many fishing locales in the last several years. When zebra mussels invaded the rivers, their shells made the bottom very sharp and jagged, which can easily slice monofilament or weaken the tippet by shredding its coating. This makes it very important to fish heavier tippet in these places. You should also choose a brand of leader material that is known for its abrasion resistance.

In general, the slower your presentation and the clearer the water, the lighter the tippet you will use. On slower drifts, 10-pound tippet is not uncommon. In the dead of winter, ice and snow absorb much of the groundwater that might come into the river. As a result, with little to disturb the river, it becomes extremely clear. As less water is coming into the river, and any precipitation is usually in the form of snow, the water not only will be clear but will be low. If the water is low, cold, and clear in the winter, I will use 8-pound tippet at times. This lighter line has a further advantage in that you will catch more resident trout and other game fish in comparison to heavier tippets. Resident fish have seen many presentations, and lighter line might add them to your catch.

We often use fluorocarbon leader, especially during the clear water periods of the year. If you are fishing in any way that presents the fly quickly, standard monofilament will work just fine. However, any time you slow down the presentation and use lighter tippet, fluorocarbon leader material might just give you the edge to be successful.

If you are using lighter tippet with a swung-fly presentation, be more cautious when lifting the fish. This is easier said than done, but fortunately winter fish don't initially pull as hard as fall fish when they take the fly. If you make it through the strike with the lighter tippet, you should be fine for landing the fish. If you are fishing in below-freezing temperatures, you will want to take extra care to keep your line and reel free of ice. If your reel or rod guides freeze, the added inertia when you hook a big fish on the lighter tippet will lose you a fish.

Whether you fish in the fall with heavy tippet for hot fish or fish in the winter with light tippet for more-lethargic fish, there is good reason not only to use good tippet but to make your terminal connections with a good knot.

Terminal Connections and Knots

You may have purchased the very best rod and reel that money can by, and it may be lined perfectly, and you have great flies and the right tippet. Now you head to the river and make a majestic cast that lands your fly in a prime lie. Suddenly, the line goes tight and there is the heavy pull of a really big fish. You lift your rod, and then . . . nothing. Hmmm, you think, I did not put much pressure on the fish—I wonder why he came off. You get your line in, only to find a small, curly loop at the end of your line. Expletives follow. This is a common scenario for those new to streamer fishing for big fish. If you have done a lot of trout or bass fishing and are now in the realm of migratory fish, you will find that it is much more important to tie really good knots.

Throughout much of the season, you may be using a traditional swing and only a short, 3- or

For wrestling big fish away from brush and timber, you better make good terminal connections. A combination of a good knot and heavy tippet were key to landing this big chrome hen.

Without winter apparel, fishing on a day like this would have been impossible. Advances in outdoor clothing technology have made winter fishing much more practical in the last few years. I just wish I had remembered to bring my rods in that night!

4-foot section of heavy tippet. Many people recommend using a loop-to-loop connection at the end of the line, incorporating a perfection loop or surgeon's loop, etc. This sort of connection is convenient if you are frequently changing leaders, but that is really its only advantage. Unfortunately, too often this connection will fail.

A better option might be to nail knot your leader directly to the end of your fly line. A nail knot tool simplifies the process, and you can add a second nail knot using the tag if you want additional security. If I am on the river and my hands are cold, and I want a secure leader/sink-tip connection, I will often use a quick but less elegant solution. What I will do is tie a perfection loop with the sink-tip material itself. At that point, I will tie the leader onto this loop directly with a good strong terminal knot, such as the Eugene bend. This solution is typically very strong, as the monofilament of the leader will bite into the coating of the line. Even if the loop knot at the end of the sink-tip fails, often the leader biting into the coating will be enough to land a fish.

If you are using a sink-tip material that is no heavier than T14, you can add a slick makeshift loop to either end of the sink-tip with a nail knot tool. This takes a little bit more time, but the results are nice. All that you need to do is fold the sink-tip over on itself and put it into the nail knot tool. At this point you will tie a nail knot with 20-pound mono over the folded-over line, forming a nice loop that can then be used as an attachment point or a secure loop-to-loop connection.

As mentioned above, a great terminal knot is the Eugene bend. Instructions for this knot can easily be found online. It is a very strong knot that is easy to tie, but it needs to be seated correctly. If you find yourself to be an avid steelhead angler, you will no doubt be fishing in the dead of winter at some point. The Eugene bend is an easy knot to tie when your hands are cold, and it can be done mostly by touch. If you tie it often enough, you can almost tie it without looking at the line at all. This makes the knot gold for me, and it is my favorite knot. I use it for all types of streamer fishing, whether stripping or swinging a fly. It is exceedingly rare to lose a fish due to this knot. There are a lot of good fishing knots out there, and everyone has their personal preference. When you decide on a knot, make sure that it is one that maintains high tensile strength when complete.

You can make a good case for giving your fly a little more action by selecting a loop knot for attaching your fly. This is a common practice while stripping flies, but it applies more broadly to any time that you are fishing a streamer. A loop knot has the advantage of imparting some extra action to a fly. Some of these knots are very strong if tied properly. A knot favored by a lot of guides is the nonslip loop knot, and it is very good. Between this knot and the Eugene bend, my knot needs are met.

Fishing Apparel

It's funny that you could easily write an entire book that covers fishing for migratory fish without covering the one thing that makes fishing for them possible year-round. That one thing is the dry gear that we use to keep us fishing in difficult conditions. Without the proper stuff, fishing in the cold would be miserable indeed. From my perspective, the real reason we have such vibrant winter fisheries is directly related to the availability of reasonably priced, warm gear. There have always been winter anglers, but modern foul-weather clothing has made fishing a lot more practical.

If you are one of those rare individuals who can wade in icy water in light waders without discomfort, I admire you a lot. Most people do not fall into that category. I have had a lot of anglers who have forgotten about the fish they caught on a trip and have only remembered one thing—how cold it was on the day that they were fishing! This basic section is for all of you who have spent a day on the river freezing your butt off.

If you get into fishing for migratory fish, you will be fishing in the cold at some point—it is unavoidable. If you are a wading angler, you are not only fighting the cold air temperatures but also the crushing of the cold water along your legs. This will slow circulation and will make the right wading gear a must.

If the air temperature is above 40 degrees, typically you can get away with casual breathable waders and separate boots. However, as the temperature gets below 40, this will be uncomfortable on your legs and your feet will become numb. In these conditions, you will need boot-foot waders to keep your feet and legs warm. If you walk great distances and cover a lot of water when you wade, a breathable boot-foot with a heavy boot will be the way to go. This type of wader is among the most expensive pieces of gear that you can buy, but is very nice to fish with.

If you are only covering smaller sections of water and are not wading far, there is a cheaper alternative that works great. Boot-foot neoprene waders are warm and significantly less expensive, but they are very heavy. If you go this route, look for waders with a boot that contains at least 1,000 grams of insulation. There is no point in combining a warm wading material, such as neoprene, with a lightweight boot.

A limited number of neoprene fishing waders are available with such a boot attached. If you are looking for a pair of warm waders that last, don't hesitate to cross the aisle and check out duck-hunting waders. Duck hunters hunt in the cold and they demand a durable product, so often these hunting waders double as great fishing waders. If you are hard on equipment, a good pair of duck-hunting waders works great. Some of the most recent duck-hunting waders incorporate neoprene and breathable fabrics. This combination is really nice to fish with. Remember, your friends may make fun of you for your duck-hunting waders, but you will have the last laugh. You will be warm, and they will be cold. As a result, you will probably catch more fish.

If you fish from a boat, your options are considerably more varied. You won't have to worry about your activity causing sweat and making you cold, and you also should not have to worry about taking water in through wading. You will likely want to remain waterproof on the exterior, however. In extreme weather in a boat, thick boot-foot neoprene waders with an insulated boot are a great option. Another popular option is a pair of bibs or snow pants with heavily insulated boots. Knee-type boots with no laces and heavy insulation make launching a boat practical and keep you very warm.

Keeping your feet as well as your other extremities warm is the primary goal. A heavy wool hat or fleece beanie will take care of your head. A neck gaiter or even a sun gaiter also will help in bitter conditions. Without a doubt, the hardest thing to keep warm is your hands, as they are the one part of your body that has to be in contact with cold fishing line.

Keeping your hands warm is extremely challenging, especially if you fish in below-freezing temperatures on a regular basis. If you are using one of the swung-fly methods with a two-handed rod, it is a lot easier to keep your hands warm. The reason for this is that by limiting your casting distance, you can eliminate the need for shooting line. This means that the longest casts that you make would be the length of your fly-line head. When you do it this way, you can use mittens to protect your hands, which are much warmer than any gloves. The only trick to using mittens is that somehow you need to remove them quickly when a fish strikes your fly.

If you choose to strip a fly in the middle of the winter, or if you want to shoot line while Spey fishing, your choices are more limited and there may be a threshold of temperature where you find the fishing to be impractical. These methods will require a lot of use of your hands. Some people fish well with gloves, others do not. If you choose to fish without gloves, keep all the other parts of your body as warm as possible, as a warm core temperature will go a long way and will buy you time with your hands.

One of the best ways to make fishing more practical in winter is to use lots of air-activated hand warmers. These won't work when wet, however. If it is just cold, they can be placed on the backs of your hands in gloves or mittens, making fishing much more civilized. If it is raining or snowing and you can't get them to work on your hands, you can put them on your wrists or anywhere else on your body to bring up your core temperatures. The large sizes of these hand warmers are much more effective than the small.

There are a lot of other products on the market that might work well for you. These include heated jackets, electric warmers, and fuel warmers. If you want to fish in the winter, use whatever it takes to keep your core temperature up, and fishing will be much more practical.

In summing up this chapter, the equipment you choose to use will reflect your choice of methods. A single-handed rod can be used for most methods and works great for stripping flies. However, there are quite a few limitations when swinging flies with a single-handed rod. These will be especially pronounced in your ability to roll cast with trees behind you. A single-handed rod will also limit the amount of sink-tip line that you can use. If you go with a two-handed rod for swinging flies, a switch rod is appropriate for small streams, with full Spey rods up to 14 feet appropriate for larger Midwest waters. These longer rods will give you the line control that is needed as you head into the winter months.

Another big decision lies in your choice of fly line. An intermediate or sinking line will keep the fly low in the water column; however, a floating bellied line will give you the line control that will be necessary with some presentations.

After all of these decisions are made, you still have to make one final decision, which is what to fly use. You can match specific baitfish, but it is also a good idea to choose the profile of your fly carefully. Narrow flies such as darters will sink well, whereas wide patterns such as sculpins are at their best in slow or shallower runs. This book contains a sampling of very effective fly patterns, but there are many more great patterns out there. Pay attention to local fly shops and guides, as they will know what is going on in their local rivers. As previously mentioned, a safe bet is earth-tone flies (olive or tan) that match the color of the riverbed. These flies can cover a lot of different forage species. If you are fishing early in the morning or in the evening, a wide, dark pattern such as a sculpin or goby might draw the vicious strike that you have been waiting for.

The following chapter contains a cross section of flies that we commonly use while fishing baitfish patterns. It is a strong starting point for the fall, winter, and spring and contains patterns that work for a variety of different resident species at other times of the year.

CHAPTER 6

Fly Patterns

In a previous chapter, we discussed how to be dynamic on the water and how to try to avoid doing the same thing day after day as an angler. There are times when you are forced to fish in water that everyone else is fishing. Perhaps the river is busy, and you can only fish in water that you know has been heavily plied by others. Or perhaps you are fishing in high water and it limits your mobility or options. There are many reasons why you might fish water that has already been fished by others or that holds very educated fish.

One thing that you can control and that you can constantly change is what is on the end of your line. This chapter covers some of the most successful patterns I have used in the Great Lakes region and includes a variety of the baitfish discussed in chapter 1. Most of the flies that we use are between 1½ and 4 inches in length. This is a good general baitfish size, and most of the baitfish fall into this size category.

As a matter of background, my personal patterns are the product of tying flies every day for many years. At this point, the flies have been refined into simple patterns that have the necessary qualities to catch fish. They are designed to be tied quickly and catch fish. However, they won't win a beauty contest. A typical day for me is spent on the river guiding until 5:00 p.m. I come home and cook dinner, and then the chaos begins. My wife arrives with our three young kids, and we have family time until they are in bed, usually around 8:30 p.m. The term "herding cats" comes to mind. After that, I tie flies while returning phone calls, etc. At this point in my life, time is very valuable. You can understand the need to be concise with the fly tying. The flies in my box are guide flies that are simple and catch fish.

Tying baitfish flies is an everyday ritual in my business. These are some sculpins tied for winter steelhead and brown trout. Often I will find a base pattern that works and vary the weight it is tied in and the color of the flash that I use. The patterns in this chapter are easy flies to tie and can serve as a base for your fly box.

Often you will find yourself fishing in a situation where there are many different types of baitfish present, and no particular one stands out as what the fish are eating. This is a good situation, believe it or not. Large migratory fish are opportunistic hunters by nature and will eat whatever looks delicious at the time. This allows you to choose your fly according to its profile. For example, if I am in a cold-water scenario and I need to get the fly to the bottom, I might choose a narrow, weighted pattern such as a darter. If I am in the tailout of a run, I might choose a big bushy sculpin to push the fish into biting. If I am fishing slow water, I would pick a pattern that has a lot of movement built in.

There are a lot of ways to weight a fly, including lead eyes, tungsten, etc. Fishing with weighted flies is covered elsewhere in this book. You can also tie unweighted flies and vary the weight of the hook. This is often done with classic patterns and Spey flies. A heavy hook, with a sparse pattern, will sink pretty well. Conversely, a more heavily dressed pattern on a light hook will ride high in the water column. If you look into an experienced streamer angler's box, the flies may all look similar but there are probably subtle differences under the hood of the patterns that help them do what they are supposed to do.

If you are using any of the swung-fly techniques, you have some options of how to rig your fly. The old-school way of doing this is to simply tie a fly to a regular hook. This has some advantages. One advantage that is frequently overlooked is that tying a fly on a regular hook is simply quick and effective. When I am getting ready for a guide trip and need a pocketful of flies in short order, a regular hook will fit the bill. Whenever possible, avoid hooks longer than a 3X. You will find that for each increment larger, you will lose more fish. However, up until 3X they have a very good landing percentage.

Right: Tying flies on shanks allows you to tie a very bulky fly and still use a short-shanked hook that grips the fish. Erik Rambo caught this great steelhead on a heavily dressed sculpin pattern. If he had tied this fly on a standard hook, it would have been a huge hook. The shank style made this fly practical.

Tying flies on a regular hook does have the disadvantage of being unable to tailor the hook to the fishing situation. You are using a heavy- or light-wire hook and there is no turning back from it. Another obvious disadvantage to using a fly tied directly on a hook is that the life span of the fly is limited to the hook. If you bend a hook or break it, there is no repair. As a side note, I will tell you that steelhead can easily bend hooks that have been previously bent. If you find a fly has a bent hook—unless you don't mind losing a fish—I would discard it. As landing a fish isn't as important to me when I am fishing alone, I carry along a graveyard box of flies whose hooks have been bent by clients. These are the flies I use when fun fishing.

It is not a bad idea if you are tying flies to vary the hook a little bit from batch to batch. Occasionally you will come across a bad box of hooks. I have had some incredibly frustrating guide trips where the flies were tied on hooks that bent too easily, even though they were manufactured by a reputable hook company.

There are two other options for tying flies for swinging. One is the tube fly. Tube flies are tied onto a tube, as you might expect. The hook is attached by a piece of tubing on the back of the fly, which serves as a bridge between the hook and body of the fly. You can use any type of hook that you would like with these flies, and they fish very well. Rather than weighting the fly with eyes, etc., you can use tubes made out of a variety of different materials, including metals. You can also concoct some pretty cheap and effective tubes from household items such as the plastic tube in Q-tips.

Personally, I go through phases where I use tube flies and find them nice to fish. However, since I am constantly tying an array of flies for guiding, I find them too time-consuming to manufacture. Typically, you need some type of apparatus for building tube flies, often in the form of a tube fly head for your vise or a needle to hold the tube. In the end, they just take longer to tie and aren't any more or less effective than normal flies or the next style of fly, flies tied on shanks.

A shank is basically a straight piece of metal with an eye. The eye can be formed up or straight; either way works just fine. There are very nice shanks on the market that are great to work with

and are very refined in appearance. I will let you in on another dirty little secret, though: You can tie using this method with cotter pins you purchased online. One year, I bought a thousand cotter pins from Amazon for 15 dollars. I tied swung flies on these for over a year and noticed no difference in the fish-catching rate whatsoever.

A shank can be placed directly into your standard vise. Once you put the shank in the vise, one of the first things that you do is attach a trailing loop to it, which will hold the hook. This can be a flexible wire or other material. I typically prefer a braided material for my flies. This gives the fly more action but it is also more prone to tangling, so you have to be careful with how flexible of material you use. For example, a 65-pound braid will be considerably less prone to tangling than a 20-pound braid. Here is another guide tip: If you are having problems with tangling loops, add a drop of UV glue to the braid after a hook has been inserted and hit it with direct sunlight or a UV light. This will stiffen the connection while still allowing hook replacement.

Heavy braid will limit the size of the hooks that you use. If you are trying to only catch migratory fish, a heavy braid and large hook will be desirable. However, if you want to catch resident trout as well as lake run fish, you will want a thinner braid that can accommodate a lighter hook. You must be also be cautious in how you attach this loop, as they can easily pull out when a big fish strikes.

I have had some embarrassing situations with flies tied with shanks. One day, I took a good client fishing and he had an amazing pull on the line. The chrome fish cartwheeled out of the water—and then, it was gone. However, there was still some part of the fly on the line. You can see where I'm going with this: The fish pulled on the hook, and totally stripped the loop off from the shank. For the next half hour we were haunted by this massive fish, as it jumped out of the water several times trying to free the hook that remained in its mouth. There was a cold silence in the boat. Fortunately, all was forgiven when we hooked the next fish.

The moral of this story is to simply attach your loop well when building shank-type flies. Don't be afraid to add a drop of glue if there is any doubt in your mind about the quality of your connection.

One way to ensure that a shank style fly does not fall apart is to tie an overhand knot in your braided loop. This will keep the loop from pulling free from the hook. I prefer to use braided material over a wire loop.

An additional safety measure when using braided loops is to add an overhand knot to the loop before tying the loop in. This knot gives your thread something to bite into and acts as a stopper when your fly tries to fall apart. When you fish for big fish on streamers, it is the little things that make all the difference between success and failure.

Shank-type flies are a perfect blend of speed and function. They don't take very long to build, and have replaceable hooks. To speed the process of tying further, prepare several loops beforehand and mass-produce your flies with them. Shank-type flies are at their best when swinging, but can also be used for stripping a streamer when paired with a stiff-enough wire juncture.

As mentioned earlier, if a hook is bent, you are better off discarding it if you want to have a good chance with your next fish. The nice thing about shank-type flies as well as tube flies is that you can easily replace a hook rather than discarding the entire fly. For added appeal, you can also replace your original hook with colored hooks, hooks with flash, or dressed hooks. These effectively change the appearance of your fly without actually changing the fly itself.

When you compare shanks and tube flies to flies tied on regular hooks, there is one other hidden advantage that is worth mentioning. If you want to pack light and not use a fly box, you can place tube flies or shank flies in a plastic bag inside your pocket and carry the hooks separately. This way, you save the space and added weight of a fly box. This is especially nice if you just want to hit the river for a short period of time and carry enough flies for a brief outing.

Regardless of the apparatus you choose to tie your flies on, the following pages detail flies for the variety of presentations highlighted in this book. These are flies that have stood the test of time and will be in my box for years to come. Something in this chapter will catch steelhead and browns wherever they are found.

Baitfish Flies That Swing

These patterns are designed to be swung at or quicker than the speed of the current. They are often buoyant, and for that reason are fished with a long sink-tip. The long sink-tip will pull the fly deeper over distance. In larger rivers they are often fished with full-sinking or intermediate lines. These patterns commonly imitate sculpins, gobies, and shiner species.

There are certain things that can give such a fly great action. For starters, you want the head to be buoyant but not too buoyant. For this reason, we avoid head materials like deer hair in favor of softer materials like Australian possum, fox tail, and various dubbings. On these imitations it is always a great idea to spread the eyes out to give the fly a wide profile. To do this, we use multiple bead-chain eyes. These eyes add a little weight to the fly and also cause a disturbance in the water.

Aquatic Nuisance

The Aquatic Nuisance has been in our box for a very long time and is a staple pattern. I have tried a lot of variations of it, but this one is the best. It is a sculpin pattern with a bulky head and a significant amount of flash. It is not an easy fly to cast—one of my longtime clients has dubbed it the "Casting Nuisance." It is best when fished with a long sink-tip. The flash combination of green and copper is a deadly one.

Due to its large profile, this fly fishes very well in the early morning and late in the day. It is also a really good choice for fishing the tailout or bottleneck in a run. This fly is aggravating to steelhead and brown trout alike.

Sculpins are active during low-light hours, so that makes them a key pattern at these times. This fly is good with a dark tail or a lighter-colored one. Unlike some of the other patterns, this one really seems to fish best when tied on a large hook versus a shank.

- **Hook:** #10 Daiichi 2461
- **Tail:** Dark olive rabbit strip
- **Body:** Olive Ice Dub
- **Wing 1:** Copper Flashabou
- **Wing 2:** Green Polar Flash
- **Wing 3 (optional):** Black Flashabou Magnum and a few strands of yellow Holographic Flashabou
- **Collar:** Large mallard feather or other large Spey hackle
- **Head:** Australian possum in a thick clump encircling the head

Drew's Low-Water Goby

Drew Rosema is a talented guide who spends his summers in Alaska and guides on the Muskegon River for the rest of the year. He has a creative mind, and his flies catch lots of fish. Drew's goby pattern is a good example of a swung baitfish pattern.

This fly is tied on a shank and incorporates squirrel strips as well as some grizzly marabou, and it can be weighted or unweighted. It always works but is especially effective at the end of winter. With its large profile, it is a good low-light fly as well. This pattern imitates a dark male goby and can also generically mimic a sculpin.

- **Hook:** Owner SSW
- **Shank:** Any short shank
- **Tail:** Black pine squirrel strip
- **Body:** Olive Ice Dub
- **Underwing:** Tan grizzly marabou
- **Wing:** Black Flashabou and bronze/copper/green Flashabou Weave
- **Fins:** Black squirrel strips
- **Head:** Peacock black Ice Dub

The Aquatic Nuisance, sarcastically dubbed the "Casting Nuisance," is a great pattern that is used when you need a big profile or you want a buoyant pattern. I use this fly when I want to maneuver over heavy structure. There is something to be said about big fly, big fish; on years that we have runs of larger fish, I lean toward big patterns such as the Nuisance.

Drew's Low-Water Goby really shines in late winter and early spring. The pattern imitates a black goby and is particularly effective in rocky areas. It is a big pattern that Drew takes fish with on a regular basis.

Jeff Hubbard's Pugsley Sculpin uses this rubber-legged sculpin pattern in smaller rivers in the winter months. Smaller rivers with good water quality, such as Jeff's home river, the Pere Marquette, hold a lot of sculpins.

Jeff Hubbard's Pugsley Sculpin

Jeff is a longtime friend and one of the best swung-fly guides in the game. He has been guiding for many years, and we spent much of our guiding youth fishing together. This is a great rubber-legged sculpin pattern that he uses on the Pere Marquette and other rivers.

- **Shank:** Of your choosing
- **Tail:** Peacock Ice Dub and olive marabou
- **Rubber legs (both sets):** Magic Perch
- **Collar:** Olive schlappen around the legs
- **Body:** Caddis green Ice Dub
- **Collar:** Olive marabou
- **Wing:** Copper Flashabou
- **Collar:** Barred wood duck flank feather
- **Head:** Australian possum and shrimp pink Ice Dub
- **Wire:** Beadalon
- **Trailer hook:** #2 Allen Octopus

Dedicated guides contribute proven patterns to the Midwest steelhead fishery. Here, Michigan guide Jeff Hubbard cradles a great buck that grabbed one of his very effective patterns.

Baitfish Flies for the Deep Swing

These fly patterns are designed to be fished deep and slow. For that reason, they are tied to be pretty accurate imitations of what they represent. They are designed to be fished close enough to the river bottom that they often touch.

Because you want these flies to fish as deeply as possible, it is a good idea to lean toward baitfish imitations that have a narrow profile. Darters are active in the cold-water periods and are a good choice for a baitfish, if you were to pick one. This is especially true for ultradeep areas or areas with moderate current.

Sculpins and gobies are effective imitations with this pattern, but getting them to the bottom can be a challenge in deep areas due to their profile. They will fish better in the shallower, slower areas. Here are four of my best—I could fish the entire winter with just variations of these.

Inside Bender

The Inside Bender, or just "Bender," is a very simple, go-to fly for fishing in the winter months all the way through the spring. It is designed to be used as a swung fly but often pulls double duty when nymph fishing deep runs in the spring. As the name implies, it works well on the slow inside bends of streams. It also works very well on seams formed by timber and in large, flat pre-spawn areas of the river.

This fly incorporates a mottled hen feather, which gives it some action in the water. It also uses olive, peacock, or peacock eye Ice Dub for the head, which is a set of materials that work great for steelhead in the winter and spring. It is also very attractive to resident trout. This fly is typically tied on a shank when specifically used for swung-fly applications. As spring approaches and I want to use it for nymphing, I will tie it on a straight Aberdeen-style hook.

If I need these flies quickly in a pinch for swinging, I will also use a straight-eye hook, as they are quick and easy to mass-produce in this format. When I do so, the flies pull double duty and I can use them with swung fly, stripping, and nymphing techniques. We use this fly in an array of color combinations that ranges from earth tones to gaudy attractors. Drew Rosema, a friend and guide, has devised a variation of this fly that is blue and yellow. Here is the most common color combination.

- **Hook:** #2–4 short shank or Daiichi 2461
- **Body:** Peacock eye Ice Dub
- **Wing:** Olive grizzly hen hackle
- **Overwing:** Cranberry Holographic Flashabou and rainbow Krystal Flash
- **Eyes:** Bead chain in either Gold or Silver
- **Head:** Peacock eye Ice Dub

Shrew Sculpin

The Shrew is a larger pattern that is mostly used on the deep swing presentation. It is also a good fly for the traditional swung-fly method. This fly has caught a lot of steelhead and brown trout, but has also taken sizable stream trout, pike, walleye, and smallmouth bass in the mix. It is the workhorse of sculpin patterns, and we fish it with a lot of weight.

Whereas many steelhead patterns use rabbit strips for action, this fly uses pine squirrel. Pine squirrel is a great material when you want the action of a strip but don't want it to absorb a lot of water. This fly is most commonly tied on a longer shank and is tied larger than a Bender, often 3 to 4 inches in length.

- **Hook or shank:** Longer (55mm) shank
- **Tail:** Olive pine squirrel strip and cranberry Flashabou
- **Body:** Olive Ice Dub, covered with a pheasant rump feather, followed by more Ice Dub
- **Flash:** Cranberry Flashabou, covered with rainbow Krystal Flash
- **Head:** Clump of dark Ice Dub covered with olive Hare's Wiggle Dub
- **Eyes:** Gold bead chain (2 or 4)

The Inside Bender is a very simple fly that imitates a darter. It is best during cold-water periods. Due to its narrow profile, this fly sinks very well. It is a smaller pattern that fishes equally well on shanks and hooks. This is a great cost/benefit fly, as it has caught many fish and is so easy to tie.

The Shrew Sculpin is a very reliable, slow-water winter pattern. It is an accurate sculpin imitation that I love to use. This fly was designed for maximum sinkability of a sculpin pattern—most sculpin patterns are buoyant; this one is not. It regularly catches steelhead, lake-run browns, and stream trout. It has also incidentally taken walleyes and some large northern pike.

Stream Punk Goby

It would be hard to understate the value of a goby in a Midwest tailwater river. This fly is another regular pattern for the winter months. It works in all scenarios, and I find myself using it as a traditional swung fly late in the fall, only to swing it deeply during the winter months. This fly utilizes Craft Fur, which is a material I use on just about every goby pattern. There is something about the slimy sheen of a goby that Craft Fur mimics very well. This fly also has a new Flashabou color, white, which works great in the winter months. It is always tied on a shank for best results.

- **Hook:** 30–50mm shank
- **Wing 1:** Salmon or tan-colored grizzly saddle feather
- **Wing 2:** Gray olive Hareline Extra Select Craft Fur
- **Flash:** White Flashabou Magnum and cranberry Holographic Flashabou Magnum
- **Wing 3:** Black-tipped feather from the body of a ringneck pheasant
- **Hackle:** Large grizzly, brown, or tan saddle or schlappen feather, wound and overwound tightly to form a makeshift head
- **Head 1:** Olive Scud Dub
- **Head 2:** Light Rainbow Scud Dub
- **Eyes:** Large pearl plastic bead chain

Veiled UV Sculpin

The Veiled UV sculpin is a newer pattern that is used when the fish prefer an earth-tone baitfish pattern that is swung faster than the current. It was initially tied for the deep swing but was found to be just as effective with traditional swung fly methods. This fly is both razzle-dazzle and natural at the same time, which makes it versatile. UV materials do work and seem to trigger predatory fish. This fly incorporates UV Crystal Flash.

- **Shank:** 35mm or Longer Up-eye Shank of your choice
- **Tail:** Olive Hen Hackle and two thin Grizzly Hackles.
- **Flash:** Magnum Holographic Cranberry Flash topped with Rainbow Krystal Flash and Black/Green/Electric Blue Flahsabou weave
- **Eyes:** Pink Bead Chain, 4 beads, tied in ¼" behind the eye
- **Head Behind Eyes:** Emerald Senyo Fusion Dub, tied in as a clump
- **Head in Front of Eyes:** Olive Creepy Crawly Dub mixed with Gray Olive Scud Dub. Usually I mix this in a coffee grinder, as it makes the texture nicer to work with.
- **Veil:** Gray UV Crystal flash is tied in between the eyes and the front head, which makes the flash flare. This gives the fly a webby feel.

The Stream Punk Goby is a pattern born out of the invasion of gobies and is deadly on steelhead and browns. Gobies have large bulbous eyes, and this is a key component of a good goby pattern. Often king salmon will bash this fly as a bonus early in the fall.

The Veiled UV Sculpin is a pattern that we use quite a bit in the spring, as the water temps are changing from the deep freeze into spring. It incorporates natural earth-tone colors in addition to more colorful synthetics.

Big Baitfish Flies for Stripping

These are large flies designed to have lots of movement both while being retrieved and at pause. More often than not, they have a large head, composed of deer hair or some other buoyant material to give them action in the water. They can be tied so that they are articulated. These flies are fished with a single-handed rod and a sink-tip. Big flies will catch big fish, but expect to have a tired arm at the end of a day of fishing. If you are fishing an area with deep water near shore, the fly will need to be weighted to draw attention to it as soon as it enters the water.

Earlier in this book, I mentioned that fish will key in on color depending on the depth of the fly. For this reason, I have included a couple of natural sculpins to be fished in slow currents closer to the river bottom, and two natural shiner patterns to be fished higher in the water column. Beyond the flies mentioned here, there are many great trout streamers that work awesome for steelhead and lake-run browns. This is a starting point, but also look for flies from Kelly Galloup, Russ Maddin, Tommy Lynch, and Blane Chocklett, to name a just a few.

River Chicken

The River Chicken is a large but very natural streamer pattern. It has a soft head and nice action in the water. Sometimes I will add copper flash to this fly, but it can stand on its own without it. Though it is usually tied large, I will tie smaller versions if I am using it in tandem with another fly.

This is a fly that has been in my box for 15 years, and it sprang from the original sculpin pattern that I used, the Emulator. Though the fly has a lot of action, one of its strengths is that it takes fish on the pause. Its head is composed of Australian possum, which gives flies a lot of action while still sinking to some degree. It is a nice step down from a deer hair head in this regard. On these larger flies, if you don't have access to Australian possum, fox fur makes a good substitute.

- **Hook:** #1–4 Daiichi 2461
- **Tail:** Australian possum
- **Body:** Yellow and shrimp pink Ice Dub, mixed
- **Wing 1:** Wood duck flank
- **Wing 2:** Chinchilla rabbit strip, sandwiched between the duck flanks
- **Wing 3:** Wood duck flank
- **Wing 4 (optional):** Copper Flashabou
- **Collar:** Large flank feather
- **Head:** Large clump of Australian possum or tan fox tail (for larger sizes)

Emulator

I frequently try different fly patterns with new materials. However, there are some flies that have remained largely unchanged for a long time. The Emulator is a fly that I started using over 20 years ago and continue to use to this day. It is a basic, lifelike sculpin pattern that can be used as a swung fly, a stripped fly, or fished as a nymph to catch just about every warm- and coldwater predatory species in our rivers. This is a fly that I often lean on when it is a bright day or when the fish don't seem active. It is also deadly during the winter months and can catch fish at any speed. Because it is truly a natural pattern, it works great deep and slow. When you tie this fly for your local river, first look at the river bottom and match that color to the color of your fly. If you do this, you can expect consistent results.

This fly can be spruced up with flash or rubber legs (I often do this with smallmouth), but it fishes just fine the way it is. It is easily one of the most versatile patterns around. It is a great generic earth-tone fly, meaning it can imitate many things, including sculpins, gobies, and crayfish.

- **Hook:** #1/0–4 Daiichi 2461
- **Tail:** Two tan or olive grizzly marabou feathers
- **Hackle:** Large brown schlappen feather
- **Body:** Emu feather wound tightly forward on the hook
- **Collar:** Large duck flank feather
- **Pectoral fins:** Olive or tan grizzly hen feather on each side
- **Head:** Thick clump of Australian possum

Duck flank gives movement to the **River Chicken**, a natural sculpin pattern. This is a pattern that has been in the box for 15 years and has not changed too much. I recommend trying it with some copper flash and without. Often I trail this fly behind a smaller, flashier pattern.

The Emulator is an old friend of a fly pattern, and it has been catching anything that will eat a sculpin for 20 years. It was one of my first tries at a sculpin pattern and has been with me ever since. It can be stripped, swung, bounced along the bottom—you name it.

Spotfin Shiner

Spotfin shiners are a baitfish that I only recently realized were playing a very large role in our local rivers, especially the larger ones. In this book we detail how to fish around wood and timber. This minnow is the most common fish I have found around the woody steelhead lies. The females are more olive and yellow, whereas the males are steely gray and yellow. They are large, typically 2 to 5 inches in length. I really like the gray and yellow color these fish exhibit, and have been very successful with that color combination for migratory, warmwater, and coldwater species.

The eyes on this fish are set back a little ways, which gives them a triangular head. When you add eyes to your pattern, make sure to set them back far enough to fit a large clump of dubbing behind the eyes and a small clump in front. This fly can be tied in gray/yellow or olive/yellow combinations.

- **Hook:** #2/0 Daiichi 2461
- **Tail:** Mustard yellow Craft Fur
- **Body:** Minnow belly Ice Dub
- **Front of belly:** Veil of shrimp pink Ripple Ice Fiber
- **Wing:** Elk mane (long fibers)
- **Overwing:** Yellow Fish Scale
- **Flash 1:** Gray UV and yellow Krystal Flash
- **Flash 2:** Strand of yellow Magnum Lateral Scale
- **Eyes:** Gold bead chain (4 or 6)
- **Head:** Senyo's Fusion Dub in Fishmas color is tied behind the eyes; a small ball of yellow Ice Dub in front

Sunnyday Shiner

When you look at shiner minnows in the water, they look very shiny, and many species are a silver or emerald color when held out of the water. However, if you get below them in the sun, you will often see that their bodies are a light pink color in the sunlight and the tops of their bodies reflect a gold color.

This pattern is meant to imitate one of our most common minnow species, the common shiner. It is abundant in many river systems, and Great Lakes fish are bound to be familiar with this type of minnow. This pattern exaggerates the yellow and pink colors that fish see when looking up at shiners.

- **Hook:** #1 Daiichi 2461
- **Tail:** Cinnamon Hareline Extra Select Craft Fur
- **Body:** Mix of yellow and shrimp pink Ice Dub
- **Wing 1:** Long blond elk mane fibers, tied on top of the hook
- **Wing 2:** Gray, Tan, or Gray-Olive Hareline Extra Select Craft Fur
- **Wing 3:** Yellow Flashabou Accent
- **Wing 4:** Gold and silver Flashabou Magnum
- **Wing 5:** Olive Fish Scale
- **Eyes:** Gold bead chain (4)
- **Head:** Brown olive Scud Dub

Large, steel-colored shiners are prevalent around brush and timber. This fly is tied with gray and yellow, an underrated color combination in my opinion. I also have grown to like gray UV Krystal Flash for a lot of patterns. Expect to encounter a large predator fish with this **Spotfin Shiner** fly!

Shiners look different when you view them from below in the sunlight. They appear silver in your hand, but this is deceptive! When viewed from below, which is where the predators are, shiners show yellow and pink. The **Sunnyday Shiner** is for just this scenario.

Small Baitfish Flies for Stripping

These patterns commonly represent shiners and fry. A sink-tip or sinking leader is used to present these flies, often along the edges of a river. They will catch steelhead or any brown trout available, whether they be lake-run or stream fish.

I find that small amounts of flash really benefit these patterns. They are often used in the spring, when colorful minnows are present. The flash preferences of fish varies from river system to river system. In West Michigan, copper is among the best colors for both steelhead and brown trout. On sunny days, hints of gold and yellow can really do the trick.

In order to catch large fish with these patterns, it is common to use two flies when presenting them. The front fly will typically have some flash, whereas the rear fly will be more subtle. Often a fish will pursue the bright fly, only to drop back and attack the rear one. Whichever fly they choose, you win!

Queen of the Muddy Waters

The Queen is my go-to dirty water streamer, and it has been producing year after year for a long time. If works well on its own but is also small enough and light enough to fish in front of another fly. It is a fry imitation and attractor pattern rolled into one. It generically imitates the shape of a fry, and in the spring, when shiners are spawning, it makes a great imitation for these fish as well. The copper flash is its best variation, but powder blue marabou is a good substitute to have in your box as well.

This fly has little weight, so a good sink-tip in front of it is a must. Fish it with short, sharp strips. This fly will only catch fish when it is moving. However, if you trail it with a more natural pattern, you will frequently get fish to follow the Queen and eat the other fly on a pause.

- **Hook:** #1–6 4XL streamer hook
- **Wing:** Two mallard flank feathers, tied two-thirds the way up the hook shank from the bend, topped with copper Flashabou
- **Collar:** Large mallard flank, palmered
- **Body:** Pink UV Ice Dub

Simple All-Purpose Shiner

This pattern works great on sunny days anywhere shiners are found. The gray-olive used in the fly's tail and wing is a color that steelhead and brown trout seem to love.

- **Hook:** #2–6 3XL streamer hook
- **Tail:** Gray-olive Craft Fur
- **Wing:** Gray-olive Craft Fur
- **Head:** Cinnamon UV Ice Dub
- **Wing:** A few strands each of silver and gold Flashabou Magnum

The Queen of the Muddy Waters is a shiner or fry imitation. Often it is used in conjunction with another pattern; it is placed in front and its attractor qualities draw fish in to strike. If you are familiar with Great Lakes spoon fishing, think of this fly as a Dodger. A lot of times a big fish will follow the front fly out, only to later strike the second fly.

The Simple All-Purpose Shiner is a flashy bait that works well not only for steelhead and brown trout but also for smallmouth bass. It has great flash properties and is well suited for sunny days. It can be fished with a variety of methods and is very easy to cast.

Baitfish Flies for Switch

These are small to midsize patterns, and the weight of the line will limit the size of the flies you can use. The fly line used should be agile so that the fly can be manipulated as it swings. These patterns will imitate darters, fry, and shiner species.

Common flies in this category feature weighted eyes or drilled beads for the head. Drilled tungsten beads work great for this, as they sink extremely quickly. Unfortunately, they can be expensive. When working with beads on streamers, always use some head cement. Spey casting can add a lot of strain to a pattern.

Copperhead Fry

This fry pattern is extremely simple to make and fishes very well along the edge of the river. It has a copper tungsten bead for a head and is tied in smaller sizes of 1 to 2 inches. It is one of the smallest flies that I use for migratory fish on the swing, and is also a very good resident trout fly in rivers with brown and rainbow trout populations. This pattern should always be tied on a hook for best results.

- **Hook:** #2–6 3XL streamer
- **Tail:** Gray olive Hareline Extra Select Craft Fur
- **Flash:** Two strands of copper Flashabou Magnum
- **Shoulder:** Ginger marabou
- **Head:** Copper tungsten bead

Queen of the Waters

The Queen of the Waters is an old traditional pattern, dating from the 1800s. This fly was guarded with secrecy among some of the old anglers I used to know, but eventually the secret got out. It is a great fly for both trout and migratory fish and works well throughout the spring. This variation of the pattern leaves the general pattern intact but updates it with modern materials. It is a traditional fly that makes for a very good fry pattern. It is easy to cast and catches lots of fish.

- **Hook:** #4–8 wet fly
- **Tail:** Two strands of rainbow Krystal Flash
- **Body:** Orange Ice dub, ribbed with silver wire (optional)
- **Wing:** Duck flank
- **Collar:** Brown hackle

The Copperhead Fry is a simple pattern for use at the conclusion of the migratory fish run. It works in any river with a fry population and should be twitched while swung. A little bit of flash helps these small flies have a big presence in the water.

The Queen of the Waters is an old fly pattern that still has applications today. It is deadly during the spring months when spruced up with synthetic materials. When tied with a black body, it is often called the King of the Waters. The black variant works well when stoneflies are hatching in early spring.

Baitfish Flies for Nymphing

These are very natural patterns, and some of the best in the Midwest imitate salmon and steelhead fry. They can imitate anything, however, such as sculpins, darters, and shiners. Wiggle nymphs are a great example of this; a Hex nymph can imitate fry patterns and other small minnows, etc.

A lot of these patterns are articulated. I tend to use a heavy front hook and a lighter, longer rear hook. The most common configuration is a heavy-wire size 4 or 6 egg hook for the front hook, followed by a lighter-wire Aberdeen-style rear hook that has a straight eye. The front hook is the one supposed to hook the fish, so the rear hook does not need to be an expensive one. Often I find myself buying simple gold Aberdeen panfish hooks for the rear hook. The gold color adds a hint of flash to an otherwise completely natural pattern.

When the front of the fly has the weight, the rear is free to wiggle. On flies like this, it is really important that the hooks are joined tightly but not so tightly that they can't wiggle. Monofilament works better for the junction than braid. The rear hook swings too loosely and tangles too frequently with braid. For many of the typical articulated patterns, I use 20-pound Maxima Ultragreen, though there are many options for this.

When the water is high and cold and the food sources are small, nymph-fishing approaches are the best road to success. Since your fly is presented close to the bottom for much for its drift, you would be imitating the top and sides of the baitfish that you are mimicking.

Australian Possum Hex

Hex wiggle nymphs are a multifunctional pattern, kind of like an SUV for your fly box. They are designed for nymphing, but can also be used for deep swung-fly methods. They work in both large and small rivers. Though they are an accurate imitation of a Hex, there is no doubt that they are mistaken for darters in the fall and salmon fry in the spring.

This pattern incorporates Australian possum for the gills. This material has a natural fish-attracting quality and is used for a lot of different types of streamer flies.

- **Rear Hook:** Size 10 3xl Streamer Hook
- **Hook:** #10 3–4XL streamer
- **Tail and body:** Three clumps of Australian possum interspersed with two sections of yellow Ice Dub
- **Junction:** 20-pound Maxima loop
- **Front Hook:** Size 6 Egg Hook, such as Daiichi 1520
- **Tail covering juncture:** Tuft of natural Australian possum fur
- **Shellback:** Brown Antron fibers
- **Legs:** Brown hen hackle
- **Thorax:** Orange Ice Dub
- **Eyes:** Black mono bead chain

Better than Spawn Holographic (BTS)

This is another pattern that has been in my box for a very long time. It is a deadly fly in the spring when salmon fry are present, and can be used in a variety of different situations.

This fly got its name in a funny way. Two good bait fishermen had just fished through a run when my clients and I slid in as they left. On the first cast, one of my clients caught a big steelhead. He then uttered, "This fly is better than spawn." He was prophetic, as from then on the fly was called Better than Spawn.

Though no fly beats well-presented real eggs, there are fish in every run that would just as soon eat something other than a protein ball. In the spring, this fly fits the bill.

- **Rear Hook:** Size 10 3xl Streamer Hook
- **Tail and body:** Grizzly marabou tied in as a tail, with the remnant wound forward for a narrow body
- **Junction:** 20-pound Maxima loop
- **Front Hook:** Size 6 Egg Hook, such as Daiichi 1520
- **Tail covering juncture:** Tuft of natural Australian possum fur
- **Flash:** Yellow Holographic Flashabou
- **Throat:** Pink UV Ice Dub
- **Eyes:** Black mono bead chain

The Australian Possum (or A.P.) Hex is another one of my creations from years ago. It can be used effectively any time steelhead are present, and works well as a nymph or for the deep swing. This fly represents a lot of different food sources in addition to a Hex. I consider it to be one of the best salmon fry imitations, and it also imitates small darters and gobies well.

The BTS is a staple in my area, and I can't imagine how many of them I have tied over many years of guiding. It is a pattern that works every year. Though time-consuming to tie, it is worth it! While keeping the body the same, try using different colors of flash such as yellow, silver holographic, and olive Krystal Flash.

This is a basic sculpin pattern that works with a variety of presentations. Bars can easily be added to its side with a permanent marker. It is without a doubt the simplest pattern in my box, but it sometimes works when others do not.

Basic Sculpin

Sculpins are not always moving much along the bottom, so it is always good to have an accurate sculpin pattern handy when you are nymph fishing. There are often times when we fish deep runs in high water in the spring for steelhead. After a long winter, these late winter/spring fish are in the mood for a large meal. Furthermore, a sculpin pattern will be easy for a large gamefish to see in high water.

Whenever fishing a sculpin pattern as a nymph, always allow the fly to swing out at the end of the drift. This goes against the perfect drift logic of traditional nymph fishing, but remember, a sculpin is not a nymph. It is so much better. This sculpin pattern is used for nymph fishing but has multiple uses. It will be recycled as a trout or smallmouth fly long after the migratory fish are out of the river.

■ **Tail:** Tan Hareline Extra Select Craft Fur
■ **Body:** Mix of yellow and shrimp pink Ice Dub
■ **Wing:** Tan Hareline Extra Select Craft Fur
■ **Eyes:** Gold or black bead chain
■ **Head:** Dark tan Senyo's Laser dubbing, tied as a clump

■ **Note:** It is a very good idea to carry a selection of Sharpie permanent markers when fishing flies made of craft fur. You can easily add mottling to the fly and change its appearance when warranted.

And so, now that you have tied some flies, you head to the river well prepared to read the water. You select a bushy sculpin pattern, and you cast it into the river. After feeling a heavy tug, a mighty gamefish is on your line. After sizzling runs, you fight the fish and bring it to net. You admire the beauty and power of this animal and realize how blessed you are to have such great and accessible resources.

Slowly you lower the fish into the water and release it head first into the river. Its tail gives a resounding splash and water hits you in the face as it goes home. Soon thereafter you think, "That was awesome! I want to catch another!" And so you resume fishing, casting your life away one step at a time. Well . . . at least this is what happened to me. It is not so bad.

Index